"The private funding of police has been a peripheral issue in criminological scholarship. Lippert and Walby's fine book shows this to be a mistake. Using a rich dataset born of meticulous investigation, they shine much needed critical light on the dark money animating police operations across North America. It is a highly illuminating and often unsettling read."

Adam White
Senior Lecturer in Criminology, University of Sheffield

"In *Police Funding, Dark Money, and the Greedy Institution*, Lippert and Walby continue their exceptional efforts to push policing scholarship into uncharted research terrain. With all eyes drawn to the public financing of police organizations through the 'defunding' debate, the surreptitious and contaminating expansion of private sponsorship of public policing has been worryingly neglected. Built upon robust investigation that breaches the blue wall and illuminates the dark money flowing into police coffers, this book spotlights the worrying implications of this disreputable public-private exchange within policing. Empirically-rich; methodologically-robust; conceptually-nuanced: this book will be of immense benefit to policing scholars, and indeed many more besides."

Conor O'Reilly
Professor in Transnational Crime and Security, University of Leeds

"This meticulous study reveals the pervasive influences of private funding in North American policing. Lippert and Walby are to be commended for uncovering many complex and potentially troubling networks of financial exchange that raise important questions about transparency, neutrality, accountability, and private influence in contemporary public administration."

Ian Warren
Senior Lecturer in Criminology, Deakin University

"Lippert and Walby have written a path-breaking book that exposes and makes sense of a deeply consequential trend: dark private money feeding the mass-policing beast. They balance rigorous research findings with incisive theoretical concepts making for an eye-opening and disquieting analysis."

Pete Kraska
Professor of Police and Justice Studies, Eastern Kentucky University

Police Funding, Dark Money, and the Greedy Institution

Police Funding, Dark Money, and the Greedy Institution is about a pervasive but little-studied phenomenon. Private funding of public police entails private entities sending resources to police through unconventional or hidden channels, sometimes for suspect reasons. The book argues police acquisition of this "dark money" befits the notion of a "greedy institution" that pursues resources beyond ample public funding and needs, and seeks ever more loyal members beyond its traditional boundaries to reproduce itself. The book focuses on private police foundations, corporate sponsorships, and paid detail arrangements primarily in North America, how these funding networks operate and are framed for audiences, and the forms and volumes of capital they generate.

Based on interviews with police representatives, sponsors, funders, and foundation representatives as well as records from over 100 police departments, this book examines key issues in private funding of public police, including corporatization, accountability, corruption, and the rule of law. It documents and analyzes the troubling explosion of police foundations and sponsors and corporate paid detail brokers unknown to the public as a social and policy issue and a potential hidden response to the global police defunding movement. The book also considers potential policy responses and community safety alternatives in a more generous society.

An accessible and compelling read, students and scholars in criminology, criminal justice, law, sociology, political science, anthropology, geography, as well as policymakers, will find this timely book revealing of a neglected, growing area of police practice spanning multiple themes and jurisdictions.

Randy K. Lippert is Professor of Criminology at the University of Windsor, Canada.

Kevin Walby is Associate Professor of Criminal Justice at the University of Winnipeg, Canada.

Routledge Studies in Crime, Security and Justice

Contemporary social scientific scholarship is being transformed by the challenges associated with the changing nature of, and responses to, questions of crime, security, and justice across the globe. Traditional disciplinary boundaries in the social sciences are being disturbed and at times broken down by the emerging scholarly analysis of both the increasing merging of issues of "crime" and "security" and the unsettling of traditional notions of justice, rights and due process in an international political and cultural climate seemingly saturated by, and obsessed with, fear, insecurity, and risk. This series showcases contemporary research studies, edited collections and works of original intellectual synthesis that contribute to this new body of scholarship both within the field of study of criminology and beyond to its connections with debates in the social sciences more broadly.

Edited by
Adam Edwards, Cardiff University
Gordon Hughes, Cardiff University
Reece Walters, Queensland University of Technology

The Algorithmic Society
Technology, Power, and Knowledge
Edited by Marc Schuilenburg and Rik Peeters

Crime and Disorder in Community Context
Edited by Rebecca Wickes and Lorraine Mazerolle

Police Funding, Dark Money, and the Greedy Institution
Randy K. Lippert and Kevin Walby

For more information about this series, please visit: https://www.routledge.com/Routledge-Studies-in-Crime-Security-and-Justice/book-series/RSCSJ

Police Funding, Dark Money, and the Greedy Institution

Randy K. Lippert and Kevin Walby

Routledge
Taylor & Francis Group
LONDON AND NEW YORK

First published 2022
by Routledge
4 Park Square, Milton Park, Abingdon, Oxon OX14 4RN

and by Routledge
605 Third Avenue, New York, NY 10158

Routledge is an imprint of the Taylor & Francis Group, an informa business

British Library Cataloguing-in-Publication Data
A catalogue record for this book is available from the British Library

Library of Congress Cataloging-in-Publication Data
A catalog record has been requested for this book

ISBN: 978-0-367-76647-4 (hbk)
ISBN: 978-0-367-76648-1 (pbk)
ISBN: 978-1-003-16791-4 (ebk)

DOI: 10.4324/9781003167914

Typeset in Bembo
by KnowledgeWorks Global Ltd.

Contents

List of Tables

List of Figures

Acknowledgements

Randy K. Lippert acknowledges support of his partner Francine throughout the long research and writing process informing this book.

Kevin Walby thanks his colleagues in Criminal Justice at University of Winnipeg.

Our special thanks to acquisition editor Thomas Sutton at Routledge for his interest and solid support of this project from the outset. We greatly enjoyed working with him again. Both authors offer our heart-felt thanks and appreciation to the two research assistants – A. Luscombe and M. Zaia – who diligently, expertly, and extensively worked on the project from which this book has drawn. We also consider ourselves fortunate to have worked with the inquisitive minds of graduate students J.C. Emery, C. Labute, and the late B. Ujevic. We would like to thank William Harrison for assistance with the figures as well as N. Necsefor, M. Held, S. Sidhu, and N. Seavers for their edits and comments. We also thank S. Treffers for generously commenting on the manuscript at a key juncture.

We acknowledge that some chapters include small portions of previously published but that this material has also been updated and revised.

Chapter Two draws from K. Walby, R. Lippert, and A. Luscombe, 2018. The Police Foundation's Rise: Implications of Public Policing's Dark Money. *British Journal of Criminology*, 58(4), pp. 827–833. Produced with permission from Oxford University Press.

Chapter Five draws from K. Walby, R. Lippert, and A. Luscombe 2020. Police Foundation Governance and Accountability: Corporate Interlocks and Private, Non-profit Influence on Public Police. *Criminology & Criminal Justice*, 20(2), p. 144. Produced with permission from Oxford University Press.

Chapter Six draws from R. Lippert, K. Walby, and M. Zaia 2019. Managing Risk and Pre-empting Immorality in Private Employment of Public Police. *Social & Legal Studies*, 28(6), pp. 803–809. Produced with permission from Sage. It also draws from R. Lippert and K. Walby 2014. Marketization, Knowledge Work and Visibility in 'Users Pay' Policing in Canada. *British Journal of Criminology*, 54(2), pp. 273–276. Produced with permission from Oxford University Press.

Introduction

Public Policing's Greed and Dark Money: Private Sponsorship and Funding of Police in North America

Like most large North American urban areas, Houston, Texas has witnessed major public protests over police surveillance, violence, and killings in racialized and poor communities in recent years. These protests grew in number, size, and intensity in 2020 following the death of George Floyd at the hands of Minneapolis police officers. With these protests have come widespread, consistent, and spirited calls to defund and eventually abolish public police departments. At one such Houston protest in May 2020, a peaceful woman protestor, Melissa Sanchez, while holding a placard was trampled from behind by an armed, uniformed, horse-mounted Houston Police Department officer donning a shielded helmet, tactical vest, and riot gear. Following this terrifying incident, Houston's mayor apologized to the injured woman on behalf of the Houston Police Department, promising to "look on how we can better deploy our resources to keep that from happening again so you or anyone else can exercise your Constitutional right and we can maintain the peace" (ABC 2020). In 2021, Sanchez filed a civil lawsuit against the Houston Police Department for harm incurred while exercising her right to protest (Houston Chronicle 2021).

Absent from media coverage of this terrible incident, official response, and related protestors' calls for social change, however, was knowledge of how the Houston Police Department had acquired resources to confront protests in the first place. Who had funded the purchase of officers' riot helmets and shields, tactical gear, horses, and mounted unit equipment that had made this disturbing incident possible? The fact that much of the funding did not flow from Houston's public police budget was neither remarked upon, nor likely known by most journalists, onlookers, protestors, and even government officials. Nor was the relevant funding the mayor publicly promised to deploy differently inevitably under her mayoral control. Rather, for the Houston Police Department, funds for these resources were sought, acquired, and channelled by an independent, private organization called the Houston Police Foundation. The Foundation's "funded projects" since inception in 2012 include "financial support for Mounted Patrol through a horse sponsorship program"; "a horse trailer and supplies... purchased to assist the Mounted

DOI: 10.4324/9781003167914-1

Unit in their daily activities"; "700 Tactical Vest Covers for the HPD officers...with their bullet proof safety gear"; "a HPD SWAT Tactical Shoot House [that] enables officers to practice in a tactical environment"; other "Tactical Equipment for Special Threat Situations... [so that] Officers are equipped with the necessary tactical gear and weapons" (Houston Police Foundation 2021a); and more. Garnering funds from myriad private sources, in this way more than ten million USD has been provided to the Houston Police Department since 2012 by this private foundation (Houston Police Foundation 2021b), the more specific sources of which remain hidden. But as intriguing as the funding's private sources, is how these arrangements, networks and relations have been framed, as well as the exchanges of capital they entail. Here and across North America, the broader police institution appears to expect to receive this funding and resources through private sponsorship and funding networks in which it is increasingly enrolled. This expectation is evident, for example, from the outset of the first North American police foundation prototype, the New York Police Foundation created in 1972. At that time New York's mayor framed the foundation for a *Times* article, asserting "it would serve as a vehicle for receiving contributions from individuals and organizations that *wish to demonstrate their support* of the city's Police Department" (Ranzal 1972; emphasis added). Indeed, the efforts of these foundations in New York, Houston and proliferating across North America to *loyally* provide and arrange these resources for the police institution seem less a gift for which the institution is grateful, and more an expectation of those presumed or persuaded to be loyal to the police.

Two months earlier in March 2020 in nearby Blanco, Texas, the Kinder Morgan corporation's massive 428-mile, $2 billion US pipeline promising to connect to the Gulf Coast near Houston, was being erected across the Texas rural landscape. A local journalist, Jody Barr, and the pipeline protestors he was interviewing, noticed something happening nearby. The chief of the local Blanco police department was seen casually unlocking the gate to the Kinder Morgan pipeline storage site adjacent the public road. When Barr approached him and asked who was paying the armed, uniformed police chief to provide pipeline security, he refused to divulge this information, incredulously claiming not to know who had negotiated his contract (Barr 2020). Keeping the source and specifics of what we call "paid detail funding" in the shadows while providing a highly visible armed and uniformed presence is common among police departments in North America. In this instance, the Blanco police chief then proceeded to snap seven photographs of Barr and his and protestors' vehicles parked on the public roadside. A few weeks later, on April 14, 2020, when Barr, for his pipeline protest story, followed two trucks carrying pipe from Blanco up Texas highway 420 to see where they were going, two police vehicles with lights flashing, one a Gillespie County constable and the other a Gillespie County Sheriff's Office deputy, suddenly pulled his car over. The trucks moved down the highway out of sight. The

Gillespie County deputy came to the car window to demand the journalist provide identification and queried him about a morning "incident" where Barr had been filming on the public road, intelligence about him obviously having been transferred to these other area police departments. Barr complied but complained he "was trying to conduct his business as a news reporter." Like Sanchez who had assembled with Black Lives Matter and other protestors to express her free speech before being violently trampled, in pursuing his investigative story, before being halted on a public highway, Barr was exercising his first amendment freedom of the press rights enshrined in the US Constitution. Neither Sanchez nor Barr were even alleged by police to have committed any criminal offence in relation to these events, much less charged with one.

The hiring of the Blanco police chief to provide security, along with many other area police department officers, including the Texas Department of Public Safety, at this and other pipeline construction sites across rural Texas was funded by the Kinder Morgan corporation, among the largest energy infrastructure corporations in North America. Remarkably, the same corporation, as revealed by a leaked memorandum, had been funding Pennsylvania police to "deter protests" at a separate pipeline construction project in 2015 on the border between Pennsylvania and New York (Federman 2015). Similar corporations have more recently funded police to arrest protestors. In the Texas case an independent, security corporation called the Athos Group, with offices in Irving, Texas, as well as other US cities, brokered this. This kind of paid detail arrangement is increasingly common. On Houston's outskirts circled by refineries, processing plants, and pipelines, in this fossil fuel industry-dominated urban region, one can observe Houston Police Department and Harris County Sheriff's officers providing paid detail too. In the Texas heat, these mostly idle, armed, and uniformed officers stand adjacent the gates to these multinational corporation-owned oil refineries and processing plants. The presence of HPD and HCS officers is not directly funded by any level – local, state, or federal – of the public purse. These officers are not dispatched by the Houston Police Department or Sheriff's Office either, but instead via an agency like Athos, called Frizell Group International headquartered in Houston. Like Blanco's police chief, the presence of Houston area officers is funded through this type of broker, which, but for Barr's reporting, would be unknown to the public. As with funding from foundations, sponsorships, and the myriad donations this book explores, here too police departments seem to expect these arrangements be made available for their officers and for entities such as the Frizell Group, and private corporations, smaller companies, and even individuals, to loyally fund them. The fact both Frizell Group and Athos Group are led by former police officers, David Frizell, "a former federal law enforcement and counterintelligence agent" (Frizell Group 2021) and Jeff Sweetin, who had "a thirty-year local and federal law enforcement career" (Athos Group 2021) respectively, coheres with this notion. The framing of these arrangements too suggests the police institution demands a loyal commitment to funding from these nominally external organizations.

The character and components of these private charitable foundations and for-profit brokers providing funds to police we argue are aligned in some ways, their networks occasionally interlinking. More importantly they simultaneously raise two vital issues that demand attention. The first is the spectre of the corporatization of public policing that is occurring apace due to the expanding flow of private funds into this institution and the problems this can create, including corruption, rule of law discrepancies, destruction of legitimacy and related scandals, and as seen above, even constitutional rights violations. In addition to the longer standing and lower-level provision of donations to police departments, in this book we explore sponsorships and other measures as well as how the flow of these monies is framed by police and endows police practices. The second issue raised is even more neglected, and centres on the other side of the equation, the greed of the police institution that demands and expects this dark money from loyal actors and all that accompanies it. By "greedy" in this book we do not primarily mean the character of individual police administrators and officers, as we explain more below. And we do not mean mere collection of economic capital either. Rather, we are referring to the institutional level, that is, to police as what Lewis Coser (1974) coined a "greedy institution," and we are referring to a broader process of aligning interests as a means of institutional reproduction.

Starting with an account of activities of the Houston Police Department, its foundation, and paid detail brokers operating in Texas, might seem a peculiar choice for a book about the police institution. This is especially so given more famous North American police departments, such as the New York Police Department and the Royal Canadian Mounted Police available for discussion. Yet, as we will demonstrate, these latter departments reflect some trends and mutations too, including the kinds of framing, exchanges, and networks we identify that make these sponsorships and funding possible. We chose to open with Texas arrangements and practices because we think they are not exceptional in North America and instead represent what is happening in large urban and rural populations elsewhere, and which demand scholarly scrutiny too. We contend the funding exchanges and measures that the Houston Police Department and Blanco's Police epitomize are at the forefront of major mutations in the police institution and are perhaps further advanced than some other departments we discuss in this book. Illuminating these private sponsorship and funding networks using the tools of investigative social science is overdue. Much of this network building and these exchanges are happening in the shadows and it is difficult to determine the extent of benefits accrued from this private funding, hence the term "dark money" in our book's title. The police institution's greedy demand for and even expectation of dark money and the networked relations that underpin them has arrived and is spreading across the US and, to a lesser extent, Canadian police departments.

There remains great variance in these private funding arrangements in North America, as we will show, but it is also true that the police institution increasingly frames itself, makes exchanges, and enters networks that variously include sponsors, funders, and brokers of paid detail services, as well as other private and external funders through more direct avenues. We also argue the police institution seeks to impose the demand for loyalty far beyond their rank-and-file recruits and the institution's formal purview, as those writing on greedy institutions have suggested. Although the arrangements are not widely known, especially among the public, private sponsorship and funding that we document is not occurring on geographical, temporal, conceptual, or other fringes. They are evident in cities like New York, Seattle, Toronto, and Vancouver. Often when police officers are patrolling in vehicles or responding to calls or a crisis and otherwise most publicly visible, their presence and some of their equipment has been funded by private rather than public sources. The idea that private sponsorship and funding of public policing is a marginal phenomenon is often part of how police frame these arrangements to avoid accountability and transparency. This book suggests private sponsorship and funding may well represent the beginning of a return to the early history of policing before the introduction of comprehensive public funding of police departments intended to serve and protect everyone consistent with the rule of law, rather than only powerful private companies and elites. But the unequal protection is only one consequence. Another is the unequal surveillance and violence that racialized and poor communities face. We thus also contend this trajectory is not inevitable and that a fundamental change in institutional spirit and mission from greed to generosity is possible and needed.

Greed and Dark Money

Police Funding, Dark Money, and the Greedy Institution is about a pervasive and fast changing but thus far little-studied or known phenomenon, the private sponsorship and funding of police. This funding typically entails not publicly disclosing its source or openness to public scrutiny. In fact, it often comes to light because of a one-off incident, criminal or otherwise, that suddenly, but temporarily, garners media attention, such as a pipeline protest. Private sponsorship and funding of public policing entails a private organization or individual providing monies directly or through a broker to a police department. In many such arrangements, the broker is a police foundation with charity status, operating between the police and funders and often masking the sponsor's identity entirely. Paid detail arrangements involving private individuals and organizations paying for police to provide security and other services are only a slightly better-known form of private funding of police. However, even these private sources are mostly kept hidden from immediate public scrutiny. For example, in the recent instance in Texas noted above, despite some officers using publicly owned department vehicles, firearms, and uniforms for paid detail on the pipeline, Barr, the journalist, discovered they were immune to freedom of information (FOI) requests (Barr 2020). Foundations are not subject to FOI law or public oversight beyond basic reporting rules of charitable organizations either, so monies given to foundations and these firms become shrouded in secrecy in the dark. In the US there is sometimes little oversight of these organizations and, as we discuss, massive holes in the policies governing private sponsorship and funding arrangements of police too. Despite controversies and scandals in the US especially, but also in Canada, and their relation to emerging calls for and debates about defunding, private sponsorship and funding of public policing remains under-researched and neglected. Sponsorship is an overlooked phenomenon in the literature about the politics of policing too (Reiner 1992). To date, there has not been comprehensive, in-depth study of these arrangements and practices in North America or elsewhere.

This book is necessarily about the complex supply side of private sponsorships and funding of the police institution, which has been taken up by media a bit of late, as well as in our earlier work. But this book is as much or more focused on the demand side that has been largely neglected or taken as self-evident in previous accounts. An institutional greed is manifested in how demand is realized through exchanges that form networks reaching beyond demands of loyalty from officers behind that traditional blue line and into external institutions. Organizations provide funding to police often through these unconventional and ill-defined channels and sometimes for suspect reasons, partially because they are expected by police to do so.

This book is therefore not about protests over police violence and killings, institutional racism, and what has emerged as the global defunding movement, as relevant as these are to understanding the current landscape in which the police institution finds itself and the need for change. But we nonetheless hope this book will lend at least some insight into issues at their centre. Private sponsorship and funding of public policing and especially the rise and spread of private police foundations and paid detail broker companies are relatively recent developments in public policing in North America and beyond. Other arrangements we examine such as donations are longer standing and tend to operate at a lower scale but nonetheless require empirical attention since little is known about their extent and features. This book examines the variable practices and issues of private sponsorship and funding of public policing. In doing so the themes of accountability, legitimacy, communication framing, relational exchanges, networks, constitutional rights, the rule of law, corporatization, and corruption manifest across numerous jurisdictions. Private sponsorship and funding of public policing, once illuminated by empirical research, lends insight into police as a greedy institution as well as these other conceptual and theoretical aspects.

We analyze the growing private sponsorship and funding of public police in North America as a significant policy issue that has been in the dark for too long, and which may be serving as a potential hidden police response to the recent global police defunding movement. As this book reveals, there is also variation in how this sponsorship is promoted and managed. For example, at time of writing we know of no Canadian police department that has entered arrangements with Frizell Group, Athos Group, or similar broker corporations, although clearly the potential now exists.

Police as Greedy Institution

Drawing from Coser (1974) and the few criminologists and other scholars who have engaged with his ideas, we argue police are a "greedy institution" (see also Peterson and Uhnoo 2012). By "greedy" we do not merely mean the desire for and acquisition of funds far beyond community and individual needs, although that is a consequence of police framing and exchanges with other organizations. Rather, we agree with Coser that greedy institutions "seek exclusive and undivided loyalty and they attempt to reduce the claims of competing roles and status positions on those they wish to encompass within their boundaries" (1973, 4). Furthermore they "tend to rely mainly on non-physical mechanisms to separate the insider from the outsider to erect symbolic boundaries between them" (6). In this book, we argue the police institution seeks to extend these boundaries and we explore how it entices, coaxes, and captures funds from external institutions beyond traditional blue lines in elaborate networks. But as a greedy institution we suggest the police seek influence beyond what most people would think of as their boundaries. Their boundaries continue to expand as a by-product of the institution constantly and sometimes aggressively attempting to replicate itself. Though this has several implications, the main one taken up in this book is the quest for sponsorship and related funds beyond the significant resources already allotted to this institution and democratically accounted for through public treasuries. It is fundamental to our argument about private sponsorship and funding that police as a greedy institution lends itself to pursuing and accepting dark money.

We also contend in any instance of framing and point of exchange in the formation of funding networks, that there may well be competition or tension among greedy institutions. Previous work, for example, has noted competition between the military and family institution as greedy institutions (Segal 1986). Where police are concerned there is undoubtedly some competition among different departments under the police institution umbrella, but also with private corporations' greed. Police expectations often include institutions like corporations that are themselves greedy institutions, in the narrow sense of desiring resources beyond their needs (i.e., surplus profit), but also in the broader loyalty sense of greedily demanding consumers embrace their brands and contrived lifestyles (e.g., Nike, Ford, Apple) via their sophisticated market framing, rather than those of rival corporations (Columbia, Toyota, Hewlett Packard) or traditional institutions. While these are secret negotiations, the exchanges between the police institution and private corporations can potentially entail conflict and negotiation over what the sponsorship will look like. Corporations might prefer the entire police cruiser sport the corporation's brand in exchange for funds for equipment, while the police might prefer only a small emblem on the cruiser's rear fender, both institutions therefore demanding loyalty of outsiders and onlookers. A mid-sized emblem in exchange for funds may become the result of a compromise. Merely because the police institution demands loyalty does not mean it is always obtained, which the increasing numbers of police recruits who leave police departments for different careers after only a few years will attest (Police Executive Research Forum 2019).

We want to repeat in this introduction something about police as a greedy institution. We are not suggesting individual officers and civilian staff in police departments as part of this institution are necessarily greedy individuals in their everyday lives. Ours is an *institutional* not an *individual* concern. This is not an attempt to let police off the hook for wrongdoing. It is simply the level of analysis we work at as sociological criminologists. As is true of everyone who occupies and contributes to social institutions, whether it be the family, military, faith-based organizations, or even universities, the individual actor is never only the institution's placid tool or dope, with all institutional discourses and practices in which they are involved and enlisted directly reflecting an institution's character. Some individual police administrators and officers may well fit the greedy bill, as members of many institutions would, including those from other greedy institutions, while others may not. For police, here one recalls the infamous "meat eater" versus "grass eater" individual distinctions in the Knapp Commission report (New York 1972) on New York Police Department corruption in the early 1970s. The former individuals consumed by delving deep into the pie, gorging themselves, exploiting all opportunities, and disregarding rules and laws. The latter individuals merely grazed off the top by more occasionally bending some rules. We think some police personnel are still corrupt meat eaters and there are many news stories and academic findings about such cases but, again, our focus in this book is on the police institution itself, which compared to others, often eats at the top of the food chain of social institutions. To follow this analogy further, in the book's conclusion we speculate on what police in a generous society might look like instead. A generous society, it would seem, would ensure the communities the police institution is supposed to serve are first munificently fed and their needs satiated, long before police would be permitted to eat, and even then, only on what meat or grass remained. This would have far-reaching implications for the size, power, and character of police agencies in our world.

Was the police institution always greedy? While our immediate focus is not historical, we nonetheless think it necessary to briefly speculate about an answer to this inevitable query in lieu of a detailed, sustained scholarly exploration, which has yet to be conducted. Thus, we think the police institution's current greedy character results from the emergence and convergence of an historical complex of other institutional discourses and practices, including those of other greedy institutions. The early influences of the military institution on the development of the police and the failure to diverge from that institution in the many years that followed suggest the incorporation of military institution features that demand not only loyalty of its members (i.e., its captains, lieutenants, sergeants, constables, recruits, and beyond) but also those external to it. Indeed, it is this insight of demands for loyalty of a greedy institution beyond itself, which is a major contribution of this book to the growing but still small and slightly stagnant greedy institution literature. Moreover, militarization of the police has become more pronounced in the last 20 years to the point it is difficult to any longer distinguish the police from the military at certain moments in North American departments (a division that never happened in more authoritarian countries). We do not think that development is easily separated from the growing greedy character of the police institution and its acquisition of dark monies. Elsewhere the emergence of the terms "extended police [or policing] family" (see Johnston 2007), a more recent development, speaks to the notion that the police institution has taken on some qualities of that greedy institution – the family – too. Indeed, there is a broader police family that includes other law enforcement personnel and practices. The role of police unions or police associations cannot be overlooked in the expansion of police power and networks either. Indeed, some kinds of financial arrangements we comment on in the following chapters have been pushed for not by police management such as chiefs and superintendents but by police unions, who are among the most aggressive appendages of police as an institution. Our point here is that there is a more complex genealogy still to be traced, however such a historical inquiry is beyond the scope of this book. We also think this genealogy, as recent mass protests over police violence, killings, and systemic racism during 2020 and since have reminded the world, must refer to complicating colonizing discourses and practices of at least the past 200 years in North America alongside the tidy, perhaps trite, story of the borrowing of Robert Peel's nine principles and features such as uniforms and discipline that show the military institution's influence. We think both are lineages and elements of the genealogy of the police institution as a greedy institution, but that neither is a complete, sufficient account on its own. We consciously use the term "genealogy" here to refer to police as a greedy institution, since it leaves open at least the possibility, more than historical accounts invoking political economic or other totalizing structures, that the police institution can change and is potentially influenced by alternative discourses and practices, specifically those characterized by generosity rather than greed, as seen in the book's conclusion.

Dark Money

Private sponsorship of public policing represents many volatilities and contradictions of policing as a dominant social institution undergoing criticism from numerous angles during a time of tremendous social change. We focus on private sponsorship of police because it straddles or implodes the conventional public-private dichotomy. In so doing, the book also shows, as noted above, that the police institution as a greedy institution extends beyond its traditional boundaries. Indeed, as we argue, the greedy institutions may upset the rule of law in efforts to extend itself and replicate. Yet, this book makes other conceptual and empirical contributions beyond the greedy institution literature, many of which are related to the police desire for and acquisition of mostly private dark money.

Focusing on private funding matters in an age of increasing exchange between private and public policing realms (Button and Wakefield 2018; White 2012) and raises questions about the influence of plural policing arrangements on the public good (van Stokkom and Terpstra 2018; O'Reilly 2015). On the one hand, for much of the 20th century the police institution was expected to receive public funds rather than operate via private monies. On the other hand, public police budgets in local US jurisdictions tend to be trimmed, and coupled with recent calls for defunding this institution, will likely step up its search for alternative sources beyond the public treasury. Long before the police defunding movement's arrival in Canada, there were taxpayer-focused efforts to reduce municipal public spending on public police. For example, in 2015 Ontario Association of Municipalities authored a major report arguing that costs of policing to municipal government budgets had become unsustainable (AMO 2015). Other data supports this. For example, a recent journalistic study found public spending on police in Canadian cities "ranges from one-tenth to nearly a third of total budgets" with a suburb of Montreal (Longueil), Winnipeg, a suburb of Vancouver (Surrey), and Vancouver proper heading the list and ranging from 21 to 29 per cent of all municipal expenditures (Cardoso and Hayes 2020). According to a recent Statistics Canada report:

> The cost of operating police services in Canada has *generally been on the increase* since 1996/1997 and continued to inch up in 2018/2019 reaching \$15.7 billion. After accounting for inflation, total operating expenditures rose by 1% from the previous year. Higher salary and non-salary costs contributed to greater operating costs overall. The cost of salaries, wages and benefits for police service personnel increased 3% in 2018/2019

> reaching $12.8 billion in 2018/2019... accounting for 81% of operating expenditures in 2018/2019 (Statistics Canada 2020; emphasis added).

This suggests public funding not only has been increasing for police but is already high compared to other services (the study noted, for example, that police outpaced costs of social services and transit). Looking at Winnipeg alone, the police budget increased 36 per cent from 2010 to 2015. Eight police officers were found to have higher public sector salaries than the sitting mayor of Winnipeg (Cardoso and Hayes 2020).

In the US, a similar picture emerges. An analysis by the Urban Institute (2021) reported: "In 2018, state and local governments spent *$119 billion on police*" (emphasis added). More journalistic research has revealed: "Over the past three decades, US cities *have allocated larger and larger shares of their budgets towards law enforcement*. Today, the US collectively spends $100 billion a year on policing" (McCarthy 2017). For these reasons, in the book's conclusion we connect our findings and arguments about police as a greedy institution to debates and movements concerning defunding police in North America.

What sponsors and donors of private funds destined for police receive in exchange for their transfer is murky and dark; whether it is a philanthropic corporate-led or individual citizenship initiative; or whether more tangible benefits are to be received in return, for example, enhanced patrols in spaces of private concern or identification of crimes that victimize a specific donor, sponsor, or industry. For paid detail arrangements this transfer of private funds to police directly leads to tangible public policing patrols to serve mostly private interests in return, although even here the perceived benefits of such patrols vary considerably and have led to controversies and scandals across North America. Other such exchanges from private to public may be disreputable (Rossman 2014). The kinds of brokers noted above, such as Houston Police Foundation or the Frizell firm, are opaque vessels that conceal what would in earlier decades be considered disreputable exchanges operating in the dark. The police institution appears here to depart from its rule of law mandate and ostensive civic, public principles and scruples (Loader 2016). When police provide a security presence for private corporations and individuals (Fleury-Steiner and Wiles 2003) their accountability, transparency and legitimacy is diminished. Police begin to appear less like public service providers and more like hired guns or, when sponsorships are created, as mobile billboards for corporations. It is worth asking what conflicts of interest and cronyism emerge (also see Maier et al. 2016; MacDonald et al. 2002). To explore this, we discern donors' identities and on what monies they provide are spent once transferred through a police foundation. Many donors are weapons and surveillance device companies, information and communication technology corporations, and real estate firms. Many expenditures are on surveillance devices and gear that can be linked to technological and militarized policing.

Public policing's dark money is not only a way for police organizations to top up their public funds. Sponsorship and donation may also lead to gradual mutations in police policies and practices. Even mundane paid detail assignments may lead to ongoing adoption of norms among officers, for example, of physical violence due to consistent exposure to the rough and tumble culture of nightclub and major league sports security scenes, while serving their private masters, rather than a public good. The coziness evident between some police departments and private sponsors raises crucial questions. Are police still adhering to the rule of law in the networks identified? Do the optics of these arrangements damage already weakened police legitimacy? Do police overlook transgressions related to sponsors' activities or expend more resources (including those provided by the sponsor or donor) on unwanted behaviour that directly harms sponsors to the neglect of less powerful victims? The potential for corruption, graft, and collusion (Jancsics 2014; Prenzler et al. 2013; Kleinig 2002; Punch 2000; Kappeler et al. 1998; New York 1972) in such arrangements raises questions about mechanisms for transparency, accountability (Walker and Archbold 2013), legitimacy (Tyler 2004), or "the public good" (Loader and Walker 2001) and about the holes or chasms in related police policies. We therefore also draw from and contribute to work on accountability, corruption, visibility (Brighenti 2007), and corporatization (McDonald 2014) in this book's analysis. Dark money alludes to the lack of transparency of private sponsorship and donor arrangements, and their potential to call the rule of law into doubt due to actual or apparent unequal treatment, which several chapters consider. Dark money also points to the creeping influence and activity of corporations in the policing realm and the effects thereof.

Another key dimension of private sponsorship and funding of police is that these arrangements raise issues ranging from the global to the granular. There is global pressure on public policing agencies to corporatize (McDonald 2014), both from the private corporate sector and sometimes governments of the day, to increase revenues and operate more like market players. From this perspective privately sponsored policing provides a case study of how police become entangled in market-based security thinking and practice (Ransley and Mazerolle 2009), which has implications for thinking about accountability (Walsh and Conway 2011; Stenning 2009) too. Private sponsorship of public policing also raises issues of officer association/union salary demands, which tend to drive up police budgets, fuelling departmental quests for alternative – private – funding sources. This quest may now be exacerbated by the defunding police movement centred on incidents of extreme police violence against racialized individuals and communities. At the granular level, the mundane, behind-the-scenes channels (galas, dinners, advertising) and organization (charitable foundations) has so far avoided scrutiny given their stark juxtaposition to the usual sense of police as action-oriented, dynamic, and visible. Police sponsorship remains invisible to the public except through visible advertising of the sponsor on police vehicles or uniforms, marketing which has avoided public scorn, as this book illustrates.

Research Design

Our research design draws from several complementary, mostly qualitative, methods to study private sponsorship and funding of police: interviews with police sponsors, police foundation representatives, brokers and other funders of paid detail services, and various police personnel, including some officers. Access to officers regarding paid detail services was especially difficult, however, due to a reluctance to speak about paid detail assignments that often-added tens of thousands of dollars to officers' annual salaries; police administrators, brokers, and funders of these services were far more willing to be interviewed. Participants were identified in media accounts of police sponsorships and paid detail policing, police service websites, and the acquired police paid duty assignment logs and sponsorship or donation records. Overall, we sought interviewees from every department that had sponsors, paid detail, and a police foundation, if only an administrator or external paid detail funder. Fundamental to our design were FOI requests for private sponsorship as well as paid detail documents, including policies and other records, government charity records; archival research into donation, sponsorship, and paid detail policies and practices of police departments; and collection and examination of accounts or reviews of private funding of police arrangements and media coverage of private sponsorship and funding of police pertaining to 104 North American departments. Our research design therefore provides an example of how to use FOI in conjunction with interviews in police research. We would also say our research was motivated by an investigative ethos not unlike that of an investigative journalist as much of these data required digging deep below the surface of these murky transaction and exchanges to try to locate patterns, themes, and connections. We anonymize our interviews and use an asterisk to refer to places in some cases to protect anonymity in the analyses below.

While private sponsorship and funding of police is burgeoning in countries like Australia and the United Kingdom (UK), which we also discuss in Chapters Two and Four, we focused on North American departments since sponsorship may well be most developed there. The US and Canada are suitable jurisdictions to explore private sponsorship and funding and to some extent compare for three reasons. First, in both countries police tend to be viewed as more significant and legitimate than private security, which may not be so in other countries. Second, both countries contain provincial/state and municipal jurisdictions. We explore this variation in these two countries in the substantive chapters of the book. Third, the US and Canada have not thus far corporatized or privatized public policing to the extent we have seen elsewhere, meaning our study investigates private police funding and sponsorship at the precipice of monumental institutional change. While North America is our research focus, in Chapter Four we provide a glimpse of police sponsorship and funding in other countries too using examples drawn from media sources with an eye to showing similarities and differences. There is variation within and across these provincial, state, and municipal jurisdictions, compared say to the UK where there are far fewer police departments and those that exist are controlled tightly by a national government. This variation in the US and Canada is rich to explore. However, there are also key differences in the two countries. One difference is that police departments and officers in Canada are typically well funded and paid at the municipal or local level, but this is less true of the US. Our sample is biased toward larger police departments since they tend to store private sponsorship and paid detail police records (some smaller departments do not) we could then acquire via FOI requests. These documents were unavailable elsewhere for research purposes, making use of FOI necessary.

Roadmap

This book is organized into seven chapters, an introduction, and a conclusion. In this introduction, we have introduced key themes and arguments, defined terms, identified some conceptual and empirical contributions, and described the design of the study on which the book is based. Below we provide a road map of how the chapters in the remainder of the book unfold.

Chapter 1 – Theorizing the Flow of Dark Money in Policing: From Gifts to the Greedy Institution situates the book conceptually. We discuss gift theory in relation to police funding and then introduce Lewis Coser's notion of the greedy institution as an alternative. We elaborate the shortcomings of viewing police sponsorship and donations as gifts in previous literature. We also discuss criminology and criminal justice literatures about the rule of law, accountability, and corporatization to theorize private sponsorship and funding of police. This chapter argues for the need to examine how police institution's claims surrounding funding are framed as well as the related exchanges of various forms of capital in networks. Next, we discuss corporatization and its relationship to police as a greedy institution to answer the question of whether there is a broader idea that anchors the chapters in this book. In this way, we suggest corporatization is preferable to neo-liberalism and that corporatization and greed go hand in hand or are mutually constitutive. The chapter then introduces police sponsorship and foundations as well as paid detail as the main forms to be interrogated in the book, in relation to the concept of police as a greedy institution.

Chapter 2 – Mapping the Police Funding Terrain: Donors, Sponsors, Foundations, Paid Detail, Forfeiture and Beyond provides details and examples of private funding of police drawn from our extensive research. For this effort we analyze FOI requests, government charity records, as well as relevant funder and police websites and interviews with funders and police. We first explain key differences and overlaps among gratuities, donations or gifts, sponsorships, and partnerships in police departments across North America. The monetary values of reported donations or gifts to police departments are found to be often modest, though they vary widely and are sometimes substantial. The level of capital stemming from other forms, such as longer-standing foundations, is decidedly more substantial. This chapter identifies and discusses history, prevalence, and size of each major funding type, that is, foundations and paid detail. The chapter also details donation and sponsorship policies of eight police departments of varying sizes and locations in North America before concluding by discussing Crime Stoppers and civil forfeiture as additional funding forms as well as overlap among the various forms and funding networks.

Chapter 3 – Glossing over the Greedy Institution: Views from Inside Police Foundations draws from FOI disclosures, interviews, and websites to explore what police foundation board members say about police foundations they create and sustain. We argue police foundations are shell corporations, and we index their features to literatures on police accountability, transparency, corruption, and legal regulation. We draw from literature on corporate philanthropy and interlocks as well as state-corporate synergies to make sense of these new entities. The chapter commences by discussing origins, goals, and motivations of police foundations in detail. Next, we explore using extensive excerpts directly from interviews with foundation personnel, how they understand foundation boards, donors, and networks. The funding for local and truly needy groups is shown to be mostly a diversion from the real transfer of economic and social capital from corporate and other private or external interests to police, thus serving as a gloss to cover over the harsh terrain of a greedy institution for audiences.

Chapter 4 – Corporate-Police Partnerships and the Extension of Greed uses websites and interviews pertaining to sponsors and donors to elaborate dark money and corporate-police partnerships. We elaborate what sponsors and donors claim to derive from their efforts as well as what they may gain in exchange. We contribute to literature on motivations of corporate donors and sponsors (Aymaliev 2017). This chapter explores what police and the proliferating organizations that increasingly extend their voices and speak on their behalf – police foundations – say about private sponsorship and funding. This chapter uses FOI disclosures and interview data as well as media accounts of police sponsorship to do so. We critically assess some claimed benefits for these individuals and organizations in the US and Canada. We also explore examples of private sponsorship of public policing beyond North America where it is nascent or entails lesser or greater volumes of exchange, with emphasis on Australia and the UK. We draw attention to similarities and differences in the organization and outcomes of these arrangements.

Chapter 5 – Shadow Figures: Paid Detail Policing as Private Funding and the New Brokers examines the widespread arrangements variously termed paid detail, paid duty, and extra duty or collectively "police moonlighting." We examine these paid detail practices and argue they are a largely hidden form of mostly private police sponsorship and funding and suggest that these funders provide "easy money" assignments for police. We document aspects of these practices including moral regulation in these lucrative assignments. We argue that police departments, in prohibiting some types of funders and particular objects such as cash or sexualized spaces they deem to be immoral in paid detail, reflect a greedy institution that seeks control over its members' conduct, even where they lack the ability to directly monitor it. We also discuss how paid detail works in these private environments that may lead, like other private funding, to troubling mutations in police practice. We also explore the influence, exchanges and framing associated with new and growing commercial paid detail brokers that arrange and funnel funding into police officer pockets well beyond their regular salaries.

Chapter 6 – Framing Dark Money as Community Benefit explores communications appearing on police foundation websites. In other chapters, we examine some emergent networks among corporations, police foundations, and police. This chapter explores the visual politics of police foundation communications to show how they seek to recruit economic and social capital for police foundations and ultimately the police institution itself. We show how these forms of framing construe dark money and the networks it engenders as community benefit. We critically assess police foundation framing that suggests the work of foundations is primarily about community development. We argue this framing is crucial to the operations of the greedy institution, as it aligns other groups, organizations, and interests with the police. We show numerous visual components of framing. In documenting how crucial this framing is to police, we connect our inquiry to literature on police engagement with media and their use of social media. The character of these communications reveals the police foundation is enlisted as part of the greedy police institution. Police foundations and police departments engage in framing to convey ideas and convince audiences of their veracity and construe the positive community value of exchanges. These police foundation communications, we argue, are meant to mainly distract from the shifting of funds from corporations to foundations and, in turn, from foundations to police. Police foundations are aware of this image of police, and they launder the reputation of police as well as social and economic capital emanating from the corporate realm that is transferred to police.

Chapter 7 – Controversies and Holes in Private Police Funding Policy discusses controversies and holes in police department policies and the need for reform across jurisdictions. We discuss key controversies in funding in Los Angeles and other cities. We contend the holes revealed in these controversies show the need for greater transparency, regulation, and enforcement to ensure adherence to the rule of law and avoid corruption and further militarization, as well as to achieve community control. One key reform would entail illuminating hidden funders for public viewing. Another reform of paid detail arrangements involves implementing random assignments of officers to avoid corruption. We then focus on two expanding holes for the future. The first is the growth in police foundations in the US. The second is the stunning growth in US commercial paid detail broker contracts with departments. Both may further darken funding networks. We remark how policies do not set an absolute limit on the level of private funding a department can receive, which is a greedy institution's dream. Considering the sobering record of police reform in North America, we assess prospects to make sponsorship and private funding of policing more accountable and suggest banning sponsorship, foundations, and paid detail from police departments all together. Finally, we argue some reform efforts have already stalled or failed, including efforts to defund the police themselves, implying reform will be difficult due to the power and size of funding networks and their framing apparatus, and the greedy institution's obsession with reproducing itself.

Conclusion: The Future of Private Sponsorship and Funding of Police: Greed to Generosity, Dark Money to Defunding, and Beyond reviews the main arguments and findings of the book. We connect these to our core concepts and trends in criminology, criminal justice, law, and sociology literatures. We review why scholars in these disciplines should find the outcomes of this research enlightening. We point to future avenues of research into private funding of police. We also discuss possible effects of the new global defunding movement in relation to private funding and sponsorship. We argue that the defunding movement points out many problems with policing, but that a greedy institution is as much about social and political capital as it is about finances, which has implications for understanding police power and how it is replicated. Finally, we consider what policing in a generous society might look like to replace a greedy institution and its dark money desires.

Chapter 1

Theorizing the Flow of Dark Money in Policing

From Gifts to the Greedy Institution

Introduction: Dark Money and the Gift

This chapter sets out to conceptualize and explain issues of police sponsorship, police foundations, and other forms of dark money in policing. Dark money is the shadowy exchange of money and other resources to expand organizations and the political footprint of those organizations (Mayer 2016). Here, dark money refers to the expanding social, political, and cultural footprint of the police and the role of private and corporate money in that process. These developments in police resource acquisition are occurring during a specific juncture in history. We are seeing rapid development of third-party policing and private security (Ransley and Mazerolle 2009). We are seeing contests over policing whereby police are more aggressively attempting to display expertise and relevance (Côté-Lussier 2013). We are also witnessing a social movement to defund and abolish police that broke through in 2020, but has roots in community struggles against police violence reaching back decades. There seems to be little question that police legitimacy is eroding. The police response entails boosting their image (Mawby and Worthington 2002), expanding their networks, as well as attracting, arranging, and even coercing more capital. We see police sponsorship, police foundations, paid detail services, and other forms of what we call dark money in policing, as more than an economic or financial issue. These issues are social and political too.

The main work conceptualizing dynamics of police resources in the 21st century is by Julie Ayling, Peter Grabosky, and Clifford Shearing (2009) entitled *Lengthening the Arm of the Law*. The book is an insightful exploration of the issue of police resources. Ayling and colleagues cover a lot of ground. They examine police as buyers of information, technologies, services, and discuss police as sellers of security and assurance. In a sense, police tout a brand, one that offers the promise of command and authority. Ayling and colleagues (2009) rely on the sociology and anthropology of the gift to conceptualize these exchanges. Relying on gift theory situates this work in a lineage of sociologists and anthropologists reaching back to Marcel Mauss. Ayling and colleagues conceptualize private sponsorship as gift giving, and

DOI: 10.4324/9781003167914-2

they dig into those elements of sponsorship that can be conceptualized as such, exploring the benefits for givers and receivers of the gift. Ayling and colleagues (2009) acknowledge an element of coercion in these relationships. They invoke an element of power in their inquiry, but ultimately rely on an idea of ambiguous exchange. They use gift theory to explain exchanges of money and other forms of capital that are ambiguous or peculiar and which police must manage. From this point of view, the sponsorship that police receive is not normatively wrong or politically misguided. It is not really a social problem or a threat to democracy. It is not bad public policy or a slippery slope leading to corruption. It is merely ambiguous, and peculiar. The possibility of a conflict of interest apparently exists, but Ayling and colleagues do not pursue it to any extent.

There are many other works that extend the anthropology and the sociology of the gift, such as Godbout's (1998) work with A. Caillé. For Godbout and A. Caillé, the gift creates what they call a "strange loop" in requiring future reciprocation. The gift creates reciprocal future indebtedness. In this sense, we have no problem with gift conceptualization. It is a useful explanation, and such exchanges are part of what we explore in the chapters that follow. Yet, we would contend that this gift framework is limited in several ways. Foremost, the idea of the gift in anthropology assumes a broader symbolic constellation of connected institutions that are committed to ensuring the success of one another's future endeavours. In policing, this could be true to the extent private individuals and corporations and police have mutually shared interests and endeavours they wish to see continue. However, the gift framework leaves out many players and actors in these relations, such as those subject to police interventions and encounters (the public) and what they gain or lose in the process.

There is also a literature in criminology and other social science disciplines examining gifts to police and the potential for graft (Prenzler et al. 2013; Coleman 2004). However, this literature assumes that the gift is about the supply from donors or givers and that the rule of law is operating relatively unimpaired. The cultural, social, and political implications are not the focus. For us, the world of the gift is important to explore and books by Ayling and colleagues and Godbout and Caillé admirably deploy this concept. However, we offer an alternative approach to theorizing the relations involved in police sponsorship and funding to move beyond the assumptions of gift theory and extend the critical analysis of these dynamics. This alternative explanation is a needed one that is not only more critical but also accounts better for the institutional power relations such exchanges entail.

As Diphoorn and Grassiani (2016) argue, policing is never only about law enforcement and is always about a broader set of relations and networks supporting a specific political and economic order. Within these relationships, organizations attempt to collect and convert various forms of capital to extend and enhance their operations. The accumulation and conversion of this economic, social, and cultural capital help to replicate that organization and similar entities. They argue what is needed is a:

> processual-relational approach that is based on the translation and conversion of other types of capital, such as economic and social, to acquire a position of power within a specific (security) 'field' (Diphoorn and Grassiani 2016, 430).

They refer to the overall process as securitizing capital. This approach obviously is indebted to Pierre Bourdieu's understanding of social, cultural, and symbolic capital, the last of which refers to the conversion of any other form of capital. The concept of securitizing capital refers to "the process whereby different security actors use various forms of capital, both intentionally and unintentionally, to acquire legitimacy and power" (431). As they argue:

> symbolic capital, especially legitimacy and authority, is the one possible end result and that other forms of capital are translated and converted for this goal… different types of capital, such as social and economic capital, are mobilized in order to acquire symbolic capital in the field of security (436).

The police foundation, a key focus of this book, is central to these processes of capital attraction and conversion. While we appreciate the attempt to reach outside criminological theory (into anthropology) to conceive these exchanges, gift theory does not interrogate and destabilize these obscure flows and disreputable relations enough. Gift theory may also have to be contorted to apply to private funding of police. As a corrective or simply novel theorization, we draw from and apply greedy institution theory to all forms of private funding of police. The notion of the greedy institution better encapsulates the drive from inside a police department to accumulate social, economic, and political capital from outside it.

From Gifts to the Greedy Institution

Lewis Coser advanced the idea of greedy institutions throughout the mid-20th century in several now-classic sociological works. For Coser (1974), a greedy institution is one that seeks exclusive and undivided loyalty. Coser argues a greedy institution does not involve as much physical control as a total institution, famously described by Goffman (1961), or as found in totalitarian societies. A greedy institution is perhaps more suited to the modern era that values individual freedom and autonomy, but nonetheless manages and manipulates freedom and autonomy in institutional forms. For Coser, the greedy institution exercises power over individuals and over the relations of persons working or living in that institution. It does so without physical barriers, and through other measures designed to secure sustained inundation by the institution and enduring loyalty. The greedy institution also tends to sever relations with other bodies or organizations that will not conform to the greedy institution's worldview. At a psycho-social level, the greedy institution attempts to consume the mental space or worldview of the individual and replace it with its own.

Many types of institutions have been studied using the greedy institution framework. Some have argued the military is an exemplar of a greedy institution that severs member relations with other types of institutions and other persons and demands absolute loyalty and conformity to the martial worldview (Vuga and Juvan 2013). Others have argued the family exemplifies a greedy institution that demands conformity and promotes the primacy of itself among all individual members (Segal 1986). The idea of a greedy institution has not disappeared with the emergence of online forms of communication which seem to erode the primacy of big institutions in our lives (Cox 2016; De Campo 2013). The concept of a greedy institution still applies to many sets of relations in our world despite the proliferation of movements against modern institutions or the fragmentation of the modern social order (Beck 1992; Giddens 1991).

Police are a greedy institution. We are not the first to claim this. However, most literature on the police as a greedy institution has tended to focus downward or inward (Cox 2016). It has been an insular-looking framework focused on the individual members of the institution and their levels of conformity. The tendency in this literature is to examine how the greedy institution manages or manipulates its own individual members and assures loyalty and conformity within the institution (De Campo 2013). Literature on police socialization and police culture shows this loyalty and conformity being manufactured through police training and interactions and workplace practices and rituals. Norman Conti (2009, 2006) points to this system of shaming those who deviate from police culture, honouring those who remain loyal, and how forms of socialization in policing replicate this police culture to assure conformity to, and in essence, replicate the greedy institution. Police members are to abide by the police culture behind the "blue wall" of silence. The greedy police institution's focus on individual members also sometimes entails a kind of moral regulation of officers as we show in Chapter Five on paid detail. Coser's (1974) work predates the moral regulation concept, perhaps best explained by Hunt (1997) as governance of the self and others driven by knowledge of morality and risk, but some of what Coser says regarding greedy institutional practices is plainly about moral regulation of members. For example, Coser (1974, 15–16) suggests greedy institutions often attend to sexual attachments of their members and we show in paid detail there are rules about officers' proximity to sexualized objects and spaces while on "easy money" assignments funded through those networks.

These are important works because Conti (2009, 2006) and many others writing about police culture show how this loyalty to policing is assembled through daily institutional practices in ways that create a uniform worldview to which police officers must be loyal or risk shame or ostracization. In this sense, police are an incredibly greedy institution; they demand everything of their members. This differs from a total institution because police officers are not physically threatened or restricted in the ways that someone might be in, for example, a mental asylum. The effect of the greedy institution can nonetheless be totalizing. Although there are mirages of choice and flexibility for the members of this police culture, as literature has explored, police culture leads to many problems such as institutionalized racism, sexism, as well as homophobia (Campeau 2015; Loftus 2010). This begins with police socialization (Van Maanen 1975) and is rehearsed and re-instilled in many ways through officers' careers. It also leads to police corruption. As many scholars of police corruption have noted, its link to police culture is strong (Punch 2000), and the foundation of police corruption is the abuse of power with impunity.

Pointing to the role of police socialization in creating the conditions for replication of the greedy institution, Abby Peterson and Sarah Uhnoo (2012) examined police as a greedy institution in research on ethnic minority police officers as outsiders within police departments. They assert ethnic minority police officers are subjected to daily trials of loyalty that are difficult to endure and have a dual function. First, they continually test the minority officers' loyalty and conformity to the greedy institution. Second, by doing so, these tests replicate the institutional form of greediness and perpetuate policing as an institution into the future. This is an important dimension of the greedy institutional framework, the idea of how police as a socially necessary institution is reproduced. For us, greediness begins with this tendency to demand conformity and loyalty of its members, and we explore this in relation to paid detail especially. But as we will also explore, and as Peterson and Uhnoo (2012) claim, the greedy institution requires its members to give preference and priority to participation in the institution's routines and how it organizes ideas and knowledge to underscore or make sense of that information. As we will argue, the networks of dark money that have emerged around policing in many ways extend this greedy institution. It is greedy in the sense that it demands conformity, loyalty, and replication of policing. It demands conformity of other organizations and their mandates to the police's own, not simply downward and inward for its own members, but outward into an expanding, extensive web of external persons and organizations. This is what makes policing and the issue of police resources one that befits the idea of a greedy institution. Second, it is a literal form of greediness too in that police demand more and more of the public purse and now corporate and other private money as well. The greediness seems to expand as well in ways we explore in later chapters.

Before further explaining this outward, extending view of the greedy institution in the policing field, we draw attention to Amanda Cox's (2016) argument that greedy institutions are only able to secure such loyalty and conformity through the operation of frames or communication mechanisms. Cox reminds us that the greedy institution attempts to minimize participation in outside social spheres and minimize associations, among other organizations, and to limit the number of associations, channelling them to the greedy institution as a vital node. Cox argues the identity of the members starts to become shaped in the image of the greedy institution, that there is a promotion of a specialness, which becomes an element of the allure of membership. Finally, there can be trials of worthiness that can eliminate members who do not display loyalty and conformity (687). All these dimensions of the greedy institution are enabled by framing and communication. These ideas are not written down in a policing handbook. It happens through police communications inside the institution but as we will show, outside, too. Police communications are meant to manipulate the interest of listeners and audiences to agree with the police view of the world and treat it as legitimate in their own future actions. More attention needs to be placed on the mechanisms by which greedy institutions operate and are replicated, and this applies downward or inward and how internal loyalty is reproduced. However, as we examine in this book, there is no shortage of connections that police have outwardly in the community, in neighbourhoods, with the state and corporations. These networks become notable in the field of sponsorship, in the arena of exchanges that police foundations enable, as well as in paid detail policing. We underscore this phenomenon in this book, although we know much more research remains to be done in this regard.

A Greedy Institution and Networks

Rather than focussing only on the flow of money in police sponsorship, police foundations, and paid detail arrangements, we want to provide a theoretical framing that accounts for the other social, political, and cultural dimensions of dark money. To do so, it is necessary to situate the police as a greedy institution in state and corporate networks, understanding that greedy networks turn outward and make similar demands of loyalty and conformity through these exchanges. The greedy institution is all about maximizing loyalty and conformity.

There is some sociological and political science literature that has explored the state-corporate symbiosis that appears in forms of governance and sponsorship (O'Reilly 2010). This symbiosis is one where the allegiances and alliances of those participating bodies are being fused. However, when one of the parties or more in that relationship is a greedy institution, that institution does not suddenly give up its tendency to demand loyalty and conformity and to cull entities lacking these qualities. That same tendency is reproduced outward and in an extending motion through the interactions and communications beyond the blue wall. In this sense, we do not see the exchanges in police sponsorship as "ambiguous" as Ayling and colleagues (2009) put it.

There is very little ambiguity in this field. Police are a greedy institution, and they are entering these exchanges to maximize the loyalty and conformity to police. This is an economic project insofar as it pertains to accumulating resources, but it is also a political and social project and perhaps that is the primary way to understand it. It is about aligning several political interests to fashion police into a more and more powerful political player in municipalities, regions, and throughout the countries where this is occurring. Policing is a cultural phenomenon to the extent people begin to associate with the police image or myth, as members of the police do inside the greedy institution. It is a social project, since it is about accumulating social capital, not only donors to police but also defenders of policing at a time when police work has never been under more criticism with the focus on defunding and even abolishing the police. Among other responses to those criticisms, such as the thin blue line metaphor, which police translate into symbols and patches used to adorn their uniforms, the accumulation of economic, social, and other kinds of capital through sponsorship and the types of exchanges that foundations engage in must be seen as a way of shoring up police power. Thus, police sponsorship, foundations, and paid detail arrangements are not only about providing police resources but also police power in our age of Black Lives Matter, Idle No More, and other movements that have made compelling and pointed critiques of police power and the police institution that has marginalized Black, Indigenous, and People of Color (BIPOC).

Understanding police as a greedy institution, looking downwardly or inwardly, is already an accepted conceptual practice in criminology and sociology (De Campo 2013). Literature on police culture and police socialization provides countless examples of this. Lewis Coser's work (1974) is invoked in some studies. There is barely any institution in our contemporary world that demands as much loyalty and conformity as police and that has endured the fragmentation of modern society with so little change. Police are dinosaurs romping around in the Anthropocene. Most other institutions have changed radically in the last 30 to 40 years. For example, the family has mutated. As Beck (1992) and Giddens (1991) point out, grand transformations of most of society's institutions have occurred. Not so with the police. This is, we contend, because police operate so effectively as a greedy institution. The emergence and expansion of new forms of police sponsorship, police foundations, paid detail, and other forms of what we call dark money in policing are mutations in this greedy endeavour. One of our main contributions is to suggest this tendency to demand conformity and loyalty does not only point downward or inward to the members. It points outward too. It is extended in all police relations. We also contend this outward extension happens through networks and is consistent – not exclusively, but to a great extent – with corporatization.

Networks, Capital, and Framing

To extend the footprint of police outward through the development of additional police resources, we argue that three main mechanisms are required: networks, capital, and framing. This focus comes from our reading of literature on police culture and police organizations. These mechanisms enable police to be a greedy institution internally and it follows that these mechanisms enable police to extend their reach outward too.

The work of securing loyalty and conformity happens in networks. Networks are channels for the conveyance of forms of capital. The expansion of networks is a manoeuvre of position as police seek to maintain or enhance their status in their respective jurisdiction. The study of security networks in criminology and criminal justice studies has expanded considerably in the past two decades (Shearing and Johnston 2010; Terpstra 2008; Dupont 2006, 2004; Gill 2006; Shearing 2005). Networks comprise "nodes" which are key actors and sites of governance. Nodes are not only public; rather, "[n]odes can be public, private or hybrid institutions and may include anything from police departments to private corporations..." (Huey et al. 2012, 84). Nodes include "individuals, groups (and parts of groups), organizations (and parts of organizations), or states" (Shearing and Johnston 2010, 501); a way of conceiving what is governed; ways of shaping conduct; operational resources; and an institutional structure enabling these elements (Burris, Drahos and Shearing 2005, 11–12; Bien 1997). These networks allow police to reach outside themselves into other organizations and agencies. Sponsorship, foundations, and paid detail create new networks to expand the reach of police. These networks are new opportunities to test loyalty and obtain conformity among organizations that become nodes in the sense above. Some are their own greedy institutions. This is true of private corporations that sponsor police, as we show in Chapter Four. They also seek brand loyalty through their corporate cultures. It is the meeting of these two greedy institutions, which appear to have shared interests, where loyalty to a brand intermix and at least temporarily gel, that makes an exploration of policing's dark money so intellectually intriguing and conceptually rich. All these nodes beyond the police entail at least some kind of exchange with police or even kinds of coercion by police, for example, regarding paid detail where laws and in some documented instances, police themselves demand funding from potentially reluctant organizations and individuals as we show in Chapters Five and Seven. This can even entail coercion of ill-fitting ideas or values until they are rendered mutual interests leading to new sponsorship or a paid detail gig, forcing disparate aims of these nodes to intermix. If there is one thing lacking in analyses of policing and security networks in ours and others' reading of the literature, as insightful as it often is – whether due to a lack of data or ignorance – the presence of kinds of coercion in networks between nodes. Our analysis of police as a greedy institution operating in and extending such networks promises to reveal coercion by and in communications with other nodes, and sometimes a decidedly more alarming kind of implied physical coercion with which police have become closely associated, and which many suggest defines them.

The communications and manoeuvres in security networks are further about exchanging social, political, and economic capital and expanding the footprint of the police in political and cultural terms. Police scholars have remarked upon police using a Bourdieusian framework. Wood (2004, 36) has noted "police have been emphasizing the specific capitals they have accumulated over time (political, cultural, symbolic) in challenging the legitimacy of non-state providers of security." Chan (2003, 36) describes police requirements for social, cultural, and other capitals. While these authors and the security network and user-pays policing literatures lend insight into themes discussed below (e.g., Lippert et al. 2016), they have not fully explored capital exchanges, save for Dupont (2004). Capital is the prize for police in these networks, but economic capital is not the foremost payoff. Social capital and political capital may be far more important to expanding the police mission and this greedy institution's sought-after treasures.

Drawing on Bourdieu's (1989) studies of capital exchange, Dupont (2004) outlines a typology of five forms of capital relevant to security networks and nodes: economic, symbolic, cultural, social, and political (also see Huey et al. 2012). First, *economic* capital refers to financial resources. Second, for Dupont (2004, 86), *symbolic* capital is about legitimacy, "power … to speak with authority to other actors." Third, *cultural* capital refers to police knowledge, proficiency, and expertise, such as in criminal intelligence and intelligence-led policing (Dupont 2004, 85–86). Fourth, *social* capital is the "set of social relations that allow the constitution, maintenance, and expansion of social networks," which is also associated with opportunities for political favours and corruption (Crawford 2006; Dupont 2004, 86). Finally, Dupont (2004, 85) indicates that *political* capital "derives from the proximity of actors to the machinery of government and their capacity to influence or direct this machinery toward their own objectives" (also see Martin 2013). In policing and security literature, study of the *volume* of capital exchanged is limited, but the same could be said about the function and purpose of this exchange. These forms of capital are the reward for successfully achieving loyalty and conformity among other agencies and organizations. We are arguing the networks established and the capital that flows as a result is not merely an economic issue but is centrally about replicating policing as a worldview.

As Cox (2016) argues, greedy institutions can only secure loyalty and conformity through communication mechanisms. Debates about frame analysis are long-standing in the social sciences (cf. Denzin and Keller 1981; Goffman 1981). Acknowledging there are more ethnomethodological and more structuralist approaches, we draw from literature that conceives of framing as human activity that organizes information to emphasize, highlight, or make sense of that information in specific ways (Kuypers 2005). As Kuypers and Cooper (2005, 2) put it, "framing thus elevates the salience of some facts over others." In other words, framing serves to "punctuate, elaborate" (Creed et al. 2002, 37) and otherwise define an issue. In this way, framing can inform what issues people think about and how they interpret events. The work of framing involves some people (e.g., police public relations officers) deciding what information to include (say, in a visual display) and what to exclude. People engaged in framing draw from cultural stocks of knowledge (VanGorp 2007), readily apparent ideas that users of the framed information can comprehend. Police communications, internal and external, are about enforcing police views and visions of the world to retain members and recruit more allegiances. The public relations machines that police have built (Lee and McGovern 2013) are designed to attract more and more allegiances to police. These frames convey the message to be loyal and to conform to the police view of the world. Consuming police frames reduces the number of other worldviews about social or other issues that will resonate in communications. Police frames are attempts to align diverse political, cultural, and economic views with the police institution, although as we show sometimes these efforts are outsourced to other entities (such as police foundations or commercial paid detail brokers) to undertake and manage. Police networks, capital, and communications are the essential components of the police as a greedy institution turned outward and facing the world.

Corporatization and Greedy Institutions

One conceptual question raised by these developments in policing is this: where did they come from? Is there a bigger idea that explains it all? While we think it is never so simple and do not intend here to offer a totalizing theoretical contribution, clearly some bigger ideas and processes are at work. It would be easy to respond by invoking "neo-liberalism." While some aspects of these economic formations no doubt have neo-liberal characteristics, they lack many others. For example, neo-liberalism as a mentality of governance calls for the shrinking of state agencies (belt-tightening, defunding of social welfare, see Brady and Lippert 2016), whereby the state shifts from "rowing" to "steering" the ship (Crawford 2006). With the police institution, we mostly see expansion in the past half century. With recent developments in policing, we see even more expansion.

O'Malley and Hutchinson (2007) argue corporatization has permeated the police institution. They contend police managers and police unions have displayed corporatized tendencies for several decades. Corporatization incorporates mechanisms of governing from the private sector and deploys them in the public sector. Corporatization is about winning. This might seem like an odd mentality to permeate the public sector. However, O'Malley and Hutchinson (2007) argue corporatization has made police more competitive. For example, they show how due to corporatization police started to view private security as competition and began to play hard ball for more contracts and greater jurisdictional coverage in North American cities. Police would attempt to discredit, deride, or distance themselves from competitors, mainly private security, but also community-based or other security providers (such as ambassador uniformed patrols, see Sleiman and Lippert 2010). In this sense, police exhibit a sort of coercive corporatization. It is a competitive outlook and worldview, and if you are not aligned with police, you are a problem. This is referred to elsewhere as police expansionism (Côté-Lussier 2013). O'Malley and Hutchinson (2007) suggest this corporatization was exhibited primarily by police executives rather than street-level police or police unions. However, we are not so certain police unions are without their own competitive outlook and worldview. As Fleming et al. (2006, 78) explain concerning Australia, "Police unions are central to the public police organisations' decision-making processes and practice" and "they are well connected and use their various networks effectively to advance their aims and objectives." Burgess (2006, 150) similarly notes police unions "are key bodies involved in the shaping of police workplace conditions and policing policy." Burpo (1971) earlier argued that police unions developed strategies for getting what they want from whomever they want it. These range from hard bargaining with municipal and other governments, to mild forms of protest, to abuse of practices like ticketing, to work stoppages, sick calls, and mass resignations (25–30). The Toronto Police Association's Operation True Blue campaign in the early 2000s that we discuss in Chapter Four is a clear example of this. Juris and Feuille (1973) likewise argue the rise of police unions in North America led to the emergence of police militancy. This militancy existed in the union against police administrators, but also against politicians and local governments (Duncan and Walby 2022). Police have positioned themselves as standing alone against competitors in security provision, but also against a supposedly hostile public. The response, however, has not been to become tyrannical in orientation. Rather, to go back to O'Malley and Hutchinson (2007), the police institution as an assembly of entities (executives, unions, officers) is corporatized to the extent they stifle competition and attempt to align the interests of others with police.

All this has required selling the police worldview more than imposing it on people. It has necessitated the development of arms-length, non-public shell corporations for moving money (police foundations), and a whole array of processes that are corporate in nature. For example, some fundraising efforts of police foundations resemble the strategies of for-profit companies rather than public, government agencies. Fundraising is one aspect of the work of police foundations that appears corporate in nature. Vancouver Police Foundation, especially, has been pushing the boundaries of police fundraising. In 2011, the organization established a relationship with the large drugstore chain London Drugs, whose customers could donate to the Vancouver Police Foundation or purchase a $20 "I Love Vancouver" t-shirt, with proceeds to the Foundation (Marketwire Canada 2011). More recently, London Drugs and Vancouver Police Foundation partnered on the Kops Shades for Kids Campaign. Aviator sunglasses – "a signature look inherently tied to police" – were sold for $20, with proceeds to the Foundation (Canadian Government News 2014). In 2016, Calgary Police Foundation copied the Aviator fundraising strategy. Enrolling a corporation to collect funds for a police foundation in a commercial context shows how foundations broker police legitimacy to arrange the reach of foundations into the private realm and expect outsiders to loyally comply by purchasing these items in support. These are corporatized strategies, spanning public and private, and aligning the interests of others with those of police.

In some government sectors, including policing, "state intervention is being withdrawn, in other areas it is redrawn, and in still others it is being extended" (Crawford 2006, 471). Corporatization of police is redrawing and extending police operations and it further institutionalizes police powers, syphoning private resources to augment state power. However, the greedy institution framework we have proposed is more cogent, we believe, in revealing how institutions compel or invite conformity with their approach and exchange capital than the corporatization model. But these models are not separate in practice; rather they feed each other and converge. Corporatization encourages greed in the sense we understand it and greed leads to more corporatization in the ways discussed above. What we explore is how corporatization amplifies or augments this greedy institutional tendency of police.

Police Sponsorship, Foundations, and Greedy Institution

It follows that police sponsorship is a key dimension of the police as a greedy institution. The request for sponsorship is part of the demand in the equation. However, the demand is not simply, or even primarily, financial, as police have already received copious amounts of funding through tax dollars. The demand is more than that. It is about loyalty and conformity to a police view of how to address social unrest, distress, and transgressions in our communities and broader society, a view that ensures the replication of police.

As suggested above regarding nodes, we also explore the supply side, which is the motivations of corporate sponsors and donors and others, and those may align very clearly with the police worldview. A few but not all reflect those of greedy institutions too, as an effort to capture police loyalty while police seek theirs. But as we examine in Chapter Four, there could be varied motivations for donating to police (Aymaliev 2017). It is possible to examine both as specific phenomena requiring investigation, both motivations for sponsoring or donating to police and the police view of those funds and donors and sponsors. In fact, we contend at least some other organizations that sponsor, donate, and purchase services, such as for-profit private corporations are also greedy institutions in the same sense as above. We will show in later chapters the degree of correspondence between some greedy institutions and the police who extend their demands for loyalty and conformity into the world and the motivations of sponsors and buyers of police services. However, our main point is the greedy institution does not simply look downward or inward, it extends outward, and, in its relations, it similarly demands conformity and loyalty.

The issue of sponsorship and the expansive growth of police foundations especially from this framework is not merely about dollars and cents. It is about politics and expanding the political and cultural footprint of the police. It is in a nutshell an attempt to replicate itself. This pertains to the more ostentatious forms such as branding on police cars, which demonstrates a manufactured alignment of police with private corporate interests and vice versa (Fleury-Steiner and Wiles 2003; also see Chapter Four), but it goes for the more surreptitious forms of sponsorship as well that are funnelled through foundations and largely obscured paid detail arrangements. What is especially fascinating about the latter arrangements, and which could not be more revealing of police as a greedy institution, is how they demand a certain morality of conduct of its officer members even as they are permitted, through department sanctioned arrangements, to provide security for external organizations (see Chapters Five and Seven). Though varied, there are some clear commonalities among the rules determining where and how officers can work as well as to what physical objects they can be in proximity. Indeed, the very notion it is an officer's "detail" or "duty", in paid detail policies and practices, even as they demand funding of these comparatively easy money jobs (sometimes through subtle coercion) in other organizations, that shows the inside and outside working together at once. These processes demand conformity and loyalty outwardly as well to recruit new members, but also to recruit people into the police point of view and social, cultural, financial resources, and relations. The processes we examine can be further theorized using the greedy institution approach, some of which we leave for subsequent chapters.

Police sponsorship entails primarily corporate and other mostly private entities transferring funds to police. Sometimes this occurs directly. But there are sometimes laws or rules that potentially prohibit too large of a single donation (albeit not an overall limit on private funds that can be received – see Chapter Seven), in direct terms. Police foundations have emerged to receive these donations and to distribute them to police. Social media describes these donations and the subsequent forms of giving as philanthropy, as gifts that produce further gifts that then produce goodness in the world (see Chapter Seven). There is a public relations dimension to this. The police foundation has emerged as a shell corporation to manage the taint that corporate money in policing might engender. The police foundation is designed to perform obfuscator work (Rossman 2014) and provide cover from critique. Non-profits and charities are excellent vessels for obfuscated exchange (Schilke and Rossman 2018), which is probably the main reason hundreds of police foundations in North America have been created (see Chapter Two) since the 1970s.

In adopting greedy institution theory, we do not see the rise of the police foundation, these forms of sponsorship and giving as mere gifts or ambiguous exchanges. For example, Grabosky (2007) views sponsorship mainly as a supply side issue that raises the problem of conflict of interest for police. Rather, we conceive sponsorship and foundations as police attempting to attract further loyalty and conformity to a police agenda irrespective of the individual motivations of donors. Grabosky (2007) raises the possibility of capture by the donor, wherein police start to represent corporate interests. However, the process of capture can go the other way too. Attracting sponsorship is a way of extending police power and influence. This understanding is evident in the policy documents on police foundations and the purpose of creating police foundations. It is about seeking to expand the police project, not only in financial terms but also in political, social, and cultural terms.

Paid Detail and the Greedy Institution

Paid detail policing also can be conceived through a greedy institution perspective. While there is now dated research (Gans 2000; Reiss 1988) on paid detail and related public safety and legal (Vaughn and Coomes; Sullivan 1987, 1995) and job satisfaction issues (Grant 1977; Miller and Presley 1973), as well as about officers' perceptions (Jenks 2009), our interest in the following chapters is paid detail as a form of funding for a greedy institution. It is possible to reduce paid detail policing to mere economic exchange, one that directly benefits individual officers. They essentially rent themselves for several hours and are paid handsomely usually through the police department to stand around as symbols of authority or as scarecrows. In most police departments in the US, "tens of thousands of officers at those agencies log millions of hours every year working for private employers" (Stoughton 2017). But from an institutional point of view, paid detail arrangements are not only about money. We think paid detail is as much or more about the greedy institution. Police executives and managers are not always thrilled with paid detail (in part because they have a bit more difficulty controlling officers on paid detail despite rules about who can fund a paid detail site or event and about what the officers do there – See Chapter Five), but they tolerate it because individual officers and police unions want these "easy money" assignments that often demand little more than being present. And because it expands the purview and operations of police and their world-view that transgressions are best reacted to via surveillance schemes, heroic demonstrations of brute force, apprehension and detention, and criminalization. For police, *real* security provision is provided by police, full stop.

For Mulone (2011), paid detail appears to reveal commercialization of policing. Police and their unions have fought hard for decades to expand paid detail policing, requiring it in settings where most members of the public would view it as a ridiculous waste of resources (also see Ayling and Shearing 2008; Gans 2000). Why would police members and unions fight so hard for paid detail policing, which seems to bring only financial benefit to individual officers and serves very myopic individual and private interests? The often-exorbitant pay for individuals is one motivation. However, from a greedy institution perspective, it is also about expanding the quest for loyalty and conformity outward in society. It is about expanding the footprint of the police in political and cultural terms, and paid detail achieves that. It puts police officers on every street corner, outside bars and nightclubs, in jewellery stores, in hospitals, on movie shoots and even at weddings, in the nooks and crannies of private space for myriad events where they would not otherwise be, and not necessarily to actively reduce transgressions there. To respond to Mulone (2011), we would suggest paid detail appears to reveal a form of commercialization of policing, but appearances can be deceiving. Police have long been interwoven with private business and have long worked at the behest of private interests (Williams 2008). Therefore, another explanation is needed beyond commercialization, privatization, or neo-liberalization, hence our discussion of corporatization above.

Greedy institution theory assists our thinking and analysis because it refers to the institutional form of police and its mission: expansive expansion. In a sense, as a process, paid detail functions to legitimize the role of police in those disparate locales and scenes in a self-serving way. Occasionally, it backfires because police guarding a pothole on a public street seems so ridiculous when visualized or the amount of money going to officers seems like double dipping when it is revealed in different investigations to be verging on corruption in some instances (Bruser and Brazao 2009). We want to emphasize these exchanges are partially about institutional replication, about the greedy institution demanding loyalty and conformity outside itself. However, at an individual level, it is also about literal greed. In purely financial terms, obviously, officers enjoy paid detail and sometimes get into trouble when they work more paid detail hours than permitted, for a few doubling their annual earnings. This is individual greed, perhaps, but our focus in this book is more on the institutional than the individual level.

Looking Ahead

We are interested in how the police, as a greedy institution, extends and replicates itself through its quest for and management of police resources. Police sponsorship, police foundations, and other forms of what we call dark money in policing are not centrally about reputation. Police care about reputation to the extent they want to keep dark money opaque, and it can be imposed to shape others' reputations in exchange. It is not even ultimately about the money. Police departments already have control of public purse strings in many cities and larger regions; it is also about demanding conformity to the police worldview. In this sense, the accumulation of economic and social capital is a political project. Police departments are like black holes that will consume as much of the social galaxies they are situated in if the tendency toward projecting loyalty, conformity, and greed can continue unmitigated. The exchanges are hardly ambiguous from this point of view. The related processes are clear and political. The exchanges are not simply economic from the greedy institutional point of view. Instead, they are social, cultural, and political too and this demands analysis at the institutional level to assess the outcomes of the greedy attempt at police replication that police sponsorship, police foundations, and paid detail policing represent. These outcomes then raise the question of possible alternatives to current arrangements, guided by the idea of generosity over greed. It is to these various inquiries, analyses, and ideas we now turn.

Chapter 2

Mapping the Police Funding Terrain

Donors, Sponsors, Foundations, Paid Detail, Forfeiture, and Beyond

The terrain of private funding and sponsorship of police is a deep dark mine striated with abundant gold seams and accessible through manifold obscured tunnels and shafts that occasionally intersect. It is a mine chock-full of loyal masked miners busily surfacing its riches through these channels for the greedy police institution. Over many years, the police institution slowly carved out the mine. Its contours and corridors are rarely publicly acknowledged, and the mine shows signs neither of imminent exhaustion nor collapse. Instead, it is growing deeper, wider, and darker underground. This chapter illuminates, explores, and maps this mine from which dark money is unearthed, unmasking some loyal miners along the way. We throw this dark terrain into relief by elaborating key types of funding networks comprising it, their histories, prevalence, and volumes, as well as providing detailed examples of several department policies and received funds in Canada and the US.

We begin by distinguishing among key funding types and drawing on specific policies for illustration and then focus on foundations and paid detail funding types. The chapter then describes private funding policies from eight departments of varying sizes and jurisdictions in the two countries: York Regional, Vancouver, Winnipeg, and Royal Newfound Constabulary in Canada, as well as Boise, Miami, Austin, and Santa Clara in the US. We conclude by exploring two other relevant forms of funding by drawing on previous research as well as suggesting these networks overlap.

Overall, this chapter shows the prevalence and variety of private police funding types, the size and power of these funding networks, as well as the volume of capital exchanged through them, are highly significant. Our archival research concerning several departments reveals internal policies and acceptance of gratuities, gifts, and donations are longstanding and have been exchanged from at least the early 20th century. Paid detail may well be as old in North America. Foundations, along with Crime Stoppers and forfeiture, became prevalent in the early 1980s. From 2016 onwards, foundations in the US spread with a rapidity never seen before, a growth which mirrors the

DOI: 10.4324/9781003167914-3

growth of commercial paid detail brokers discussed in Chapter Five. This chapter reveals departmental rules governing gratuities, gifts, donations, and sponsorships specifically for the greedy institution are varied but also often outdated, contradictory, pithy, or non-existent across Canada and the US. While several laws are relevant to some funding types, there is limited active legal governance of these dark funding networks – there are lots of miners but few mine inspections. If there is a quality of this terrain, it is a lack of consistency in the volume of capital extracted as well as in departmental rules governing it, even within one North American jurisdiction.

Private Police Funding Definitions and Types: Gratuities, Gifts, Donations, Sponsorships, Partnerships, Foundations, and Paid Detail

There are key differences among private and external funding types. While literature has explored gratuities and gifts transferred to officers while on duty (Ruiz and Bono 2004; Macintyre and Prenzler 1999; Prenzler and Mackay 1995; Kania 1988), much less is known about gifts, donations, sponsorships, and partnerships at the department level. These two levels of exchange to officers and to the department threaten to undermine the rule of law and accountability (Luscombe et al. 2018, 561).

Gratuities, gifts, and donations are typically one-off contributions of cash, services, or goods. Services can include training of kinds, and goods can entail tactical gear and weapons or even food for police dogs. Gratuities are essentially tips for services rendered and assumed to be of symbolic and minimal monetary value. Sometimes these are discounts on services or goods purchased by officers using their own money or personal favours for officers. These are not usually recorded by police departments and are largely untraceable. No department to which we made FOI requests provided information about received gratuities, presumably in part because the information is not reported, recorded, or otherwise available. When department policies mention gratuities, they refer to rules pertaining to officers rather than departments. One does not typically tip a police department. Moose Jaw Police (Saskatchewan) policy, for example, prohibits officer acceptance of any gratuity. Hamilton Police Service's policy states: "Members should not accept any gifts, favours, or gratuities, which could be perceived as capable of influencing a Member's judgment in the discharge of his/her duties."

Gratuities

Gratuities are by no means a new development. Our archival research into the Vancouver Police Department (VPD) yielded a telling memorandum referring to a $10 "gratuity" for the recovery of a stolen vehicle by Vancouver Police. The memorandum from Chief Constable Bingham to the Major of Vancouver and the Police Commission, dated January 2, 1930, reads:

> the practice of giving rewards to the police... is in vogue in other Forces. The public is prone to appreciate the recovery of stolen property and other services rendered to them by Police... and sometimes enclose a small gratuity... [I]t is better that a straightforward open method be adopted than that men should be secretly approached by generous-minded citizens. By receiving and placing before the commission such rewards each case will be gone into on its own merits, and the source of the reward, and services rendered carefully checked up. The rewards now before the Commission, I respectfully ask [to] be handed to the officers... I would recommend, in future, that all such rewards be brought to the attention of the Commission. Finally, I would add that this has always been the practice... (Vancouver Archives 1929).

This memo suggests gratuities were commonly received by many police departments (they were "in vogue") as early as the 1930s and moreover that in Vancouver at least there was some effort to account for them before providing officers with the funds. This is a practice that has shifted in many departments to allowing the individual officer to decide whether a gratuity is acceptable on their own with no recording or oversight, as we show later in this chapter. Consistent with a greedy institution, the excerpt above also reveals the 1930s police view of citizens, who are apparently expected to occasionally be "tippers" or are at least "prone to appreciate" via tips for services officers are already paid to perform. Here it is worthwhile comparing police to surgeons and professors, both of whose salaries in Canada at least are paid mostly with public funds. Neither professional would admit to or otherwise expect patients or students, respectively, to provide them with a monetary gratuity for their work or deem these persons prone to do so. Gratuities, despite appearing as low value funding, should not be construed as insignificant or not ubiquitous in the greedy police institution. Simply because they are not recorded at the department level or otherwise does not mean they are rare or are without implications. As the 1972 Knapp Commission investigation found of the NYPD:

> By far the most widespread form of misconduct the Commission found in the Police Department was the acceptance by police officers of gratuities in the form of free meals, free goods, and cash payments. Almost all policemen either solicited or accepted such favors in one form or another, and the practice was widely accepted by both the police and the citizenry, with many feeling that it wasn't corruption at all, but a natural perquisite of the job (New York 1972, 170).

We more fully discuss controversies including corruption stemming from such police funding and its relationship to the rule of law in Chapter Seven, but here again, "widely accepted" and "natural perquisite" mirrors the earlier assumption of Vancouver's Chief Constable. There was a deep-seated expectation of citizen loyalty and conformity to transfer these funds, an anticipation these private miners will regularly dig and carry tiny treasures up from the dark mine under wraps – meals, hotel stays, cash – to lay at the police institution's feet.

Gifts and Donations

In previous research on police with our colleague Alex Luscombe, we explained:

> Gifts are free, insofar as they appear voluntary and based on the generous wills of givers, but also obligatory, in part because rejecting a gift would result in harm to existing or potential social relations. In contrast to market transactions, gifts are about creating and strengthening bonds between parties (Luscombe et al. 2018, 562).

Unlike sponsorships discussed below, gifts and donations are not transferred with explicit expectation of something in return; there is no necessary quid-pro-quo (Luscombe et al. 2018, 562). Receiving something in return, however, can happen in practice. A donation implies dealing with an organization rather than an individual. Ultimately, we contend there is no convincing distinction among gratuities, gifts, and the like, on the one hand, and donations, on the other hand since one could gift a service to a department as well as donate goods to an officer. The only difference between them is whether and how they are recognized in tax laws of any given jurisdiction. Tax laws are relevant to these policies and practices as we later show, allowing different forms of tax reductions and receipt assignments to gift-givers or donors, although none to "tippers."

In one Canadian police department in Delta, BC, gifts, and donations are defined as goods and services that are "received or offered" and not required by the department, whereas procured goods and services are required and sought in a fair competitive process. This definition was evident, for example, in the nearby West Vancouver Police department too that defined money, services, or goods as gifts received "in any manner other than through a designated acquisition procedure."

Often departments require or otherwise keep a log or registry of gifts and donations, including the date the gift or donation was received, its source, use, and value. These logs reveal reported monetary values of donations or gifts to police departments are often modest and vary widely, but sometimes are substantial. FOI acquired data shows in Ontario, Amherstburg Police and York Regional Police (YRP) received $1700 and $258,269 CDN in cash donations in 2015, respectively. This difference is undoubtedly partially due to the former department being a fraction of the size of the latter, but also differing policies.

Some departments receive gifts and donations with no formal policy in existence, but they claim to adhere to conflict of interest policies pertaining to individuals from local government, such as with the Royal Newfoundland Constabulary (RNC). Long-standing department rules tend to focus on the conduct of individual officers in relation to gifts and donations, rather than department-level practices.

Sponsorships and Partnerships

In contrast to gratuities, donations, gifts, and sponsorships are long-term arrangements of exchange or reciprocity entailing an external entity entering an agreement with a police department to provide something in return. Smaller departments we studied were without formal policies concerning sponsorship and foundations. Sponsorship arrangements, where they exist, are more defined. This does not mean what a police department receives in return for being sponsored is limited to the formal written agreement. In practice, therefore, the distinction between gift-giving/donating and sponsoring may be absent. We found if there was a sponsorship policy in place, it was always from a larger police department, perhaps because smaller ones would have much less to exchange with would-be sponsors. Hamilton (Ontario) and Vancouver, for example, have policies that explicitly refer to sponsorship. These sponsorships are varied; they may involve a sponsor receiving marketing space on police property, access to police administrators, permission to advertise they support the police department. Two exemplars of police sponsorship uncovered through research with our colleague Alex Luscombe pertain to galas and conferences (Luscombe et al. 2018) and K-9 units (Walby et al. 2018). We refer readers to this work rather than delve into them here. However, later in this chapter we discuss department policies that include sponsorship.

Here we also wish to distinguish sponsorships from partnerships, which are also long-term arrangements of exchange. The former is a marketing strategy for the sponsor. The benefits tend to be about using the police to further corporate brands and perspectives. Partnerships, however, can include marketing but go beyond whereby several key interests of two institutions converge in an enterprise, for example, to reduce a kind of transgression. The Insurance Corporation of BC, for example, partners with various local police departments in that province, such as Abbotsford Police, for initiatives related to driver conduct and automobiles, thus reducing payouts for accidents and thefts and therefore reducing profit losses. Partnership, a business term, was popularized in our neo-liberal era to refer to any joining of organizations, public or private, to pursue a common or converging interest. Put simply,

> the term 'partner' has acquired moral overtones. Partnering has become the proper, civilized way to relate. Good associations are those based on good partnerships, whereas bad associations are those involving bad partnerships (Lippert 2006, 62).

The distinction between sponsorships and partnership, however, is not watertight, as we show in Chapter Four about police-corporate ventures.

All this funding is subject to various laws, including overarching provincial legislation in Canada governing the operation of police departments such as the British Columbia Police Act. This and similar legislation such as local ordinances or municipal by-laws have sections on "conflict of interest" that prohibit police from engaging in certain actions too. Tax laws surrounding charitable and non-profit organizations and the capacity for a foundation or other funding form to issue tax receipts is overseen by the Internal Revenue Service (US) and Canada Revenue Agency. A police department does not qualify as a charitable organization on its own. If there are department policies in place about this varied funding, they tend to refer to donations and gifts or both and to have been established decades ago. Reference to sponsorships, foundations, or other arrangements like forfeitures discussed below are only rarely mentioned in these policies. When they are it is usually a relatively recent development.

We present Tables 2.1 and 2.2 to provide summary information about donations. Table 2.1 reports on donations in 20 police departments based on FOI request disclosures available for 2014 and 2015. As can be seen, the amounts very dramatically among departments. Most can be seen to receive in-kind donations at a minimum. The other notable detail is that some police departments with affiliated foundations – New York, Vancouver, Calgary especially – discussed later in this chapter, tend to receive larger cash donations.

Table 2.2 below breaks down the donations and gifts received in six police departments based on FOI disclosures, for which this information was available for a two-year period. Even considering six departments, the types of in-kind gifts vary significantly. Besides the "other goods" category, the most consistent donation across the six departments was at least one vehicle, which would be a high value donation compared to the next two common types, food and drink, and clothing.

Foundations: History, Prevalence, and Size

Police foundations are the first of two major funding types we explore in this book. These are non-profit, charitable organizations with legal standing

Table 2.1 2014 and 2015 Cash/In-kind Donations for 20 Police Departments

State/Province	*Department*	*Total Cash Donations 2014*	*Total Cash Donations 2015*	*Cash/In-Kind or Both*
New York	New York	[b]$662,031.05	[c]$716,023.72	Both
California	San Francisco	$26,352.00	$65,422.09	Both
British Columbia	Delta	$3,214.05	$800.00	Cash
British Columbia	Vancouver	[a]$1,037,000.00		Cash
British Columbia	Victoria	$5,000.00	$7,500.00	Both
Alberta	Calgary	$472,300.31	$291,869.43	Both
Alberta	Lethbridge	$14,800.00	$14,160.00	Cash
Alberta	St Albert (RCMP)	$30,000.00	$40,000.00	Both
Manitoba	Winnipeg	$29,660.00	$60,841.00	Both
Nova Scotia	Amherst	$2,252.00	$1,700.00	Cash
Nova Scotia	Cape Breton	$15,250.00	N/A	Both
Nova Scotia	New Glasgow	$7,750.00	$5,850.00	Both
Ontario	Amherstburg	$2,252.00	$1,700.00	Both
Ontario	Barrie	N/A	N/A	Both
Ontario	Guelph	$11,575.00	$16,014.22	Cash
Ontario	Halton Regional	$25,550.00	N/A	Both
Ontario	London	N/A	N/A	Both
Ontario	Orangeville	$2,050.00	$1,500.00	Both
Ontario	Saugeen Shores	N/A	$3,335.00	Cash
Ontario	York Regional	$276,342.00	$258,269.00	Both

a Denotes total estimated Corporate Partner and Individual Member cash donations acquired by the Vancouver Police Foundation. Estimates were calculated using the Vancouver Police Foundation's four donation categories. 1) Chiefs Circle: $25,000 + 2) Executive Circle: $15,000–$24,999 3) Partner: $5,000–$14,999 4) Supporter: $500–$4,999. The median dollar value of each category was used on a per donor basis. 1) Chiefs Circle: $25,000 2) Executive Circle: $20,000 3) Partner: $10,000 4) Supporter: $2,750.

b Denotes total cash donations from six-month period, October 1, 2013 to March 31, 2014.

c Denotes total cash donations from six-month period October 1, 2014 to March 31, 2015 and April 1, 2015 to September 30, 2015.

focused exclusively on the police. These organizations garner funds from private and other external sources and then transfer them to police departments. The first major police foundation in North America was created in New York City in 1971, the New York City Police Foundation (NYCPF 2017a). Two small foundations preceded it in 1966 (Manchester Police Foundation, NH) and 1968 (Glendale Police Foundation, CA), but did not achieve the international recognition or standing of the NYCP Foundation. According to the NYCP Foundation's company history, it was created during a time of transition when the NYPD was undergoing corruption investigations (NYCPF 2017a; see also the New York 1972). In 1971, the foundation was "established to reduce corruption and support innovative programs that the NYPD could not readily fund" (NYCPF 2017a). The foundation in these early stages granted scholarships to officers, donated horses to the NYPD's Mounted Unit, and provided the department's first bulletproof vests. During the 1980s, the foundation broadened its responsibilities, taking over

Table 2.2 Type of In-Kind Gifts in Six North American Police Departments - 2014 and 2015

Type/Dept.	*St Albert, AB*	*Fredericton, NB*	*St. John's, NL*	*London, ON*	*San Francisco, CA*	*New York, NY*[a]
Training	0	0	1	37	0	0
Vehicles	1	0	2	1	2	2
Animals	0	0	1	0	2	0
Safety Equipment	1	0	5	0	1	0
Firearms	0	0	1	0	0	0
Food & Drink	10	5	0	0	2	1
Clothing	29	2	1	0	0	1
Travel	3	0	0	0	0	5
Entertainment	46	2	0	0	1	1
Fitness Equipment	0	0	0	0	1	1
Electronics	3	0	0	0	1	0
Other Goods	45	7	0	2	2	17
Other Services	7	0	0	0	0	2
Total	145	16	11	40	12	30

a Based on data from one NYPD precinct.

New York City's Crime Stoppers program, a separate funding arrangement discussed below, and increasingly provided the NYPD with training, equipment provision, technology upgrades, and community outreach. According to the foundation's former executive director, projects initiated or concluded in 1986 include the enhancement of SPECDA [the School Program to Educate and Control Drug Abuse], an opinion survey of the public and the police, the creation of a pilot cardiovascular health program [for officers], and an expansion of a training program of the police cadet corps (Delaney 1987, 7).

In the 1990s, the character of the programs and initiatives reveals a qualitative shift towards funding police operations in some manner. In this decade, the foundation donated the first CompStat system to the NYPD. After 9/11, "a clear role for the Police Foundation emerged: modernizing the NYPD to meet the challenges of policing a post 9/11 New York City" (ibid.). The NYCP Foundation went on to support upgrades to the NYPD's surveillance and technological infrastructure and supported the NYPD's counterterrorism initiatives. Due to Foundation funding, the NYPD even "posted detectives overseas, taught others exotic languages and acquired a mobile lab to detect chemical or biological attacks" (Weissenstein 2003). The NYCP Foundation helped fund the NYPD's Real Time Crime Center that opened in 2005 (NYCPF 2017b). The history section of NYCP Foundation's website concludes: "As we look to the future, we are more committed than ever to supporting new strategies and enhancing technical capacities. The foundation will continue to uphold the NYPD's reputation as the paragon for 21st century law enforcement" (NYCPF 2017b). Typically, a police foundation seeks and provides funds or makes purchases for only one police department.

Thus, the NYPDF works only on the NYPD's behalf, rather than generating funds for other police agencies in New York City or environs or at higher state or federal levels. As we show in detail in Chapter Three, some police foundations provide funds for police priorities best characterized, as with Houston's priorities noted earlier, as the militarization of police.

In principle, police foundations are no different from foundations operating in myriad other domains such as medical research or community building. Our archival research revealed some community foundations have provided funding to police departments through much of the 20th century. Perhaps the best example in the US is the Cleveland Foundation. Created in 1914, the Cleveland Foundation (2021) is said to be the prototype of the world's community foundations. A 1975 report by this foundation aptly titled "Private Sector Assistance to the Cleveland Police Department" reads:

> Recognizing the important role of the Cleveland Police Department... the Cleveland Foundation has long sponsored projects and made grants to assist the Department to become more effective in the discharge of its public duties and responsibilities. In 1922 a nationally acclaimed Foundation survey of Criminal Justice in Cleveland [and]...a similar report in 1966 was... Foundation sponsored... The Foundation has sponsored or participated in... forming the Administration of Justice Committee to... formulate police projects; providing college tuition to police cadets; funding a civilian police administrator to serve as Administrative Assistant to the Chief of Police; and funding a department newsletter. Most notable... has been its emphasis on police training; recruit and in-service training, a police library, and managerial supervisor training throughout the country (Maddox and Firstenberg 1975, 3–4).

Precisely what the foundation deemed to be police "duties and responsibilities" were not specified in this report, but these have certainly shifted over time.

By 1926, there were 55 similar organizations in the US. These were emulated a short time after inception in Winnipeg, Manitoba where the first such foundation in Canada appeared in 1921 (Cleveland Foundation 2021). The Winnipeg Foundation today maintains links with the Winnipeg Police Service (WPS) by offering a portal to would-be donors to the Winnipeg Police Endowment Fund, as it does for numerous other Winnipeg based charitable organizations. This police fund was created in 2012 by a Winnipeg by-law as a "permanent endowment fund established to support crime prevention through social development and the well-being of the community" (Winnipeg Foundation 2021). The fund provides monies to outside charitable or non-profit organizations via a committee of three police administrators including the Chief and two Deputy Chiefs of Winnipeg Police Service (Winnipeg City by-law no. 138/2013). According to the by-law, these funds are to be managed by the Winnipeg Foundation. This arrangement does not equate to a police foundation, where funds are earmarked for police use in some manner. Rather, this entails having the police decide which local external organizations seeking to engage in crime prevention will receive funding. For some time there has been, however, serious consideration of developing a Winnipeg police foundation (see Scott 2006).

The full extent of similar community foundation support of the police institution in other US and Canadian areas during the 20th century before the rapid growth of police-specific foundations in the 2000s, remains unknown, although it plainly takes place in addition to the work of the latter. Thus, we found ample evidence of other foundations recently and regularly providing funds to police beyond or separate from police foundations. For example, the West Vancouver Police Department receives cash donations from the West Vancouver Community Foundation directly, as well as from its closely associated West Vancouver Police Foundation. Regarding the former, the Department explained:

> Donations are mainly made to the West Vancouver Community Foundation and at that time the donor can 'ear-mark' the funds for the police, however, the WVPD often has no knowledge of where the funds come from/who the donor is. All donations through the foundation are in the form of cash, there are no 'in-kind' donations (West Vancouver Police 2016).

The Detroit Public Safety Foundation is devoted to acquiring and transferring funds to the Police Department but also other Detroit "first responder" organizations, which includes the Fire Department. However, this foundation also receives funds from grant monies provided by other private foundations. An example of this is the Detroit Medical Centre (DMC) Foundation that provided funding to the police, in one case, for First Aid training for all Detroit officers (Detroit Sponsor 1). A final example is the Boise Community Foundation that provides funding directly to the Boise Police Department (BPD), including funds to commence a separate Canine Police Foundation.

We contend the rise of police-specific foundations is historically new and reflects a greedy police institution's appetite for more resources and connections. Police foundation growth has happened against a background of cuts to municipal police department budgets in many North American jurisdictions commencing in the 1980s consistent with neo-liberalism's rise and the related embrace of corporatized solutions (although funding cuts to police in North America are not as deep as in the UK which seem to have led to pervasive privatization, see Ellison and Brogden 2012). Across the US, there were large cuts to public funding of police linked to the 2008 financial crisis too. While the trend of police foundation growth commenced much

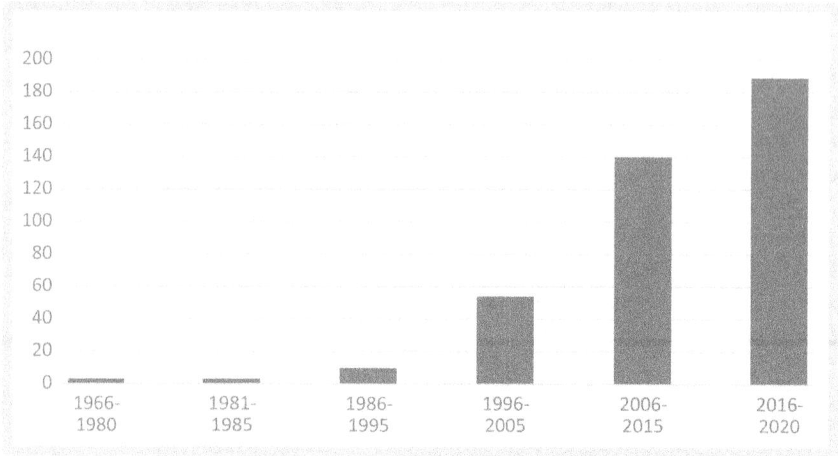

Figure 2.1 Growth of US Foundations by Year Created

earlier (Figure 2.1), 2009 marks the beginning of its acceleration. A report focusing on police foundations and economic capital flows published during the production of this book also provides important insights in the volume of corporate funds pouring into police departments through foundations in the US (see LittleSis/Color of Change and Public Accountability Initiative/Little 2021).

Police foundation growth has emerged in lockstep with cuts to public funding, but which has been neither as deep nor as wide in Canada where public funding of police has been more stable than in the US. This is reflected in, for example, much higher municipal police officer salaries in Canada (AMO 2015, 13). The effects of the COVID-19-related recession and de-funding movements on police budgets have yet to be fully realized, and thus their effects on more foundation growth remains unclear. A few US police departments, including those in Austin, New York, Seattle, Los Angeles, San Francisco, Portland, Philadelphia, and Baltimore, have undergone public funding reductions since 2020 (McEvoy 2020). We speculate this dual set of additional drivers will result in more police foundations or larger foundation networks and thus more funds transferred to police via the foundations already in place.

Beyond this, there are two key sources of police foundation growth and "isomorphism" (DiMaggio and Powell 1983) in North America. The first is foundation-specific entities such as the NYCP Foundation and the National Police Foundations Network (NPFN) and broader police networks such as the International Association of Chiefs of Police.[1] Since its establishment in 1971, the NYCP Foundation has furthered establishment of police foundations elsewhere. Only in the late 1990s did some US cities become interested in police foundations, and many modelled the NYCP Foundation. In the five years preceding 2003, partially due to that foundation's seminars, "at least 10 foundations were launched in cities nationwide" including Oakland, Atlanta, Detroit, Omaha, and Portland (Weissenstein 2003). In 2004, the NYCP Foundation published its "Starting a Police Foundation Guidebook," a lengthy step-by-step manual about how to create a police foundation, and began distributing these free of charge upon request. In 2013, Pamela Delaney, who had served as the president of the NYCP Foundation from 1983–2009, started the NPFN. Through the NPFN, Delaney uses her NYCP Foundation experience to encourage the spread of mostly municipal police foundations throughout the US. On the NPFN's website, one finds a growing body of resources on police foundation best practices, strategies and notices of workshop, training and networking opportunities for police, foundation officials, or anyone interested in starting a foundation. Second, federal agencies and professional associations such as the International Association of Chiefs of Police (IACP) have spearheaded police foundation expansion too. The IACP has a "Police Foundations Section" with a mission "to promote networking and the exchange of ideas and best practices among executives and police foundation professionals" (IACP 2017). The IACP accordingly hosts meetings and conferences for police foundation professionals, police officials, and business executives; conducts research on police foundation practices and ethics and encourages "discussion for the establishment of standards and best practices for police foundations" (IACP 2017). In 2010, the IACP's in-house publication, "The Police Chief," featured several articles on police foundations (Davis 2010; Butler and Delaney 2010; Delaney 2007).[2] The US Department of Justice's Office of Community Oriented Policing Services (COPS) has also actively promoted police foundation creation across the US. In September 2010, the COPS office joined with the Target Corporation to launch the National Police Foundations Project, providing "training workshops and technical assistance to communities to sustain community policing crime reduction and crime prevention efforts by establishing or expanding existing police foundations" (Delaney 2011). Foundations emerged first in larger cities like Los Angeles and then smaller jurisdictions followed. As two members of the Ottawa Police Foundation in Kansas wrote: "In the past, many chief executives felt that a police foundation was only for big cities like Los Angeles and Atlanta" (Butler and Delaney 2010). Foundations are now established in cities as small as Los Gatos, CA, Amherst, NY, and Ottawa, KS.

As designated charitable or non-profit organizations, foundations have reporting standards to which all must adhere to be able to issue tax receipts to donors. To lend further insight into this funding type and its networks, we used GuideStar's National Database of Charitable Organizations, the similar ProPublica and Charity Navigator databases, and data from the National Centre for Charitable Statistics (NCCS) in the US, to identify 399 mostly municipal and regional police foundations. We excluded from this sample police sports, pipe band, memorial, canine, police history/museum, officer scholarship and award, and police youth foundations. In contrast to police foundations' broad mandates and funding capabilities, these other foundations focus their funding and only rarely if ever contribute to police procurement or operational support, which is our core concern. We also excluded US state- and national-level foundations (e.g., American Police Foundation, Illinois Association of Chiefs of Police Foundation). We found the largest number of US police foundations was established in the five-year period from 2016 to 2020 (47 per cent or 189 foundations). By 2017, California, Virginia, and Florida had the most foundations. We could identify no relevant police foundations in only four of 50 states, plus Washington, DC: West Virginia, New Mexico, Vermont, and Alaska.

The IRS Form 990 available in the databases above reveals most police foundations we identified, despite being structurally modelled after larger foundations like New York's, were not yet receiving high levels of private and/or corporate donations. In 2017, for the 251 foundations we researched in the US, 27.1 per cent (68 foundations) had a reported income of > $100,000 USD, 28.3 per cent (71 foundations) reported < $100,000 USD in income, and 44.6 per cent (112 foundations) reported an income of zero. Of 112 foundations reporting zero income, 53 per cent were relatively new. We discerned 13 foundations (3 per cent of the 399) reported incomes of > $1,000,000 USD by 2018-2019, with the NYCP Foundation reporting more than $9 million USD in 2019 (Table 2.3).

To lend further insight into how the NYCP Foundation arrived at this extraordinary amount and discern its network size and donor identities, we located and analyzed data reported in its exclusive annual print journal

Table 2.3 US Police Foundations with >$1 Million USD Reported Revenue in 2018 or 2019[A]

Police Foundation	*Income (Revenue)*	*Year Established*
Atlanta Police Foundation	$10,848,654	2003
New York City Police Foundation	$9,744,791	1971
Los Angeles Police Foundation	$5,519,887	1998
Houston Police Foundation	$2,513,996	2004
St. Louis Police Foundation	$2,498,511	2007
Palm Beach Police Foundation	$2,329,790	2006
Detroit Public Safety Foundation	$1,879,822	2003
New Orleans Police and Justice Foundation	$1,492,842	1996
San Diego Police Foundation	$1,219,854	2000
Seattle Police Foundation	$1,019,266	2002
Louisville Metro Police Foundation	$1,010,867	2006
Police Foundation of Kansas City	$1,009,214	2010
Washington DC Police Foundation	$1,001,571	2007

A Last reported year of foundation's revenue on Internal Revenue Service's Form 990.

(1987–2005).[3] This journal with evocatively themed volumes (e.g., "Honor" (1987), "Partners" (1989), "True Blue" (1990), "Commitment" (1991), and "Pride" (1993) – all of which arguably speak to loyalty consistent with a greedy institution) is primarily a corporate venue comprising revenue-generating advertisements by transnational corporations or their key brand names. As we reveal in Chapter Seven, the identities of these and other donors to the police foundations remain in the dark, except for glimpses in some foundation documents like this journal. Police foundations do not routinely report how many donors and their identities. Foundations are designed to avoid doing so, and as private organizations they are immune to FOI requests as well.

The NYCP Foundation sponsors included Budweiser, Revlon, Smith and Wesson, and Philip Morris, as well as iconic firms such as the New York Yankees Baseball Club. They also included firms like Motorola that sells technology to the NYPD and many other departments, as we discuss in a later chapter. Many advertisements involved the corporation "saluting" the NYPD, a pledge of loyalty if there ever was one. Even the Trump Organization in a 1987 full-page advertisement gave "their deep appreciation to New York's Finest" unbeknownst that some 30 years later the NYPD would be spending considerable resources ($308,000 USD daily) providing protection for Trump Tower and its occupants from regular street protests in Manhattan (Reuters 2017) before the Trump administration exited the White House in 2021. These advertisement-based sponsorships grew over time. The 1990 volume of the NYCP Foundation's journal displays advertisements from 60 major corporations in its network, the 2001 volume has 84 and the 2016 volume (the last volume available on the NYPCP Foundation website) lists 96. Speaking to its network arrangements and funding volume, by the 1990s the NYCP Foundation had commenced – mimicking practices well established in the larger charitable fundraising world – publication in this journal of a donor hierarchy of Major 3 Star Donors ($75k and over US), 2 star ($25–75k US), 1 Star ($10–25k), Gold Shields ($10–5k US), and Silver Shields ($1–5k US), with each year the number of donors in the three-Star category steadily increasing after 1992. In 1997, a new four-star donor level appears ($100k to 1 million US and over), later called "platinum," that includes 10 corporations and corporate foundations. In 2011–2012 fiscal year, the last year this information was reported, there are 14 platinum donors of $100k or more (followed by numerous listed as gold, silver, and bronze benefactors). This hierarchical system of incentivizing sponsor rewards (i.e., stars, shields, various precious metals) has been emulated by other police foundations throughout the US and Canada (e.g., Vancouver Police Foundation).

In another example revealing the identities of a foundation's donors and size of its network, Washington DC Police Foundation's 2019 annual report's "sponsors" page, a montage of corporation logos, reveals at least 63 funder nodes (WCDPF 2019, 14), making this too a sizeable, powerful network (Figure 2.2). These nodes include among the most well-known and largest

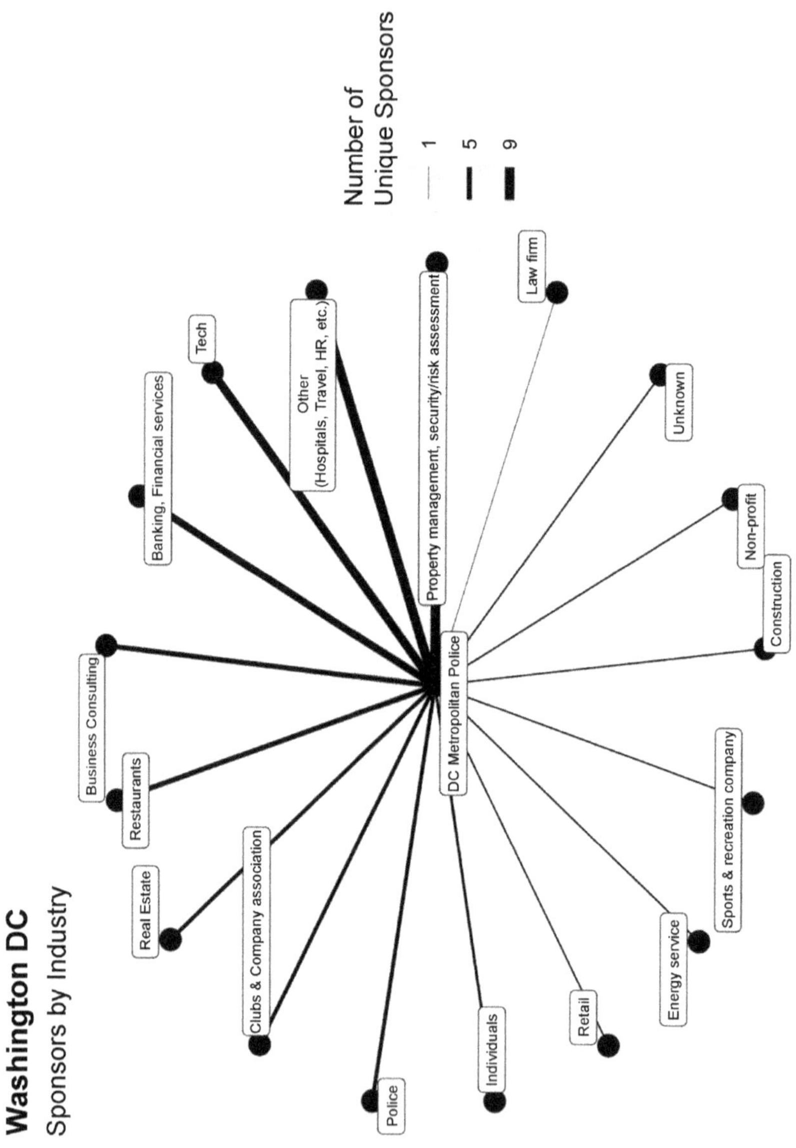

Figure 2.2 A Foundation Funding Network

Table 2.4 Canadian Police Foundations with Reported Revenue in 2018 or 2019[A]

Police Foundation	*Revenue (CDN)*	*Year Established*
Vancouver Police Foundation	$1,844,654	1976
Calgary Police Foundation	$1,200,743	2010
Edmonton Police Foundation	$440,811	2000
RCMP Foundation	$310,583	1994
SPVM (Montreal) Foundation	$235,963	2008
Saskatoon Police Service Foundation	$31,169	2018
Delta Police Foundation	$25,813	2004
Abbotsford Police Foundation	$25,432	2005

A Line 4700 of last reported year of foundation's Canada Revenue Agency's Tax Return.

corporations in North America such as Walmart, Pepco, Royal Bank of Canada, Lyft, and Thomson Reuters. They also include firms like Axon, maker of body worn cameras, that sell these technologies to police departments.

The idea of a police foundation of the NYCP Foundation type spread to Canada in subsequent decades. While the IACP has some relevance for influencing growth in Canada since it is international, the lack of a similar NPFN and Department of Justice program in Canada helps explain slower foundation growth. Using the online Charities Listing database of Canada Revenue Agency, we identified eight municipal police foundations (Table 2.4): Abbotsford, Calgary, Delta, Edmonton, Saskatoon, Vancouver, RCMP Foundation (formerly Mounted Police Foundation), and the Fondation du service de la Ville de Montreal (SPVM Foundation).

The first foundation in Canada was created in Vancouver in 1995 (though Vancouver Police Foundation claims to have commenced operations in 1976) and the last one appearing was in Saskatoon in 2018. Typical of other police foundations, the Calgary Police Foundation Board of Directors, for example, comprises persons from major corporations including Cenovus, Shaw, and PricewaterhouseCoopers. Police foundations in Canada continue to grow in number and in annual budget, but they are fewer in number compared to the US (Table 2.3). However, more are being established. For example, the Chief Constable of the new, large police department in Surrey, BC announced a police foundation will be "full on" by 2022 (Zytaruk 2021). The nearby Vancouver Foundation began modestly, receiving only about $20,000 CDN from donors in its first months (Vancouver 1976), but since has undergone exponential growth in private funds. Canadian police foundations' revenue is one of the relevant statistics available from Canada Revenue Agency's charity database. Based on this, since 2011 the Vancouver Police Foundation has reported about $1,000,000 CDN in annual revenues, over $3,000,000 CDN in 2014, and a peak of roughly $8.2 million CDN in 2015. In 2019 its revenues were $1.8 million CDN (Table 2.4). Other foundations have generated more modest revenue levels. The province of BC has seen the most (three) police foundations emerge thus far.

The database also revealed that in Canada in the fiscal period 2019 to 2020, the primary Vancouver Police Foundation donee was the Vancouver Police Department which received $929,822. The trend is similar with other police foundations. In 2019, Calgary Police Service received from the Calgary Police Foundation more than twice as much or $839,201. In 2014, Calgary Police Service received $400,000 from the foundation. Compare this to 2012, when Calgary Police Service received $220,907. In 2019 Edmonton Police Foundation transferred $240,300 to the Edmonton Police Service. Edmonton Police Service is the primary donee in each year for which there are records. Donations to police foundations can be sizeable in ways that direct donations or sponsorship of police cannot. For example, in one year the Edmonton Police Foundation accepted donations from Enbridge ($25,000), Northlands ($10,000), and several other $10,000 donations from provincially based companies. In 2014, Calgary Police Foundation embarked on a funding drive and secured several large donations from energy companies headquartered in Calgary totalling more than $1 million. Foundations also need to spend funds to raise funds. In 2016, Vancouver Police Foundation spent $60,231 on advertising and $133,782 on fundraising. Calgary Police Foundation spent $139,512 on advertising and $88,262 on fundraising. Edmonton Police Foundation spent $240,983 on fundraising. Galas require funding to host. Each year the Edmonton Police Foundation hosts the "True Blue Gala." For a table of eight persons, the cost is $2200–2700. At these galas, donors receive privileged access to key police decision-makers at their tables (Luscombe et al. 2018). Other forms of fundraising include the selling of police calendars, such as in Calgary in 2014 when all sales of the Police Service Canine Unit charity calendar went to the Calgary Police Foundation. Sales of the calendar had raised more than $30,000 for the Calgary Police Foundation the year earlier. Like other police foundations, the Vancouver Police Foundation raises funds through print and radio advertisements, fundraising dinners, galas, targeted corporate donations and sponsorships, and targeted personal contacts. They do so in ways documented more in the next three chapters.

Paid Detail Funding: History, Prevalence, and Size

Paid detail is another major funding type and network examined in this book. Paid detail[4] entails private and external entities transferring funding to police officers in exchange for a presence in North America. These are rarely one-off exchanges; instead, entities become enrolled into networks as nodes to have recurring exchanges with police (see also Whelan and Dupont 2017). In this way they are a form of partnership. Paid detail is also sometimes referred to as extra duty, special duty, special policing, paid duty, contract duty, off-duty, additional constables, among other monikers. Collectively, but with less precision, paid detail is also called "moonlighting" or "user-pays" policing. We have used both terms in our previous research, but the former is a colloquial term that is misleading since paid detail happens at all times of the day and not only at night on the temporal fringes (i.e., in the moonlight). "User-pays" policing is a broader term that also encompasses, for example, criminal record checks of teachers on behalf of schools (see, for example, Dellora and Beck 2021 on Australia) and also actual investigations on behalf of corporations as discussed in Chapter Four. Interestingly, almost no police representatives or funders interviewed conceived of paid detail as "cost recovery" either, and for this reason such funding seems to have much more to do with loyalty and tradition and to provide "easy money" for officers. We use the term paid detail in this book since it is easily the most common form of "user-pays" policing in North America. Paid detail funders in North America are typically private organizations but they also occasionally involve public and quasi-public (e.g., crown or publicly owned corporations) agencies of one kind or other, as well as individuals. The arrangement of these exchanges is varied and changing as discussed in Chapter Five. One change discussed there is the rise of for-profit commercial brokers that promote a police presence and arrange mostly lucrative funding for officers on behalf of departments and funders.

Paid detail is old, as old as the modern police institution itself it appears. In the UK, from which the police institution in North America has drawn some influence, Williams (2008, 191) writes a paid detail

> system was referred to as 'additional constables' in the nineteenth century, and increasingly as 'special policing duties' in the twentieth. Many historians of British policing have happened upon a few instances of this practice, and given them a brief mention… Its relative invisibility in current theories of policing is thus easy to understand.

Thus, paid detail has been in place in the UK for greater than a century. Currently paid detail arrangements can be found in the UK (Button and Wakefield 2018; McLelland 2016), Ireland (Garda Inspectorate 2015), and Australia (Robertson 2013; Ayling and Shearing 2008) for private businesses, concerts, festivals, sporting, and like events too. But we agree with Williams paid detail has been peculiarly left in the shadows in theories of policing in relation to greedy institutions and corporatization too. However, precisely when paid detail funding began in the US and Canada remains unclear. The two major Hillcrest Reports (Cunningham et al. 1990, 1986) show paid detail was widespread by 1981, more than 40 years ago, in the US. Our archival research concerning some jurisdictions suggests paid detail is even older and there have been at least some paid detail-like arrangements in many North American police departments even earlier in the 20th century. In the municipal archives, we found multiple references to paid detail in Calgary in the 1950s including for the Calgary Stampede (a giant rodeo) and for security at parades and for visiting dignitaries. A January 7, 1972 letter from the Chief of Seattle Police in response to a complaint letter from a private security company owner alleging paid detail practices violated the city's ethics ordinance reads:

> [T]he practice that you refer to does not constitute a violation of this [ethics] ordinance...The fact that an officer is uniformed and... armed while employed in an off-duty capacity does not affect this conclusion. The uniform symbolizes that he is a peace officer and is representative of his authority as such which he possesses... throughout his career as a sworn officer... His being armed is clearly consistent with his responsibility and authority under the law and is proper both when he is on duty and off-duty in either an employed or non-employed context. It therefore seems clear that the language and spirit of the Ethics code was not intended to prohibit an officer's off-duty employment... (Seattle Archives 1972).

Thus, more than 50 years ago, Seattle officers were uniformed, armed, and regularly receiving paid detail funding. The Chief's response also reflects the greedy institutional character of police, whereby police officers are seen as the institution's members "at all times", whether "on duty and off-duty", "employed or non-employed", and a kind of moral regulation we elaborate in Chapter Five. Toronto Police Services Board minutes from a January 22, 2009 meeting to discuss a paid detail controversy, similarly, indicate these practices were widespread in Toronto in the 1950s, though it remained uncertain whether they predated that decade in that city:

> Since the formation of the MTPF [Metropolitan Toronto Police Force] in 1957, paid duties have been part of the Uniform Collective Agreement (UCA) between the MTPF and the Metropolitan Toronto Police Association (MTPA). The 1957 Collective Agreement... set the rate for "Special Services" (now known as paid duties). There is no information available that would confirm if the decision to allow "Special Services" was a continuation of a practice from any of the police agencies that amalgamated in 1957 to form the Metropolitan Toronto Police Force or a new initiative (Toronto Police Services Board 2009).

The paid detail funders of various kinds whom we interviewed typically could not recall when such exchanges had commenced for their organization. Almost all police representatives we interviewed suggested paid detail was in place before their time. The comment of a police coordinator from a major city in Western Canada is typical, relating that paid detail is

> a regular function that we participate in. Exactly when it started or how long we've been doing it I can't tell you that but it's something that we do and we've been doing it as long as I've been involved in the police

> department which is 30 years at least so I'm sure it was going on before that (Western Canadian Police 1).

The lack of attention to its origins by those comprising and operating this funding network speaks to its mundaneness as well as conformity to the police institution. In 1990, the well-known Hall Crest Report II on private security trends, by drawing on survey research available at the time, showed paid detail was already growing "dramatically":

> [T]he number of moonlighting police increased dramatically in the 1980s. The Hallcrest 1981-82 national surveys indicated that about 20% of law enforcement officers were regularly engaged in off-duty security work. By 1987, Professor Reiss found 47% of Seattle's police officers moonlighting, and 53% in Colorado Springs. Hallcrest's field study in 1989 revealed moonlighting by more than 50% of the law enforcement officers in Seattle, in the Washington, D.C. area, and in Dade and Lee Counties in Florida... (Cunningham et al. 1990, 289–290).

In a few cities, the year of the arrival of a departmentally administered paid detail program – one of several models in operation discussed in Chapter Five – is clear. For example, we know the NYPD's paid detail program began in 1998 (NYPD 2016). However, here, and elsewhere there was likely paid detail long before this, albeit arranged by individual officers for approval by police administrators or the Chief for all subsequent assignments and transfer of funds, a second model being or already replaced in US jurisdictions, as we discuss in Chapter Five.

Paid detail predates current discussions of corporatization and predates the idea and the process of neo-liberalism. We contend nonetheless that the way paid detail is transforming is more and more consistent with these broader political and economic processes (see Chapter One). Thus, corporatization characterizes many funders and brokers since various nodes are increasingly corporations. It also predates proposals to defund the police but has managed to avoid the attention of such proposals and related protests that grew dramatically in 2020 after the killing of George Floyd.

Paid detail is not on the funding fringe. Rather, it comprises a robust set of funding networks, the size of which cannot be understated. In most departments, it provides a significant flow of capital that adds to some officers' already very high public salaries. In large departments, it also provides capital directly to the department's coffers in the form of percentage fees. These fees have been increasing as a percentage in recent years in some departments. For example, York Regional Police increased this paid detail fee to 20 per cent in 2015. We could discern no police department among the more than one hundred from which we requested FOI information that prohibited paid detail, although as we show in Chapter Five, it is still regulated in special ways consistent with a greedy institution. Similarly, a rare survey of non-federal police departments in the US, together employing 143,000 officers, revealed 80 per cent allow or arrange for officers to accept funds for security-related service (Stoughton 2017, 1847). In one major southern US police department with more than 5000 officers, a police union official in an interview asserted: "we have thousands of extra jobs." In a six-month period in 2014 York Regional Police had 3,417 separate assignments for officers. The Hall Crest Report II noted above estimated using modest assumptions, paid detail involved massive exchanges of capital already by 1990:

> If, as the staff estimated earlier, 150,000 law enforcement officers are engaged in private security work just 15 hours per week at $15 per hour (the low end of the off-duty pay range), total annual earnings would be about *$1.8 billion* (Cunningham et al. 1990, 289; emphasis added).

We present the volume of some paid detail networks below in Table 2.5.

Speaking to the size of these funding networks, using FOI acquired data we determined over a six-month period from the most updated data available Detroit's paid detail network comprised 48 different funder nodes, including Greektown Casino Hotel, Renaissance Village Apartments, as well as West Vernor and Springwells Business Improvement District (Figure 2.3). Other paid detail networks are considerably larger. Miami lists 207 different funder nodes in its paid detail network (Figure 2.3), more than 4 times the size of Detroit's. York Regional Police in Ontario had 550 different nodes (Figure 2.3), which is 11 times the size, and which includes funders as varied as Ward Funeral Home, Galleria Supermarket, and Douglas Hunter Developments. Within each paid detail funding network, some nodes exchanged decidedly more capital than others (Figure 2.3). The NYPD and LAPD did not disclose paid detail assignment logs that would likely have revealed larger networks given the size of these departments and respective

Table 2.5 Paid Detail Funding Volumes in Six North American Police Departments in 2015 or 2016

Department	*Paid Detail Funding Volume*	*City or Regional Population*
Boston, MA	$46,442,536 (USD)[a]	650,281
San Francisco, CA	$12,309,942 (USD)[b]	879,961
Ottawa, ON	$7,254,251[c]	934,240
York Regional, ON	$2,285,175	1,100,000
Hamilton, ON	$1,604,448	536,915
London, ON	$949,344	383,825

a Estimate for 2015 based on six months of data multiplied by a factor of two.
b Estimate for 2015 based on 119,514 hours × $103/hour.
c Estimate for 2015 based on dividing total by 21 months of non-demarcated data and multiplying by 12.

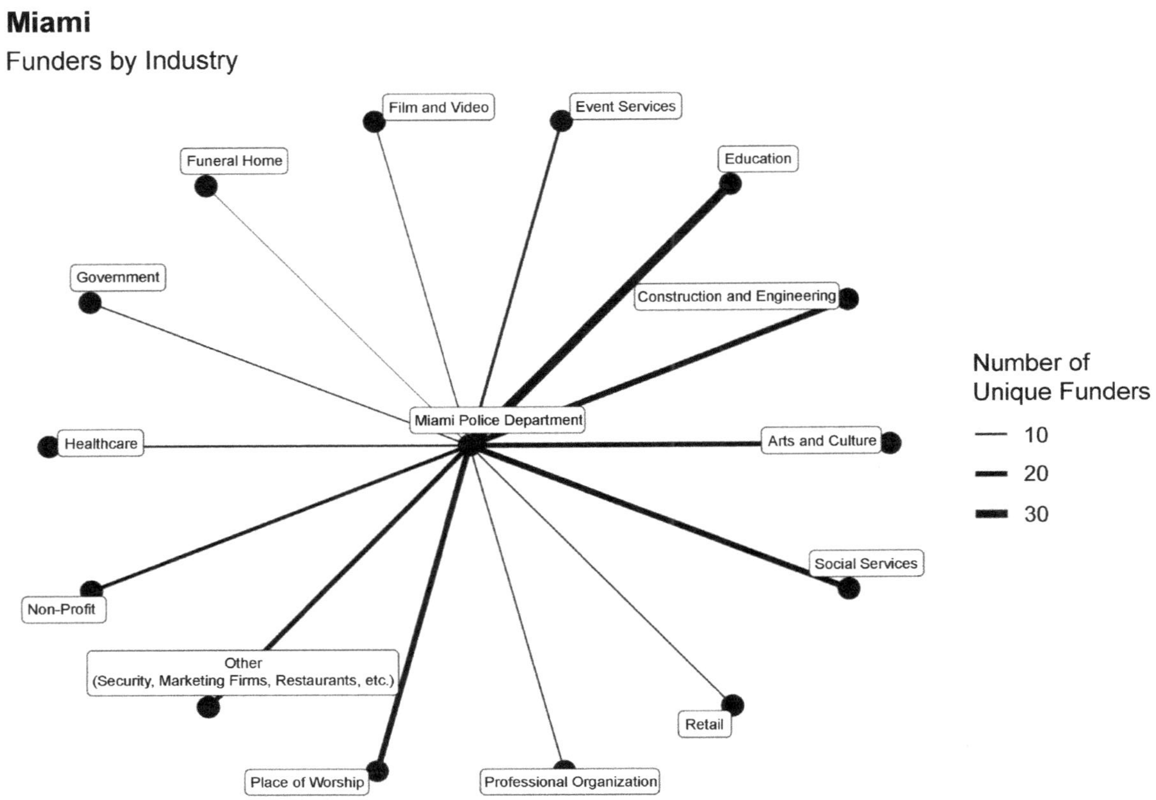

Figure 2.3 Four Paid Detail Funding Networks (*Continued*)

Figure 2.3 (Continued)

Figure 2.3 (Continued)

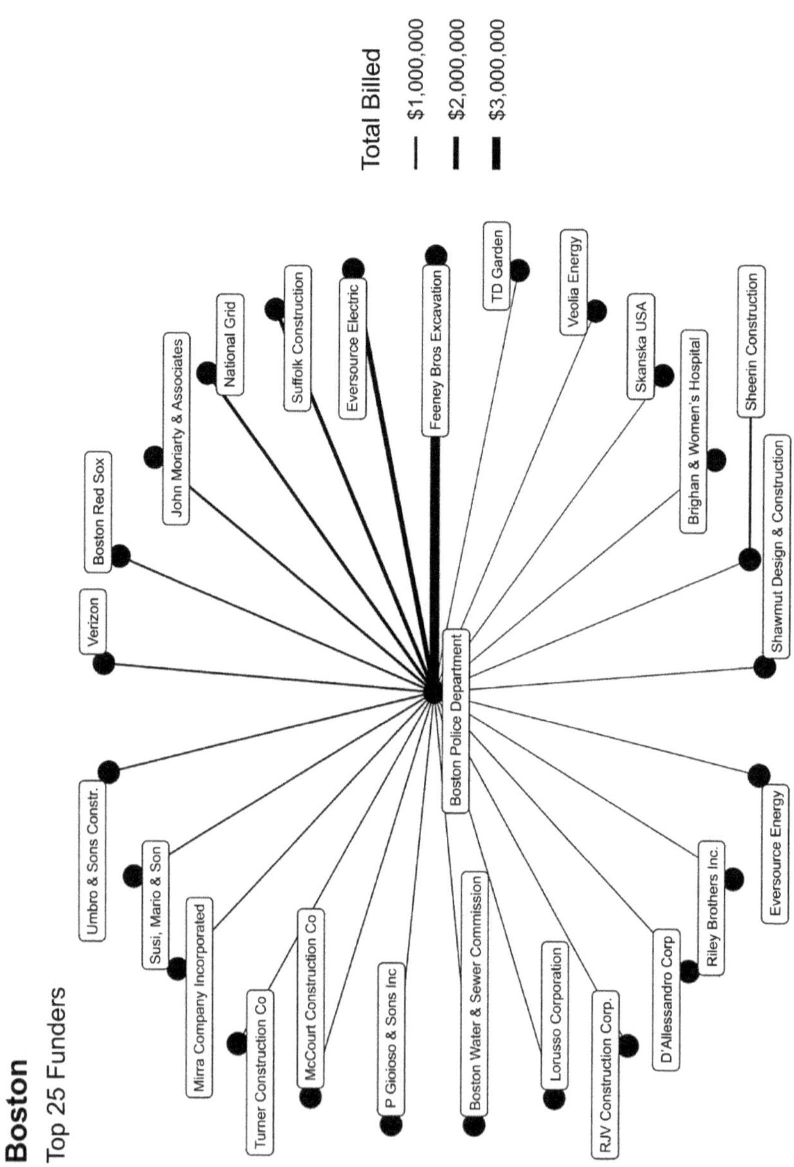

Figure 2.3 (Continued)

cities. The largest we discerned from acquired FOI data was Boston's with no less than 1102 unique funder nodes over only a six-month period (Figure 2.3). Compared to other police departments in North America, Boston's is a massive, and due to its numerous nodes, powerful funding network.

Greedy institutions create networks of which they are the central and commanding node. This is the case with the greedy police institutional complex we examine in this book and the paid detail networks that have been enacted. These network figures show the centrality of police but also the density of some flows from some funders and sectors.

The growth and size of newer corporate paid detail brokered funding networks is discussed in Chapter Five, which has vital implications for the overall size and power of paid detail funding networks too. Overall, we understand paid detail as a significant form of funding type that generates many networks spanning the public/private divide and raising many questions about the rule of law that we examine in this book. It is a funding type the police as a greedy institution but especially its members covet.

Case Studies of Donation and Sponsorship Policies

Having discussed gifts and sponsorships as well as foundation and paid detail types and networks, as well as their histories, prevalence, and size, below we describe private funding policies from eight departments of varying sizes in multiple provinces (ON, BC, MB, and NL) and states (ID, FL, TX, and CA): York Regional, Vancouver, Winnipeg, and the Royal Newfoundland Constabulary in Canada and Boise, Miami, Austin, and Santa Clara in the US. We chose these cases because each one has at least one rare or unique or decidedly typical feature or for which sponsorships and not only donations and gifts would be relevant. Assessing these policies provides an empirical basis for understanding private funding policies police have created, which also serves to highlight some of the gaps, discrepancies, and controversies we look at in subsequent chapters. We return to these features in Chapter Seven that discusses holes in policies as well as controversies and corruption.

Boise Police Department, ID, United States – 2016

Boise Police Department (BPD) serves a city of 226,000 and is the largest in the state of Idaho and the capital. It has about 300 sworn officers. The BPD's policy manual has two short sections on gifts and donations (BPD Policy Manual 2015). The first deals with gratuities and gifts at the interpersonal level; the second governs gifts at the institutional level, which it calls donations. At the department level, the BPD can accept donations, and officers are allowed to solicit donations with the permission of the Deputy Chief. The latter provision is rare in police departments.

The first (s. 11.23, 71) is called "Bribes, Discounts, Gratuities, Rewards, and Gifts." This section applies to the actions of individual officers on duty and prohibits officers from soliciting or accepting any of the listed actions (gifts, discounts, etc.) if they

> could, in the public mind, be interpreted as capable of influencing an employee's judgement in the discharge of duties or that would reflect favoritism by the employee or Department towards any particular subject, group, or business.

This section of the Boise Police Department policy on gifts, gratuities refers to the Boise City Code sections 1–21 too, thus deferring to the broader city policy, which is a common arrangement. The second (s. 11.24, 71) is about donations to the department and it indicates officers are allowed to solicit only if they have the approval of the Deputy Chief.

We additionally obtained two City of Boise resolutions on donations. One from 2014 covers two donations and one from 2015 refers to one donation. The first resolution is on two "unsolicited donations" of $1,000 US to the Department from Westat, a research company in Rockville, Maryland, and a $40 US donation from a private citizen (City of Boise 2016a). Westat provided the "donation" after interviewing the Chief, another department official, and some members of the motor unit for research it conducted. The resolution states that the gift was given "in appreciation of the BPD's cooperation" with the firm's research. The funds were used to buy new helmets for the motor unit officers: "When asked what BPD might do with the funds, Westat representatives were pleased with us of [*sic.*] the funds to purchase helmets for Motors Unit officers" (1). The private donation of $40.00 US was given because the donor "had a positive experience with a police officer and wanted to provide a donation" (City of Boise 2016a, 1). Both donations were approved. The second resolution is about a donation from Intacto Arms LLC of four TREK 5.56 Suppressors to the BPD Special Operations Unit (City of Boise 2016b). The resolution is from 2015, but this donation was received in October 2014. Suppressors are used on weapons to reduce their sound. "Intacto Arms donated the suppressors to support local law enforcement" (1). The four suppressors were valued at $2,200 US and were approved by the City of Boise.

Miami-Dade Police Department, FL, United States – 2016

The Miami Police Department (MPD) has approximately 1300 sworn officers. The MPD has a policy on "private contributions" to its Community Relations Section (Miami-Dade Police Department 2016). The purpose of the policy is: "To establish guidelines whereby Community Relations personnel may accept private contributions of monies, goods, or services toward any project or program officially sponsored by the Community Relations Section and the Miami Police Department" (13). The reason for the policy and allowing private funding is: "Many of the projects and programs coordinated by the Community Relations Section are very costly to operate" (13). In this case, donations and private contributions are deemed acceptable due to the nature of the programs the Community Relations Section operate, which "benefit the community as a whole, and not any particular individual or group" (13). For this reason, "contributions from private sources to offset expenses are welcome" (13).

Private contributions are reviewed by the Major of the Community Relations Section before they can be approved (14). There are three forms of "private contribution" distinguished in the policy: money, goods, and services. All can be accepted with various limitations on cash and cheque. Cheque/cash can be accepted but "The contributor must be made to understand that the contribution will be used to offset expenses for the project or program, and not toward any specific purchase" (13). Goods can be contributed to any project or program, examples being "toys, food, supplies necessary to complete a project, equipment, etc." (13). Services can also be given to any program or project, examples being "volunteers, entertainment, catering services, printing, photographic and video services, and other form of professional services necessary to complete a project" (13). Section employees are "prohibited from accepting contributions for personal gain or enrichment" (13). Section employees are also "prohibited from making promises or assurances of preferential treatment to potential contributors" (13).

There is a list of "some" programs private contributions can fund but it is not exhaustive (14): The Police Athletic League, National Night Out, Open House, Children's Holiday Celebration, Thanksgiving Giveaway, Peace Walk and Rally, Take Your Children to Work, Sponsors Recognition and Volunteer Program, and Gun Buy Back (14).

Donations are accepted but only for more "community-oriented" programs run by the Community Relations Unit of the MPD. The policy argues this makes outside donations acceptable because these programs benefit the community as a whole and so the MPD can avoid looking like private donors are buying them off. The policy generally frames private contributions as benign. At the same time, it recognizes problems can still emerge. Sections prohibiting officers from using these relations for private gain or promising special treatment acknowledge these problems are inherent in the exchanges.

This is very similar to the way other departments frame and handle outside donations, but without a police foundation as part of the picture. Donations go straight to the Community Relations Unit. The policy does not use the word sponsorship and none of the types of "private contribution" fit the definition of sponsorship. They are more donation-like. Private contributors can give goods or services, but when they give money they must relinquish control over its use: it can only be used to fund the program "generally" and not be directed by the donor for a particular use (this practice is called "earmarking" in the fundraising world and is being restricted here to earmarking for particular Community Relations programs but no further).

Austin Police Department, TX, US – 2016

The Austin Police Department (APD) has about 1,900 sworn officers. The APD policy indicates it accepts gifts and donations, but only minor ones can be accepted by individuals (Austin Police Department 2016). The APD redirects donations from outside parties to its "partner" charity organization. The Chief is allowed to communicate with this organization about police needs but other APD employees are not to contact official police charity organizations without the Chief's permission. The policy is primarily about donations to the department and gifts to individual officers but neither uses the terms sponsorship or partnership, nor explicitly discusses corporate sponsorship. We found this omission is typical of most North American departments. The purpose of the policy is to "establish procedures concerning the solicitation and acceptance of gifts and donations made to the Department" (1). The policy states it does not apply to grants or inter-agency contracts or "the loan of items from vendors in use for evaluation and testing" (1); "A gift or other benefit conferred on account of kinship or a personal, professional, or business relationship independent of the official status of the recipient" (1); or employee discount programs "afforded to all employees of a business" and that APD officers are given as part of a paid detail arrangement (1). The first exclusion, about the policy not covering grants, contracts, or loans, could be deemed to be referring to corporate sponsorship without stating such. A "loan of items from vendors in use for evaluation and testing" is considered a kind of sponsorship in some departments, and "inter-agency contracts," unless this is strictly between government agencies, could be seen as corporate sponsorship too.

The policy also states the Chief Constable may accept gifts on behalf of the department as long it "would provide a significant public benefit and that the acceptance would not influence, or reasonably appear to influence, the department in the performance of its duties" (1). There are three conditions a donation must meet: 1) it must advance the achievement of department "goals and duties"; 2) the donor is not "a party to a pending criminal or civil case brought by an officer or employee of the Department"; and 3) the donor is not "subject to Department licensing or regulation, or interested in any contract, purchase, payment, or claim with or against the Department" (1). Of course, "goals and duties" in the first condition could not be vaguer, with many donations potentially befitting this criterion. In the third condition, the department explicitly acknowledges the potential for donations to conflict with procurement contract bidding and other activities where the department is supposed to have an "unbiased" and "fair approach." This juxtaposition of fair procurement and donations is apparent with many other department policies too.

The next section of the policy states the department's preference for donations to be channelled through private non-profit organizations. This is a common approach and can be found in cities such as New York and Vancouver and now typically is arranged through a police foundation. If a person wants to donate to the APD, they are referred to: a) the APD Liaison for the Greater Austin Crime Commission; or b) if the donation is valued at $5,000 USD or less, a "non-profit corporation administered by the APD Office of Community Liaison (OCL)..." (1).

APD employees are prohibited from soliciting or accepting "donations or loans of property, funds, or services for use by the Department, or in carrying out its duties, except as otherwise provided in this policy" (2). APD members cannot use their APD affiliation to solicit funds "without the express approval of the Chief or designee" (2). This last exemption presumably exists because there are conceivable situations where police would want to use their status to solicit funds, like for fundraising for Cops for Cancer or another large charitable event in which many police departments routinely participate. The policy then lays out various prohibitions regarding acceptance of gifts and gratuities by individual APD members. One part invokes a condition like Boise's use of the "reasonable person" test: "Employees shall not accept or solicit any gift or favor that might reasonably tend to influence that individual in the performance of official duties, or that the employee knows or should know has been offered with the intent to influence or reward official conduct" (2).

When the donation is earmarked, the department is required to do its best to use the donation in the way the donor wanted: "The donor's request as to the use of the donation will be honored to the extent possible" (3). This differs from, for example, Miami's policy, which prohibits this. When property is donated to the APD, it is inventoried through the APD's Property Management department (3). The policy states the Chief Constable may accept gifts to the Department as long it "would provide a significant public benefit and that the acceptance would not influence, or reasonably appear to influence, the Department in the performance of its duties" (1). APD employees are prohibited from soliciting or accepting "donations or loans of property, funds, or services for use by the Department, or in carrying out its duties, except as otherwise provided in this policy" (2).

Santa Clara Police Department, CA, United States – 2017

Santa Clara has approximately 160 sworn officers. According to their policies, the department can accept gifts, but they must be vetted by City Council who has final say on acceptance or rejection. A gift to City Council can be redirected to a specific department/function/individual in the City which presumably would include the Police Department. The policy that regulates Gifts to the City is City Manager's Direction (CMD) No. 70 (Santa Clara 2017). It does not mention sponsorship, but some donations are likely to mirror sponsor-like arrangements and parts of the policy would seem to acknowledge this (e.g., where City Manager must review what donor expects from the City in return). CMD 70 states "only the City Council, at a Council meeting, may accept gifts to the city" (1). Gifts may be "tangible or intangible" (1). This means a service rendered free for the city can be considered a gift under this policy. Gifts are reviewed before accepted and assessed in terms of how "burdensome" they would be to the City. In addition, if the City Council finds that

> the donor may be coming before Council in the near future for action or a decision, plus to avoid the potential for a quid-pro-quo situation, or to avoid even the potential appearance on any impropriety, the gift should not be accepted (Santa Clara 2017, 1).

Gifts are accepted by the City itself, and then disbursed to a particular department or function:

> Under this directive, gifts are accepted as gifts to the City overall, not to a specific Department or individual. If City Council approves acceptance of the gift, the City Manager determines to what Department/function/individual the gift will be applied. The City Manager cannot be the end-recipient of the gift (Santa Clara 2017, 1).

This control by the City or municipal government differs from most other departments, whereby the department's Chief and/or a police board of some kind typically approves donations and gifts. Here when gifts are directed from the City to a specific function or individual, a special form is to be completed in addition to "memorializing the receipt of the gift in 'a written public record' (accomplished through an Agenda Report, as described in the Procedure section)" (1). Presumably then, gifts directed to the police, if there were any, would require a form and Agenda Report to be completed.

The procedure for accepting gifts is that gifts are offered to the City or a city department (e.g., police); the City Manager forwards a report about the gift to City Council with extensive information, including the reason the gift is being offered, the conditions attached to it, potential liability, benefits and drawbacks of accepting or rejecting the gift, added costs to the city of accepting gift, and public perception, suggested conditions on which gift could be accepted, and recommendation whether it should accept or reject in City Manager's opinion (1-2). This department also has a policy called "Gifts and

Favors to Individuals." The more relevant policy, however, referenced on page 3, is "CMD 70 – Gifts to the City (in contrast to individuals)" (Santa Clara 2017).

Santa Clara City policy on gifts to the city acknowledges the difficulties that can be associated with donations from third parties (in terms of optics, conflict of interest, obligations to donor, and beyond). Gifts are risky in this sense but can be accepted if the gift passes council review/deliberation and a risk assessment by the City Manager. Policy does not discuss sponsorship, but the notion of "conditions attached to gift" that City Manager considers in procedures could mean some gifts are offered with some conditions of reciprocity. Such gifts could be considered closer to sponsorship than donations. Having discussed US departments, below we now describe the donation/sponsorship policies of York Regional, Royal Newfoundland Constabulary, Vancouver, and Winnipeg from four Canadian provinces.

York Regional Police, ON, Canada – 2016

York Regional Police (YRP) (serving the Greater Toronto Area beyond the core) has about 1,600 sworn officers. The YRP Directive (York Regional Police 2016) outlines guidance of members involved in "solicitations, donations and gifts to maintain the highest ethical standards." The Directive is very detailed as to who controls each part of the donation process (i.e., receiving the request, forwarding to the Chief of Police, etc.). All donations require the approval of either the Chief of Police or the Board's approval (depending on the donation's value). A donation is defined as "financial contributions, equipment, vehicles, goods or services" that do not include donations for specific investigations. YRP also offers a definition of a "volunteer group" which is a group that, without compensation, performs tasks on behalf of YRP. This department does not have a sponsorship policy.

Members are not to solicit or accept a donation from anyone who is not a member of YRP, unless otherwise authorized by the Chief. All donations received must be accounted for by completing a "YRP360 Donation and Solicitation Information" form. In some cases, "volunteer groups" can receive donations as compensation such as the need to attend an event outside the Region of York. However, compensation for the service of volunteer groups is restricted in where a volunteer group is providing a service to a charitable or not-for-profit community event. In receiving a proposal for a donation, a District Commander must forward the above form to the Chief of Police. Prior to submitting this form, the Commander needs to examine the impact on the communities of York Region, the additional resources needed to accept the donation, the limit of any benefit to the donor (e.g., requested access to the donated item), the particulars of the donor, and an agreement specifying the disposal or return of the donated item. Donations less than $5,000.00 require the approval from the Chief of

Police, and donations with a cumulative value of $5,000.00 or more require approval of the Board. If a donation is rejected, the Chief of Police is to notify the District Commander of the reasons for rejection, and the Commander then needs to provide a letter to the donor that includes the purpose of rejection.

All members are restricted from managing private bank accounts, directly or indirectly for the purpose of accepting donations to YRP. No donations can be accepted that, in the opinion of the Chief, would bring the reputation of the YRP into disrepute. The Chief of Police also needs to ensure the donor or donation will not embarrass YRP. Under section F(1), the Directive states

> no public donation shall be accepted from an anonymous source or donor, and in all circumstances the identity of the donor shall be made known to the Chief of Police and the Chair or Vice-Chair of the Police Services Board.

The YRP Financial Services Manager must manage all monetary donations in a Regional bank account.

Vancouver Police Department, BC, Canada – 2016

Vancouver Police Department (VPD) has about 1,300 sworn officers. VPD's elaborate policies are especially instructive in showing how a larger police department frames donations and sponsorships. While most departments in North America have some policies about donations, gifts and/or gratuities, our research revealed most departments do not have policies that specify sponsorship. There are several VPD policies relevant to both donations and sponsorship. VPD policy distinguishes between donation and sponsorship by defining these two practices via the presence or absence of *quid pro quo* and expectations of reciprocity. Officially recognized police charities, or police foundations, are defined as "arms-length" sources of private funding. VPD Policy 2.6.4 (Vancouver Police Department 2016) contains the guidelines that a police charity must meet to officially partner with the VPD. However, as of 2016, the VP Foundation was the only partner.

VPD's core policy on sponsorship and donations (Vancouver Police Department 2016) acknowledges that sponsorship and donations

> can be legitimate sources of funding for equipment and initiatives that benefit the police department and the community. It is imperative that the VPD maintains the highest ethical standards and this policy establishes a process by which the VPD may effectively and ethically accept donations and participate in sponsorship arrangements (1).

For North American police departments this reference to "and the community" is typical and the claim that it "can be legitimate" shows recognition that some such arrangements are not so. The policy then defines donations and sponsorships. A donation "occurs when the VPD receives money, goods or services without any obligation being created (with the exception where the donation has been provided and accepted for a specific project or initiative)" (1). They contrast this with sponsorship, which

> occurs when the VPD forms a relationship with another party whereby both sides have specific obligations (for example, a company provides new computers, and in turn, the VPD allows the company to advertise itself as a supplier to the VPD). Sponsorship often involves a *quid pro quo* relationship (1).

The VPD policy then lays out procedures for managing and accepting donations. The first section acknowledges police foundations as "arm's length" sources of private donations. The policy also specifies that donations over $500 in value require the donor to complete a Donor Information and Application Form (1). Donors are then subjected to a background check. If this check reveals that accepting the donation would put the VPD into a "real or perceived conflict of interest or reveals serious concerns of integrity or ethics related to the donor" (2), then it is to be returned without explanation; "No explanation will be provided for declining a donation" (2). Also, donors can remain anonymous (2), presumably only if their donation is under $500.

VPD members are prohibited from soliciting donations or fundraising as members of VPD without express approval of the Chief Constable (2). They can, however, request access to funds from a police foundation or another recognized society to use for a specific program or initiative (only the VPDF is recognized). Members can request this funding by submitting a proposal form. The proposal is then reviewed for how well the program would support VPD objectives, whether it will "compromise police impartiality or objectivity" (3) or whether it will "benefit the VPD or the community without preference to the donor" (4), among other principles. Funding requests are forwarded to the Chief Constables office for review/approval. According to an interview with a trustee, the ability of VPD members to request funds accounts for the most use of foundation acquired funds.

The next section in this policy concerns sponsorship. The same principles for reviewing VPD member proposals for donation funding noted above are used to review sponsorship proposals from private companies including corporations (3). Sponsors are required to complete a form (3). Another form is also filled out and the same background check procedure for donations is used to review potential sponsor and then accept or reject it. As with donors, if and when rejected: "No explanation will be provided for declining a sponsorship" (3). Sponsorships are always "assessed on an individual basis" (3).

Unlike most other department policies regarding sponsorship, this one goes into some detail regarding eligibility. To become a VPD sponsor

a an endorsement of products and/or services is not required;
b the public image of the sponsor must be positive and have a reputation of integrity and ethical *standing that would reflect in a positive manner on the VPD*. The public image and reputation of the sponsor's business values *must reflect the core values of the VPD*;
c present and past activities of the sponsor must not be in a real or perceived conflict with, nor compromise, the VPD;
d there can be no direct benefit to the sponsor other than formal recognition for the sponsorship and/or a tax receipt may be issued to a sponsor where circumstances are appropriate;
e principles of fairness and competition must be considered when assessing a sponsorship proposal;
f the allocation of all goods and services resulting from a sponsorship is at the sole discretion of the Chief Constable; and
g the use and scope of any advertisement related to a sponsorship agreement is at the sole discretion of the Chief Constable (3–4; emphasis added).

Significant in these criteria is the demand that the company or corporation "reflect" not only positively on the VPD but must reflect the VPD's core values. In other words, the sponsor is to extend the police institution's footprint and worldview, consistent with what we have described as the greedy institution outlook of contemporary police.

The policy goes on to require equipment loans to the department be treated as sponsorships (4). If loaned from a government or other police department, a memorandum of understanding must be established "that clearly defines its purpose, all terms of the loan, use of the equipment and liability issues" (4). The final section concerns donations and sponsorship (4). If a potential conflict of interest is perceived, the Chief Constable can consult outside sources for an independent review or opinion with the VPD's ethics advisor (4). Donations and sponsorships over $5,000 are reported to the Police Board. It is the duty of the Executive Officer to the Chief Constable to develop a list at the end of every calendar year of all donations and sponsorships accepted. The report is then forwarded to the Vancouver Police Board at year end.

The next policy is "2.6.4 Police Foundations and Organizations" (Vancouver Police Department 2016). The policy defines the mission of a police foundation

> is to improve public safety by providing resources and support to municipal police departments that are not readily available through existing budgets, and are not encompassed within those services and projects which are considered the core responsibilities of a police department (1).

A recognized police foundation is to be provided with a document called the "police foundation guidelines" prepared by the Ministry of Public Safety and Solicitor General of British Columbia. To be officially recognized by the VPD, police foundations must adhere to these guidelines. Mention of police foundations in police department policies like this is extremely rare in North American police departments.

Next the policy lists 12 guidelines that a charitable organization must meet to "begin or continue a relationship with the Vancouver Police Board (VPB) and the VPD" (1). These include: "should not engage in political activity"; "should not engage in advocacy on behalf of" VPD; must operate with "utmost discretion ensuring the integrity of the VPD is not compromised or seen to be compromised, and must itself act in a manner which avoids any implication or allegation of impropriety" (1); "members/trustees of the foundation cannot appear to be using the foundation to promote themselves or business interests" (2) and "trustees of foundation or organization must undergo yearly criminal record checks; trustees cannot receive any benefit from their affiliation with the police foundation or charity."

Winnipeg Police Service, MB, Canada – 2016

Winnipeg Police Service (WPS) has over 1,100 sworn officers. WPS has a long and extensive policy on donations and sponsorship. Compared to almost all other departments, WPS's policy is unique because it seems to allow members to solicit potential donors and sponsors. The WPS defines a large donation/sponsorship as exceeding $20,000. As discussed above, the WPS does not yet have an official police foundation that channels private funds into the department although they receive funds via the Winnipeg Foundation.

WPS has a formal policy called "Donations and Sponsorship" (Winnipeg Police 2016). In referring to sponsorship, this differs from most other North American police departments. The policy opens with a general statement similar to ones in Vancouver, Victoria, and other jurisdictions accepting donations and sponsorship based on their importance in funding community initiatives outside the regular budget:

> The Service promotes the use of donations and sponsorships as a means to involve the community in police programs, to respond to the needs considered important to the community and to provide the community programs that are beyond the ability of the Service to provide independently (1).

We return to the notion of community and framing in Chapter Six. The department allows both sponsorship and donations: "External organizations may sponsor/donate funds, goods or services which cover portions of, or entire programs, events or activities conducted by the Service" (1). Donors and sponsors can provide funds in exchange for recognition/acknowledgement, for no return, or do so anonymously:

> The sponsorship/donation may be made in return for a form of recognition or acknowledgment, or no return or anonymously. Any recognition or acknowledgment received by the sponsor/donor must be agreed upon with the Service prior to the acceptance of the sponsorship/donation (1).

Sponsorships are reviewed and authorized by the Service and the City of Winnipeg. Review by the City in addition to the department is rare too. Only certain kinds of events and programs, first approved by the department, can be funded by donations and sponsorship (1). In accordance with the opening statement of the policy and in line with other departments that accept donations and sponsorships, it is plausible that only community-oriented programs would be approved.

WPS members, with approval from their Division Commander, can solicit donations/sponsorship. Police departments usually strictly prohibit this. It is also a main motive for police departments to create external foundations that can solicit, while most police departments cannot and are careful to prohibit it. But WPS policy allows solicitation by members. This request for approval to solicit donations and sponsorship must include a long series of details, including: the program the donation/sponsorship is to support, what the solicited person/organization will be providing to the police, what the solicited donor/sponsor will receive in return, a list of potential donors/sponsors, what will be done with equipment after a sponsorship arrangement is complete (i.e., kept or returned), and other conditions (2). There is then a list of factors/conditions in the policy to be used by the Division Commander when assessing a request for solicited donations/sponsorships. These include: the program/event/activity to be funded is a formally approved one; the program/event/activity "is one for which the Service receives no or inadequate funding" (3); "the total value of the sponsorship/donations… including incidentals" (3); "the funds, gifts or services will not compromise the objectivity or integrity of the Service" (3); and others (see 2–3).

Donations/sponsorships valued at over $20,000 must be acknowledged in writing and the request must be sent to the member's Commander with their recommendation (3). Here the WPS is setting a high threshold for large gifts/sponsorships at $20,000, whereas other departments (e.g., Vancouver) set it at or near $5,000 or less. This is evidence of the varying and arbitrary nature of what constitutes a large and small gift/sponsorship, and which gifts/sponsorships require added oversight/accountability across departments. Unsolicited donations can be anonymous (no police representative knows the donee) or confidential (only certain police representatives know the identity and keep it confidential) (3–4). For each unsolicited donation, the receiving member of the WPS creates a memorandum covering what was donated, the donor (if known), as well as the circumstances of offering (3). There is a section for sponsorship/donation of vehicles and vehicle equipment (4–5). Donated/sponsorship vehicles are "examined by the Vehicle Services Unit" to assess whether it is "roadworthy" (4).

Donations and sponsorship are defined as "extras" to the regular budget and as being used for community programs and initiatives. The policy opens with a general statement – similar to the one in Vancouver, Victoria, and other jurisdictions accepting donations/sponsorship – about the importance of donations/sponsorships in funding community programs and initiatives outside the regular budget.

Royal Newfoundland Constabulary, NL, Canada – 2016

The Royal Newfoundland Constabulary (RNC), Newfoundland, Canada has about 420 sworn officers. RNC apparently accepts donations from public and private organizations as well as private citizens but is without a formal policy apart from the Province of NL Conflict of Interest policy. This policy has a section covering gifts and donations, but only to individual officers, not to the department. The RNC does not have a police foundation like those in Vancouver, Delta, and Edmonton, but does have an Officer Memorial Association. The Memorial Association collects monetary donations to maintain a memorial and hold an annual service. We were told the "Royal Newfoundland Constabulary is not responsible for the management of information (records) of RNC affiliated foundations, therefore cannot provide any records in relation to these affiliated foundations" (Royal Newfoundland Constabulary 2015).

The RNC receives donations from third parties but is without any formal internal policy on donations apart from the Government of Newfoundland and Labrador Conflict of Interest Act, 1995. This is unique in referring to provincial legislation rather than a municipal or city policy in the absence of a similar department policy. Aside from general provisions in the policy about conflict of interest, there is only one small section on gifts/donations, but it applies to individual officers on duty rather than donations/sponsorship to the department (5). The section prohibits officers from accepting fees, gifts, or personal benefits except those "received as an incident of the protocol or social obligations that normally accompany the duties or responsibilities of the public office holder" (5). RNC accepts donations, but like most other departments its policy does not use the word sponsorship. Bridgewater (NS), New Glasgow (NS), and Brandon (MB) Police Services, to mention only three examples of many smaller departments we examined, all claimed to be without a sponsorship policy in responses to FOI requests. It is conceivable, however, that some donations are sponsorship-like. The RNC maintains a list of donations to the department. The list describes the donation, its value, the year acquired, and the source (mostly companies but includes one private citizen).

Other Private Types of Police Funding: Crime Stoppers and Civil Forfeiture

The police funding terrain includes types beyond those discussed above, which we cannot fully explore in this book, but nonetheless are noteworthy. We describe two we contend are consistent with police as a greedy institution, extending the police worldview into and demanding loyalty of other organizations through specific framing. These are Crime Stoppers and civil forfeiture. We provide an example of the size of their respective networks too. These two types of private funding are relatively well-covered in the literature compared to other funding channels we explore, although more research in relation to police as a greedy institution is required, a point we return to in the conclusion. Both these funding arrangements, rather than representing an alternative or even more generous view of police, are instead consistent with extending loyalty demands through funding discussed in later chapters beyond the regular police institution. The practices and related objects of both are consistent with and underpin reactive and aggressive policing aimed at a narrow range of transgressions, but especially those related to drugs. The funding is imagined therefore to target a narrow range of what police deem to be their "duties and responsibilities." Despite their wide prevalence, the effectiveness of these forms in reducing transgressions in general, however, is either dubious, or merely presumed, raising questions about the rule of law.

Crime Stoppers

One of the two noteworthy types is the longstanding and networked Crime Stoppers programs. Crime Stoppers consists of a private, non-profit, registered charitable organization in Canada and the US. It therefore shares this status with foundations in North America. Even more than foundations, Crime Stoppers trumpets aiding police in crime control over other established functions such as order-maintenance or community service. These allegedly independent programs narrowly frame transgressions as street crime and the proper reaction to it as necessarily involving police force (formal arrests and charges using intelligence) accordingly (Lippert and Walby 2017; Lippert and Wilkinson 2010; Lippert 2002; Carriere and Ericson 1989). This is done rather than via crime prevention programs consistent with ideals of community policing. Like foundations, Crime Stoppers organizations usually have charitable status and therefore a governing board and are legally separate from police departments. Research has revealed these programs are often not only staffed by a sworn police officer seconded to the role of coordinator, but often operate in police department buildings for free or at dramatically reduced rent (Lippert 2002). The programs and their personnel are involved in exchanging with and forming extensive networks.

Crime Stoppers (CS) has become a ubiquitous program operated locally. Local programs are networked with regional (or provincial), national, and international umbrella organizations and a long list and wide-ranging network of funders and "partners" who enter into formal sponsorships or partnerships, such as trucking and insurance industry lobbying organizations that promise to provide reward monies based on whether tips that serve their industries interests (e.g., theft of trucks or insurance fraud) led to arrests and charges (Lippert 2002). As a local program CS purports to be "a partnership between the police, the media and the community that enables concerned members of the public to anonymously provide information on the identity of a criminal or incidents of criminal activity" (Toronto Crime Stoppers 2021a). As with charitable foundations in North America Crime Stoppers programs are overseen by boards. One Crime Stoppers program indicates it is "a volunteer civilian Board of Directors" (Toronto Crime Stoppers 2021a). Crime Stoppers attempts to mobilize the citizenry to seek out and submit information about crime in the form of a "tip" in exchange for anonymity and variable cash rewards (Lippert 2002). If this information leads to an arrest or seizure of property or illegal drugs, the informant, or "tipster", is offered this cash reward. Since its inception in the US in 1976, and fostered by widely touted (e.g., Canadian Crime Stoppers 2021) and grandiose, but somewhat dubious (Lippert 2002; Carriere and Ericson 1989) claims of success internationally, Crime Stoppers has also garnered public legitimacy (Pfuhl 1992). Crime Stoppers is now the most popular police driven crime reduction program in North America and has expanded to more than 30 other countries, including the UK, Australia, India, and South Africa. In addition to the 100 local Crime Stoppers funding networks in Canada and about 291 networks in the US (Crime Stoppers USA 2021), Crime Stoppers International (2021a) also claims there are hundreds of local programs worldwide. This international umbrella organization is itself a foundation with non-profit status in the Netherlands (Crime Stoppers International 2021b).

To illustrate the size of one local crime stoppers funding network using accessible data, Toronto Crime Stoppers has 31 "sponsors" including Canada's largest bank corporations such as Toronto Dominion Bank and Scotia Bank as well as several private security firms such as Paragon Security, 3-Sixty, and ADT with links on this Crime Stoppers webpage (Toronto Crime Stoppers 2021b). A subset of 17 of these same sponsors are listed as "partners" on another page, which likely means they have provided more funding than regular sponsors for Crime Stoppers (Toronto Crime Stoppers 2021c). The provincial Ontario Association of Crime Stoppers (OACS) umbrella organization has 11 major sponsors in its network, including the Insurance Bureau of Canada, a private security firm, the oil and gas giant Suncor, as well as two provincial enforcement-oriented government ministries, and several which, such as the financial transaction corporation Interac, are also nodes in the Toronto Crime Stoppers funding network (OACS 2021). Because of their promise of anonymity, Crime Stoppers actively promotes a clear separation from police. Despite the popularity of Crime Stoppers in North America and globally, the effectiveness in reducing crime has never been tested using an experimental design to determine, for example, whether citizens would relay actionable information to police regardless of promises of anonymity and cash (Lippert 2002).

Civil Forfeitures

Police forfeitures are the other noteworthy form of private funding of police. Forfeitures involve acquiring private property of those associated with criminal activity. Police then use the funds from this asset confiscation for their priorities. Forfeiture is strongly associated in the public eye with the "War on Drugs" in the US (Worrall 2001) and is less significant and more strictly regulated in Canada. In a sense, this is reward-oriented policing that entails the funds being funnelled back into police operations. All but two Canadian provinces passed forfeiture laws through the 2000s beginning with Ontario and Alberta in 2001 (Canadian Justice Review Board 2017). For forfeitures how police spend these acquired funds is not unlike the priorities supported by police foundations in that they include purchases of military-related equipment, rather than proven crime prevention strategies consistent with community demands and community policing. Police auctions are a similarly greedy practice, as the sales often go back to police instead of the community (from whom the seized items originate). Forfeiture involving police has been widely criticized as "policing for profit" (Holcomb et al. 2011; Williams et al. 2010; Williams 2002). Rasmussen (2018, 98) explains "police agencies will increase effort in activities that have a higher probability of generating forfeited assets and, because of limited personnel, cut back on non-revenue-enhancing activities. This is policing for profit."

Forfeiture has generated its own small literature that seeks to explore benefits and the downside of these practices (see Baumer 2008; Miller and Selva 1994). Forfeiture has not been shown to result in crime reduction, neither of drug related crime, nor crime broadly (Rasmussen 2018). While there have been limits placed on some practices in some US states, these are often avoided by what is called "equitable sharing" (Holcomb et al. 2011). This "sharing" occurs when federal police agencies, such as the Federal Bureau of Investigations, work with local or state police departments to share profits by "adopting" a case as federal for 20 per cent of "the take", and local and state police can then avoid the limits on forfeiture cases by receiving the majority balance of these funds (Rasmussen 2018, 98; Holcomb et al. 2018). Many criticisms focus on taking private property from persons charged but not convicted of crimes, which is then transformed into police funds in the US (Rasmussen 2018, 98). In Canada, while remediation of victims is the aim of forfeiture networks that entail police, crown prosecutors, the courts and involuntary funders, many drug transactions have no victim. Moreover,

> it is difficult to know how much money collected by successful civil forfeiture applications goes towards compensating victims. Instead, it seems that much is used to purchase equipment for the police... While some provinces have made limited efforts to provide compensation for victims, much of the money collected is granted to unrelated third-party non-profit and charitable organizations (Canadian Justice Review Board 2017).

Precisely like the framing strategies of police foundations discussed in subsequent chapters,

> [t]his can lead to what is known as a 'charity wash'... when a provincial civil forfeiture office attempts to insulate itself from criticism by making it seem that those opposed to civil forfeiture also oppose the charitable work of the grant recipient (Criminal Justice Review Board 2017).

The size of forfeitures is significant too. The US government does not keep statistics on the number of asset seizures through forfeiture. However,

> one common measure of the practice is the amount of money in the asset forfeiture funds of the Department of Justice and the U.S. Treasury, the two agencies that typically perform forfeitures at the federal level. In 2008, there were less than $1.5 billion in the combined asset forfeiture funds of the Justice Department and the U.S. Treasury, according to the report. But by 2014, that number had tripled, to roughly *$4.5 billion* (Ingraham 2015; emphasis added).

Although figures are not widely available in Canada either, and this is a provincial measure, in 2013 to 2014, for example, in Ontario $22.9 million CDN was acquired this way (Canadian Justice Review Board 2017). The seizures are framed as dealing with the lucrative illegal drug trade. Forfeiture and related seizure practices are more advanced and extensive in the US. In Canada, they are also used and there has been some research focused upon it (Nicholson-Crotty et al. 2020; Gallant and King 2013). Eight Canadian provinces enacted civil forfeiture regimes after 2001 (Gallant et al. 2014).

Both Crime Stoppers and forfeitures have been found to likely influence police practices, that is, to set priorities or push police to enforce specific types of criminal offences, especially those that are drug related. Thus, most "tips" that are advertised through, for example, the longstanding Crime Stoppers

Crime of the Week campaigns, concern property crimes, and crimes related in some way to business interests, such as retail theft and robberies (Lippert and Wilkinson 2010; Lippert 2002). Many other kinds of transgressions as or more relevant to the well-being of communities are left out of intelligence seeking, such as white-collar, corporate, state crimes, crimes against the environment, or racially motivated and other unwarranted police violence, as well as those related to intimate partner violence. Crime Stoppers is said to entail mostly garnering tips about the drug trade (Lippert 2002). This narrow focus in Crime Stoppers is seen in police forfeiture practices too where drug-related offences or "enterprise" crimes are targeted. This is a long-standing critique of police and criminal justice and the little attention paid to corporate and governmental transgressions that are often as much or more harmful (Bittle and Snider 2006; Goff and Reasons 1978). We would ask: where is the advertising for tips about corporate malfeasance and fraud in Crime Stoppers, where are the police foundation transfers to departments for purchase of training and audits for officers to conduct deep investigations of "crime in the suites" or "eco crimes", and where is the seizure of assets of private corporations and other businesses immediately following preventable deaths of workers (in Canada available since the 2004 amendment to the Criminal Code called the Westray Law but which is almost never enacted)? Are these not priorities of communities too? Even research after legal reforms of forfeiture practices (see Moores 2009) has shown abuses and questionable returns (Rasmussen 2018) and how forfeiture influences police practices, especially in the US (Holcomb et al. 2018).

Here loyalty extends not so much to those submitting "tips", albeit with wheels greased by promises of anonymity and cash in exchange (see Lippert 2002), but instead to donors of various kinds, for example, through long-standing versions of "jail and bail" that involve Crime Stoppers "arresting" a prominent, often political or corporate figure, and placing them into a mock "jail" and "behind bars" and then encouraging donations to arrange their "release" (CTV 2019). These donors are then brought into the police fold. Similarly, those bidding on seized or forfeited items can be rest assured that any profits will go to future police enforcement of conventional street crimes rather than other kinds such as white collar or corporate crime (or to the public treasury) or for acquiring more private property for future bidding.

Overlap in Funding Networks and Funders

Funding involving independent organizations such as the local Crime Stoppers and police foundation also overlap. In other words, the funding networks could be viewed as not only entrenched or dug deep into this terrain but integrated and interlinked with all kinds of ramps and raises between them. The latter sometimes generates and transfers funding to the former, with both working on behalf of police departments to provide intelligence and other resources, respectively. For example, the influence of the insurance industry on Crime Stoppers is evident in formal sponsorships of local organizations across Canada (Lippert 2002). Similarly, the NYCP Foundation not only transfers monies to Crime Stoppers for rewards for relevant information for police investigators but has been a full partner in the Crime Stoppers enterprise for decades. This partnership the NYPD describes as "an invaluable crime-fighting tool since the program's inception in 1983." In this case the foundation "administers the program, distributes rewards, and coordinates media campaigns to encourage public awareness" (NYPD 2021). The Insurance Corporation of British Columbia, the public automobile insurance corporation in that province, regularly provides funding to the Delta Police Department for various projects. In another example of overlap, a commercial paid detail broker, Seattle's Finest, advertises they donate to a Seattle police-specific charity, "Stand with those Who Serve", a moniker showing the police institution's aim to reproduce and extend itself *par excellence.* The "Stand with" charity also lists one of its few main sponsors as the Seattle Police Foundation (SWTWS 2021), and thus three organizations from at least two different funding networks are currently interlinked extensions of the greedy police institution.

There was also a tendency for private and public organizations to provide funding through not one but two means: donations and paid detail. Table 2.6 shows overlap in two funding networks of York Regional Police for which data was acquired.

Conclusion

From crime scene investigators armed with hi-tech tools, to special gang and drug units deploying surveillance technology to monitor suspects, to patrol officers responding to calls using their body-worn cameras, to police investigators actioning anonymous tips about street crime from Crime Stoppers call centres, to the latest armoured car and protective gear for the militarized SWAT team, to training and conferences, much policing today is knowledge and technologically dependent. However, these types of institutional priorities must be resourced and increasingly this tends to be through mostly hidden private funding. The police as a greedy institution are content to receive these funds, and as we have already shown there are many channels for receiving these monies and moving them around. Some of the channels are obscured and the resources must remain underground. The policies that regulate these exchanges are inconsistent and incomplete. They are like a tiny, vague, rusty warning sign posted at the entrance to a dark lucrative mine in lieu of gates and inspectors, or an impenetrable concrete seal. This chapter explored and mapped the private funding mine of the police institution used for these and other purposes. It is an incomplete map of this expansive terrain of these resources coming to police but one that

Table 2.6 Overlap in Donation and Paid Detail Networks in York Regional Police-2012 to 2015

Donor/Funder	*Total Donations*	*Donation Purpose*	*Donation Dates*	*Paid Detail Hours*	*Year of Paid Detail Use*
Scotiabank	$31,800	Jamaica Adopt-a-Mission/ Police Appreciation Night	2012 & 2013	24	2012 & 2013
Saint Joan of Arc High School	$1,500	Jamaica Adopt-a-Mission	2012	9	2014
Liberty Development	$25,000	2013 Special Olympics	2013	12	2012
City of Vaughn	$20,000	2013 Special Olympics	2013	65	2014 & 2015
Powerstream	$13,000	2013 Special Olympics	2013	171	2014 & 2015
Con-Drain Company	$12,500	2013 Special Olympics	2013	820	2012 to 2015
Miller Paving Limited	$5,000	2013 Special Olympics	2013	1369.5	2012 to 2015
Brennan Paving & Construction Ltd.	$58,495	Community Safety Village	2013	4956.5	2012 to 2015
Sheraton Parkway Hotel	$50,000	2013 Special Olympics	2013	25	2012 & 2015
Town of Newmarket	$12,200	2013 Special Olympics	2013	65.5	2012, 2013 & 2015
Peter & Paul's Catering	$10,000	2013 Special Olympics	2013	4.5	2015
Town of East Gwillimbury	$5,000	2013 Special Olympics	2013	170	2012 to 2015

begins to illuminate many of the various channels and shafts. This terrain lacks consistency and standardization, which can make it difficult to traverse and which is one reason why it has received such little academic, journalistic or public scrutiny.

We provided key definitions and distinctions among types of funding before elaborating on the history, prevalence, and size of these funding networks, as well as showing detailed examples of policies and practices from six specific departments in Canada and the US. Each type has a distinct history. Additionally, the prevalence and size of the different forms and networks was found to be significant too. Foundations have grown dramatically across the US and to a lesser extent in Canada. We could discern only four of the 50 states that did not have at least one municipal police foundation although only three of the 10 provinces have them so far. It has become the exception for a police department not to allow paid detail funding rather than the rule in Canada and the US. We could not locate a state or province where a paid detail funding network was not operating. The size of foundation and paid detail networks vary considerably, but in some jurisdictions, they are quite large with many nodes. The largest we could discern was in Boston although they are likely larger in bigger US cities such as New York and Los Angeles. The chapter then explored policies and private funding donations and from several departments of varying size from Canada and the US. These were found to vary regarding reference to sponsorship and allowing officers to solicit funds from would-be donors. Many invoked community in framing their policies. Most departments in the US and Canada either have an associated local Crime Stoppers program or share one with one or more other police departments, which are in turn linked to umbrella organizations. Forfeiture funding regimes are very prevalent in the US and in Canada. Some of these networks – foundations, paid detail, Crime Stoppers, and forfeiture – overlap as well. This chapter has illuminated and mapped the dark mine that is private funding of police. These developments might mutate in the future as well, further creating private influence in the criminal justice sector (also see Rosemont 2014). For example, in June of 2021, an entity called the Victims' Assistance Community Grants Incorporated was created to funnel money to crime victims. Police foundations were some of the first of these shell corporations to be established in the criminal justice sector, but they will not be the last. Chapters that follow explore foundations, sponsorships and partnerships, and paid detail funding in greater detail before proceeding to an analysis of controversies and corruption and the sometimes-yawning holes in existing policies from which problematic intentions of the police institution and its loyal miners are unmasked and begin to be seen in the light of day.

Notes

1 One source of emulation was the Washington, DC-based American Police Foundation (Vancouver 1976).

2 These articles, since removed from the IACP's website, can be accessed by copying the URLs in the bibliographic entries into the internet database's "Wayback Machine." https://archive.org/web/.

3 Only these years of the journal were available and were acquired in person from John Jay College library in New York. This journal is not typically available to the public or otherwise online.

4 In excerpts from interviews, but not from documents, in this chapter we have replaced "paid duty" with "paid detail" for consistency.

Chapter 3

Glossing Over the Greedy Institution

Views from Inside Police Foundations

Introduction

In this book, we conceive of police as a greedy institution demanding loyalty, conformity, and resources. There are constraints on the resources the police institution can access due to concerns around conflict of interest in Canada and the US. Chapter Two, for example, identified some typical rules or laws governing the size of direct donations to police. While some direct donations still happen, more and more they are funnelled through a relatively new organization adjacent to police called a police foundation. This organization takes a specific form and is legally defined as a charity or non-profit. The public may assume non-profit organizations and charities are neutral and benign entities. However, there is a sizeable literature on conflicts of interest and corruption in these kinds of organizations (Bar-Nir and Gal 2010; Weisbrod 1997). The non-profit and charitable sector is not without influence from corporations, meaning corporatization is evident even in charities (Bromley and Meyer 2017; Baines 2010; Eikenberry and Kluver 2004; Young and Salamon 2002). This creates a leeway for disreputable exchanges (Rossman 2014) when conjoined with the greedy institution of police. The police foundation allows greed to influence public policy without reprimand or conflict of interest allegations, which is one reason we have seen such a proliferation of police foundations in North America.

As Fridman and Luscombe (2017) argue, police foundations can (1) claim separation from police, (2) deny reciprocity and *quid pro quos*, and (3) claim to be returning these funds from donors to community. All these mechanisms make police foundations the perfect broker between the corporate world and police. In Chapter Two, we discussed the size and history of police foundations among several other key private funding forms. In this chapter, we more closely examine the police foundation's role in relation to police departments. We draw from interviews with board members and staff of police foundations to explore the work police foundations do to support police with economic and social capital. We draw from critical literatures on non-profits and charities (Oelberger 2018; Eikenberry and Kluver 2004) as

DOI: 10.4324/9781003167914-4

well as nepotism and cronyism (Copeman and Banerjee 2020; Rossman 2014) to interpret the claims of respondents about the work of police foundations and the exchanges they are describing. We suggest the police foundation can be conceptualized as an extension of police as a greedy institution. We provide details on foundations' establishment and activities and detail their work as fundamental to the operation of police as a greedy institution. The police foundation is not only a shell corporation for moving private monies into policing, but also a vehicle to attract – through rhetorical framing – economic capital and social capital. The foundation is a cash cow, which political scientists Jancsics and Jávor (2012) define as a network node that due to legal loopholes acts as a consolidation and relay point for economic capital. Jancsics and Jávor (2012) contend these cash cows resemble organized crime hubs in terms of levels of secrecy and mechanisms of operation although they are appearing more and more in government and partnerships between public and private sectors. The police foundation is a perfect cash cow according to this definition. The foundation has the effect of aligning economic, social, and political capital of other groups and organizations with the police mission. Extending and supporting the police mission, the role of the police foundation is thus pivotal in the operations of police as a greedy institution.

Views from Inside Police Foundations

Origins, Goals, Motivations

Police foundations are relatively new organizations, although as noted in a previous chapter, the New York City Police Foundation (NYCPF) can be traced to the 1970s. Most police foundations in North America were established in the 2000s in cities from Charlottesville to Cleveland, Indianapolis to New Orleans, Omaha to Kansas City, and for police foundations across Canada as well. The 2000s was a decade when police foundations were being widely established. This growth was due to intensified advocacy of police foundation proponents. Former NYCPF staff went on to establish a larger US organization that assembled an instructional kit for police and local stakeholders on how to create a police foundation and its benefits. The more this kit was circulated, the more popular foundations became, including eventually in Canada. The rhetorical mission of police foundations, as stated in this kit, was to prevent corruption and economic malfeasance in policing. When the NYCPF was established, the New York City Police Department was still reeling from the Knapp Commission investigation that had discovered rampant corruption (New York 1972). The police foundation then provided cover or camouflage from the scrutiny of investigators concerned about economic malfeasance. Its rhetorical mission was to prevent police organizations and personnel from engaging with private money. There is an irony here.

The police foundation, as an arm's length but non-profit or charitable organization, can liaise with corporations and receive their donations and distribute this funding as the foundation's board sees fit. Another stated mission of police foundations for many of their representatives who we interviewed is to support the police and support the community in which they are situated. These claims about support and philanthropy are part of the rhetorical framing of police foundations. Generally, the mission of foundations is to support police departments by raising funds that are funnelled mostly into policing. Donations made to police foundations are put towards purchasing equipment and operating police-centric programming. Police foundations are considered non-profits or charities under most jurisdictions' laws.

Some interviewees from police foundations discussed their foundations' origins and how they were established. Many relied on venture capitalists and people with "deep pockets" to start. As the interviewee from a North-eastern US police foundation remarked:

> So back in 2003 … a local venture capitalist walked into the office of the police chief and said, 'what can I do to help support you and your department?' And so they came up with the police foundation (Northeastern Foundation 1).

A Canadian police foundation representative echoed:

> So we had a big, giant garage sale. Well, that didn't raise much money, …so the Chief said, 'what are we going to do?' I said, 'I guess we better form a foundation.' And that's how it started. We just phoned up people that we thought had deep pockets in *, and that's how we started (Canadian Foundation 1).

The idea of police foundations, along with its rationales, is circulated at police conferences and in police networks. As the interviewee from a US Midwest police foundation put it: "It got started in 2010. Then Chief * I think had been to a conference and heard about other police foundations in existence and thought it'd be a great opportunity" (Midwest Foundation 1). Since most police foundations take the form of charities or non-profits, this bestows them with special legal and financial status. As the interviewee from another US Midwest police foundation related:

> We incorporated in 1999 as a non-profit. It's a not for profit or 501(c)3, that's a US internal revenue service designation which allows the foundation and other non-profits with that designation to collect or receive… donations from individuals, corporations, other foundations, things like that. And then it allows those organizations or individuals to receive a tax deduction based on their tax situation. But it is the best designation in the US for a non-profit organization (Midwest Foundation 2).

That structure is important for understanding how police foundations can evade scrutiny and operate smoothly as a shell corporation for police departments. Conflicts of interest can emerge readily in charities, in part because these organizations are often subject to fewer oversight mechanisms (MacDonald et al. 2002). One would never know this from the communications of foundations themselves, which are framed to make foundations appear benign.

Some interviewees reflected on the foundation's mission and were not shy about stating the goal is benefiting the local police department rather than community groups or marginalized populations. As the interviewee from Charlottesville Police Foundation put it, the mission is: "Support the Police Department." This is an unambiguous statement and many other foundations echoed it. For example, an interviewee from a Canadian police foundation remarked:

> What we do is provide positive benefit to police initiatives that aren't funded by the city and help those agencies who are not directly part of the police service like the Legal Aid Society of Alberta, or the Arbitration Society of Alberta, or the like who are involved in policing or in issues that could lead to policing if they don't get settled correctly (Canadian Foundation 2).

One Canadian foundation's representative explained their purpose is "to help raise funds to make policing in * easier for our police officers to keep our community safe" (Canadian Foundation 1). These activities are linked directly to policing rather than being a form of community charity. For example, the New Orleans Police and Justice Foundation implemented an online camera registry which allows businesses and citizens alike to register cameras on their buildings, allowing police departments to access that footage for investigation purposes. The mission is to support police and the criminal justice apparatus. An interviewee from a US Midwest police foundation noted:

> the intent was really to create an opportunity to support police agencies throughout central [the state] so not just * but our... seven counties around us so supporting those agencies as well with a particular emphasis on supporting the law enforcement officer as an individual but also their efforts in community policing so how they impact their communities (Midwest Foundation 3).

As the interviewee from a Southern US foundation similarly explained:

> It is one thing to assist the police department but to really approach and try to solve our crime problem, there were many more players we needed to engage with so we officially changed our name to '* Police and Justice Foundation' with the intention of providing support to the public defendant, the district internee, the sheriff's office, community

> service programs, anyone and everyone who engaged with criminal justice (Southern Foundation 1).

These claims about assisting police were a constant, despite most foundation communications and websites focusing on charitable-giving to community rather than indirect funding of police. As the interviewee from a Midwest foundation quoted earlier noted, their goal is to provide funding for

> everything the police foundation purchases has to have access to for reducing violent crimes. We buy cameras, technology. We had a big camera project that we rolled out. We worked closely with the police department to identify where they want technology, where they have the highest amount of violent crime (Midwest Foundation 1).

And as the interviewee from another US Northeast foundation noted:

> Our goal is to support the * Police Department and public safety needs in the District... although we work with a lot of other agencies and informally help some others with some different initiatives (Northeast Foundation 2).

These claims clarify the role of police foundations is first and foremost to support police. Indeed, the fact these organizations label themselves "*police* foundations," as opposed to simply community or some other kind of foundation that happens to provide some funding to police, supports this notion. An example of the latter kind was the Cleveland Foundation, remarked upon in Chapter Two, that had this generic name, and happened to provide funding to Cleveland Police, but mostly contributed funds to other causes in that city through the 20th century. Thus, the fact there is now an organization called Cleveland Police Foundation is a significant, new development. The second purpose is to align the views and resources of the community with those of police. A representative from a Midwest police foundation explained that they were:

> founded to support several of the police charities but also to support the members of the * Police... Our mission is just to forge stronger bonds, to assist members... to forge stronger bonds with the community (Midwest Foundation 4).

The interviewee from a Northeast foundation quoted earlier also noted:

> one thing we're looking at is ... a lot more grassroots initiatives. Rather than just corporate sponsorships work with individual citizens even if it's smaller donations to get them involved (Northeast Foundation 2).

This expansive, network-based alignment effort is another explicit purpose. No interviewees spoke much about supporting community or community charities, which is interesting given that much rhetorical framing on foundation websites suggests community charitable giving is paramount. Instead, foundation interviewees revealed most activities are about bringing in partners, economic capital, social capital, and supporting the police mission.

Boards, Donors, Networks

Police foundations comprise a board of directors and sometimes a small staff. Some interviewees further elaborated the goals of the foundation or their goals as a board member. Board composition varies from foundation to foundation. We examined the board membership of the foundations. For the most part, board positions are all volunteer rather than paid. Some foundations prefer board members to be non-police affiliated, although as we show below this is a guideline that is not always followed. Others are mixed or comprised of police-affiliated members. All boards have men and women, yet the board members' number remains small, the smallest board being five members. To provide a sense of board member characteristics, we looked at the backgrounds of police board members in Abbotsford, Calgary, Delta, Edmonton and Vancouver in Canada, and Los Angeles, New York City, Philadelphia, Phoenix, San Diego, San Jose, Seattle, as well as St. Louis in the USA. There are 282 people identified in this 2018 snapshot of police foundation boards. Only 232 of the board member's home organizations were available, while the background of other board members was not entirely clear. Some of the sectors represented (e.g., financial service, banking, and investment management) are interrelated. The technology sector and the investment sector are the main categories represented accounting for 59.8 per cent of available board member types. These types include technology companies, investment companies, business companies, and financial service companies. Among them, technology companies and investment companies are the most common (10.8 per cent each). Law firms, police, construction companies, and energy companies are other sectors and types featuring prominently. Finally, there are people from local business enterprises that offer services like film companies, hotels, insurance companies, consultant companies, auto service companies, healthcare providers, recreation companies and construction companies, as well as non-profit organizations. While this is a limited sample, what it starts to show is the community is severely under-represented on the boards of these police foundations, with nearly 60 per cent of board members representing technology companies, investment companies, business companies, and financial service companies, then followed by law firms, police, construction companies, and energy companies. Given these connections and the flow of dark money we describe in this book, more research into police foundation board membership is needed. More research into the backgrounds of board members and the subsequent contracts that police sign for technologies and other gear and services tendered is much needed to explore these murky relations and exchanges facilitated by police foundations as well.

The board of directors attempt to attract economic and social capital to the police foundation. However, they are attracting this economic and social capital for police and filtering or brokering or laundering those forms of capital before they are transferred over to the police. The idea of capital laundering is not hyperbolic. We would suggest this is a laundering of economic capital but also social capital. Direct ties to police would create disreputable exchanges, but the go-between of the foundation creates a buffer between donors and police and therefore makes the donors loose or distant network ties. Corporations make donations to police foundations. The police foundations then decide how to distribute the monies to local groups. But in many cases, the police are the main local group who are recipients of the funds. Thus, the laundering idea is an apt description. There is some variation in the types of police foundations by state in the US. There is variation depending on tax law and the same goes for the foundation types in Canadian provinces. No matter the type, the police foundation attempts to recruit board members who will be in a good position to attract economic and social capital to the police foundation.

The interviewees discussed strategies used to recruit new members to the foundation board. All boards are different, but one commonality is the presence of business professionals. As a Northeast foundation representative explained, this included:

> [O]ne from a CPA firm and then there's a gentleman who had been part of our [National Football League team]... and he has since gone into business but he still maintains ties in that arena so I think they work to be strategic in the people they included, but they've been at it for four years now so I think they're really looking forward to kind of expanding their reach (Northeast Foundation 1).

Regarding board members, the advantage of having business professionals is deep pockets and many network connections. Community members can be involved if they bring with them network connections. As an interviewee from a Canadian police foundation noted:

> We're building up our sponsorship list and targeting people we feel that would be a good annual giver and giving them reasons why. So we don't just go out and target them... We need people from all three areas [of the city]. You can't have them all come from the business community. We have people from North * that are in business but live up there, and people know them...and when we lose a member we say, 'well look

> we're really short on somebody in the industrial area', or… try and target where you might be able to get a few more people interested. It's not because you want to be on the foundation you get to be on the foundation…. we want worker bees and we want people that are connected so that we can get into the different three areas and the industrial area (Canadian Foundation 1).

As the interviewee from one of the US Northeast foundations put it:

> There are two co-chairs of the board that have in place sometime that are heavy hitters in the business community and that play a role in coordinating other board members and most of our board members are private and affiliated with corporate sponsors (Northeast Foundation 2).

Concerning recruitment, board members from the business community tend to bring in other businesspersons to serve on the board. This same interviewee explained:

> Our major initiative in recruiting board members… might be referrals from other board members or people that we meet that introduce us to folks that would like to be involved. As far as project approval for major initiatives, we'll run it through the board if it's a big heavy funding initiative (Northeast Foundation 2).

A Midwest police foundation representative added:

> It's all civic minded business owners in *. They're prominent business owners I would surmise that all but I have 19 board members they all own their own companies or way up in the organization as executives they have the ability to spend money. They donate their own money as well as their business foundation money so we get you know it's not uncommon for my board members to give $35,000 every year (Midwest Foundation 1).

As the quotation indicates, board members must be ready and able to put their own money into funding the police in addition to attracting financial and social capital for the foundation and ultimately the entire greedy institution.

Many police foundations have high-status financial elites as board directors, although sometimes they have a designated community member on the board to help direct some funds to local community groups in need of resources too. Recruiting is the responsibility of the current board. Often this responsibility is pursued through a nomination process, and here the votes of current board members are paramount. Another foundation strategy was to build a sponsorship list and target people they thought would annually provide funds. The board of directors also varies in terms of members who are police.

For several foundations, police members played a central role on the foundation board. This was surprising since foundations are often legally required or at least expected to be at arms-length from police departments. Another Midwest foundation representative related: “11 board members and it’s almost 50/50 in terms of who are affiliated with police and who are not.” This interviewee continued:

> We’ve got one representative from it’s called * Cops which is, there’s the National Cops organization which concerns police survivors, we have a member from our F.O.P and my office is actually housed in the F.O.P building and then there’s the local F.O.P and we also have the president of the state F.O.P on our board so there’s that (Midwest Foundation 3).

As the interviewee from a different Midwest foundation explained: “We have one retired officer who owns a pretty good-sized security company” (Midwest Foundation 4). Again, the policing and security networks engendered by this institutional formation are the key feature of foundations. And current police are a central node in the network. A Canadian foundation representative explained:

> Although the Chief of police is a member of our board, and they get to appoint someone to sit on our board as well, so we always have a police constable [or] officer sitting on our board, and the Chief can come any time he wants. And he’ll come to a couple meetings here but normally he’s so busy we don’t see him that often. But we do have… the Chief’s executive assistant, at this current time (Canadian Foundation 2).

Even when advised not to, foundations still put police on their boards. As the interviewee from another Southern US foundation noted:

> The Department of Justice highly recommend that no police staff at all on the board and be it independent persons in the community. I did agree to put one police officer person on the board (Southern Foundation 2).

A Midwest police foundation representative described similar practices:

> So the current Chief comes to the board meetings [and] contributes but he can’t vote… he has no final say, but he can advise or whatever. So we were doing that. Every Chief has been an advisor or an ex officio. Well then they were letting all of them stay on, so we have two ex-Chiefs on the board (Midwest Foundation 2).

Most foundation representatives we interviewed indicated that police members (retired or otherwise) are current board members. Several boards comprise mixed board members, officers, business owners, and other community members; the Lakeland Police Foundation remains the only board not recommending having current officers sit as board members. In comparison, one confidential informant suggests their board comprises only currently employed police officers. Some police foundation boards, like Omaha's, have multiple police serving on their board. Some have only the police chief, and others have no police as board directors. In instances where police are sitting on the board of the foundation this bursts the bubbly rhetoric of transparency and limiting police engagement with private bodies because in those instances, police are situated in ways to direct the corporate funding into whatever police units they desire. There are often still several other board members at the table making decisions about from whom to request funds and who should receive donations in the community.

Pennings (1980) argues corporate boards ruthlessly compete with one another. Corporate boards also tend to try to co-opt other players in the field (Burt 1983). Police foundations emulate corporate boards, yet there is no competition or co-option. The boards if anything engage in policy learning and cooperation. This may be due in part because they tend to have police foundation monopolies – we came across no instances of there being more than one police foundation operating in the same city or locale and thus in a position to compete or co-opt the other. However, the bigger picture here is that large corporations could place multiple members on multiple police boards. This further supports our argument that the police foundation is an extension of the greedy institution and replicates the police institution overall.

Foundation donors that provide police funding vary. Some are large corporations such as energy and oil and gas giants and banks; some are wealthy individuals. Others are corporations with a stake in certain kinds of policing, such as weapons and technology companies. Without strict policies that mitigate or prohibit donations and sponsorship, as well as halt police being intimately involved on their boards in some manner, powerful corporate entities are free to attempt to garner as much influence as possible (Copeman and Banerjee 2020). These events for fundraising may foster disreputable exchanges (Rossman 2014), a point we return to in Chapter Seven, with the foundations brokering these flows from corporations and elites to police.

Some police foundations check the status of the donors to ensure they are – from the police point of view – credible and legitimate. Interviewees describe their relations with donors and their desire to enhance the reputation of both police and their foundation. Police foundations make requests of donors, and again, the economic and social capital of the members of the board of directors plays a pivotal role in attracting more economic and social capital from potential donors. As the interviewee from a Southern US foundation put it:

> I've declined donations on that basis before. They're not going to use our reputation and our association with the police department to help their business. Now I will send them a letter acknowledging their donation and tell them that it's tax exempt to Federal Law, but I…have to go on to say that no promise has been made to you and we receive no services from you. Those are the two representations that I have to make by law every time I acknowledge receipt of a donation and that's federal law and that's for anything over $250, I believe (Southern Foundation 2).

Similarly, the interviewee from another Midwest foundation noted:

> rarely but we do have, every now and then we'll have people express an interest in like I would like to buy, like for example that transport van, like a vehicle of some sort, and I would like my name on it or my company name like on the side, like "donated by," and we can't do that. So we can do donated by the * Police Foundation. You can't be like commercial advertising. Umm…we have a program at that luncheon, and we do recognize our donors in that program and then we do some signage at the luncheon as well where we recognize our donors (Midwest Foundation 2).

Some foundations at least report navigating this tricky terrain of conflict of interest and nepotism, although it is worth repeating that they constructed this terrain in the first instance due to the demands of a greedy rather than a needy institution.

The police foundations may also organize fundraising events. Hosting a certain kind of an event associated with certain groups could taint the police image. Police impartiality may be questioned if they are seen to have a direct relationship with some private sector or other external entity. Therefore, the relationship must be indirect, hence the foundation's existence. This semblance of distance in the network is a key function of the foundation (Fridman and Luscombe 2017). Having the police foundation organize such an event and liaise with private entities creates a broker, so that police do not appear to be directly related to these private entities or corporate players. Some events could include dinners or galas. Police themselves previously organized these types of events, but foundations have now assumed most of these tasks to serve as a buffer between (sometimes equally greedy) corporate and other private donors and police. When such events are held, it is a time when corporate interests in police such as those selling technology can connect and donors to police foundations may have a direct opportunity to influence police decision-making.

Interviewees describe some donors to their police foundation. One from a Midwest foundation explained:

> If an insurance company wants to donate a car, like a big car for show in autos, okay, so for a police department it's actually the division of police who accept that. It has to go through city council and an order has to be passed. You put that in, it gets accepted as a gift and add it to the police, it can be done and it is done. We donated a cargo truck to the Bureau of Community Policing to help with… taking their equipment out of the community special events (Midwest Foundation 4).

An interviewee from another foundation explained where funds come from:

> Is it individuals, are they companies, are they bigger corporations, where do most of the funds come from? All of the above… We had a $50,000 donation this year single donation from… a major corporation it's well known all over the US that's headquartered here. My board members give individually, you know like I said earlier… I had three of them give $25,000 out of their personal cheque book and then I have a couple that work for like banks and they'll give a certain amount and their company will match it. I have a couple of attorneys who will do the same thing. They'll give $2,500 and their firm will donate $2,500, so all of the above (Midwest Foundation 1).

In these ways, police foundation board members are also regular donors, funnelling their own money and money from their companies into the foundation and by extension into the police. These kinds of relations are ripe for what Jancsics (2015) calls low-level corruption, which begins with nepotism and cronyism. We return to a discussion of corruption as well as implication of the idea of rule of law in Chapter Seven.

Interviewees also commented on background checks on donors and some considerations in the process. As an interviewee from a Canadian foundation put it:

> I have a policy about that and I'm not aware of turning down money from anybody [laughter]. I mean I certainly, if we became aware that some terrorist organization or somebody who's trying to buy police influence or some such thing (Canadian Foundation 2).

Here foundations are aware of blatant conflicts of interest and cronyism but are not monitoring these too closely or carefully. A Southern US foundation representative explained:

> we look for a lot of things to make sure that donation is clean and you know without any potential for conflict. We don't even want the

> perception of conflict because obviously we are very, very concerned about protecting our corporate image, our image which is a non-profit (Southern Foundation 2).

Several respondents spoke about ensuring the donation or the money is "clean." The interviewee from a Midwest foundation explained his approach:

> before I accept money from this organization that called out of the blue …I went on and did my research [and] made sure they were a good organization and they were and at that time I called them back and gave them the information and they might donate two years in a row. We've had two people like that done that out of the area. Looking for on the research any controversial groups (Midwest Foundation 1).

The interviewee from a US Northeast foundation related:

> Essentially, we will work with the police department on that as a lot of them are guiding through that, but we will do some open-source vetting and online to make sure they don't have any baggage or issues with them. That could be some political groups… Would there be groups we would not be willing to accept donations or sponsorships from? Obviously, a hate group or a similar controversial group let's say the Ku Klux Klan… or group like that offered to give funding obviously we would not take funding from any group that's contrary to our mission of public service and the good in society (Northeast Foundation 2).

Note both interviewees use the term "good," which is consistent with moral regulation of paid detail funders, which are often pre-empted, as in Chapter Five. Most foundations do some vetting of donors and pre-empt at least some. Through vetting and voting, board members of the foundation wield incredible power and influence. Foundations devoid of a formal screening policy or process will often research donors. Foundations that vet donors, on occasion, screen through background checks for conflicts and how involved in the community they may be. Foundations who subject donors to a "check" seek to ensure the donations they receive are clean enough and free of controversy should they come to light. However, rather than a check on "bad" or immoral or even criminalized outside actors, one way to read this vetting is to exclude people they think may "rock the boat" in one way or another. In the foundation, corporate influence sits at the table with the police chief and police-friendly operators. The conjunction between corporate power and police power that allows networks to expand happens in the police foundation (as well as in paid detail, see Chapter Seven). Vetting donors may be less about making principled decisions and more about protecting this conjunction of capital and police power taking place inside the foundation to ensure networks expand.

Putting Gloss on the Greedy Institution

As noted above, police boards vary. Some have more community members than others, some have more paid members than others, and ostensibly, police foundations could benefit the community, by leveraging the social capital and the cultural relevance of police to raise funds for needy local groups. Some work of police foundations does this and much of their framing focuses on this. However, most funding that police foundations raise either through donations or events is transferred to the not so needy police. The funding for local and truly needy groups then is mostly a diversion from the real transfer of economic and social capital from corporate and other private or external interests to police.

Of the police foundations we interviewed, none reported experiencing any controversies or criticisms. However, there have been several controversies regarding police foundations in the US, for example, in Los Angeles (see Chapter Seven). Most police foundation representatives interviewed believed that no controversies or criticisms existed; for those who did, it was specific to their foundation. For those who did answer, they pointed to issues of bureaucracy or administration rather than core problems such as conflict of interest or nepotism.

Some police foundation representatives we interviewed were aware of the political role police foundations play while brokering and the potential for bad press and criticism to emerge. However, most tried to mitigate these potential conflicts of interest by carefully managing their relations and donation information and the funding transferred to police. Police foundations are not encased behind secretive corporate fencing. Their framing work involves websites and social media and they attempt to engage the public in many ways (see Crump 2011). This is, we note, in contrast to the way police frame paid detail funding as discussed Chapter Five. While foundations must report to revenue agencies (such as Canada Revenue Agency in Canada), these disclosures are limited. Foundations are not forthcoming with data on their exchanges or flows of economic capital, which makes them an apt shell corporation. Our point is it is as much the social capital (network connections) police foundations are trying to attract and launder as it is economic capital, and both befit the notion of police as a greedy institution.

Raising funds for police foundations entails varied methods. Some foundations rely on traditional methods such as solicitation, which includes knocking on doors, sending emails, or advertising on social media and other platforms (websites, signs, radio, etc.), whereas other foundations execute more strategic plans. These include hosting several sponsored events like galas, breakfasts, and other ceremonies where attendees pay a set ticket price, bring friends, and raise awareness about the foundation, thus gaining sponsors from attendees. Interviewees talk about strategies to locate donors as well as the communication formats they deploy. As an interviewee from a Northeast foundation put it:

> We have some social media presence when we have events coming up. I typically get on the radio sometimes, our TV stations will pick us up, where I'll talk about what we're doing and if you want to donate to go to our website and donate and sometimes people do sometimes. People will sign on for our newsletter or our e-newsletter and I'll send out emails and they'll have links to donate (Northeast Foundation 1).

An interviewee from another US foundation elaborated that their methods involve:

> sending emails, an existing donor database based on people who bought a T-Shirt really in 2014, an event in November... will be the first kind of major fundraiser that they've had and it'll be a breakfast, it's being sponsored through our [National Football League team]. They're very generous in helping us the sponsors...Our basketball team [and]... our football team both have committed $50,000 each over 3 years (Midwest Foundation 3).

A Southern US police foundation representative explained:

> We have done some solicitation. We've gone to some big corporations that have a lot of money that are local like we have... a big shopping centre, food shopping, and they've been extremely successful in *, multi-million dollars (Southern Foundation 2).

An interviewee from a Northeast police foundation elaborated their strategies:

> Our biggest event of the year is our awards ceremony where potential donors would come out to and see what we do to support the police department and then we'll run a number of events throughout the year. Cocktail parties..., a breakfast with the Chief that's a paid breakfast to bring people into. They'll pay 200 dollars a ticket and they'll bring in comrades that are potential sponsors as well and hopefully try and get them engaged and listen to what the Chief has to say. He'll talk about the foundation a little bit and our mission and our need for support our mission and then he will... hopefully discern some interest in those groups and we'll follow up with them to support foundation (Northeast Foundation 2).

The interviewee from a Midwest foundation related still other strategies:

> We're doing our Tribute to the * Celebration in September, and we have an awards program that we recognize officers. We have an officer-of-the-month program, the foundation does. That program is for officers who go above and beyond in community engagement… we recognize those types of acts that really aren't part of the job. In essence they are, but one guy gave a homeless guy his boots during the winter… [and] one guy crawled down a sewer to rescue a lady's dog (Midwest Foundation 4).

These kinds of fundraising double as a mechanism for boosting public views and the legitimacy of the police. Some foundation activity is oriented towards community, but we argue this activity doubles to benefit police by garnering positive views of police. As the interviewee from a Northeast foundation put it:

> Cops for Kids Day, that's my favourite. We get like 400 kids from the community. A lot of times it's kids that otherwise wouldn't be around police officers in a positive way and…we have just dozens and dozens of police officers and this like super fun event that we put on with the boys and girls club. I love that relationship partnership that we have and I always feel like it's this super positive event (Northeast Foundation 1).

Such events and links raise funds and tout community philanthropy, but the bigger picture has to do with the legitimacy of a greedy police institution, which such events enhance.

There are many foundation-led events that portray police in a positive or benevolent light while raising funds for the foundation and, by extension, for police. As the interviewee from one of the Midwest police foundations put it:

> The officer-of-the-month program is real… what we're trying to do is hey look we're recognizing these officers not because they do great work, because they do, but what's happening is other officers are seeing it and it's contagious (Midwest Foundation 4).

As the interviewee from another Midwest foundation noted that

> the luncheon's pretty cool, because we present all of the ribbons and medals earned the year before, so it's an amazing opportunity for a group of community people, like three to 400, that come to the luncheon to hear these stories and to recognize and appreciate the daily work of police officers and what they deal with (Midwest Foundation 2).

The event is a way of raising funds but also softening the police image overall among community and other local groups. As we note elsewhere (Walby et al. 2018), and as we explore further in Chapter Six, police foundations use multiple strategies to soften the image of police. One such strategy is associating the monies flowing from corporations to foundations to police with police dogs, often puppies. Associating the funds with police dogs, and framing the donation using puppy images, is a way of avoiding controversy and softening the image of police and their work at the same time. Peculiarly, police are using animals rather than humans to humanize their image. In turn, this framing about doing good and being benevolent might rub off on board members of the foundations. As the interviewee from a Midwest foundation noted, the main thing they appreciate about their work is:

> the opportunity to give back to the police department… for 27 years. I was over there 20 of those years. I was a [police] commander and I would get request after request over the years for equipment, technology just to stay current with… our peers in outlying areas and… and it'd come back disapproved, no funding (Midwest Foundation 1).

Now the former officer enjoys the ability to sign a blank foundation cheque for current police. This was the case in Cleveland too and no doubt elsewhere. Overall, interviewees reflect on the need to enhance the operations of their foundations and to enhance the overall relations people have with the police too. Several foundations discuss their proudest moment as an initiative rooted in philanthropy, such as Cops for Kids, Luncheons, and working with youth and the public. Others highlight programs that have benefitted police departments, the city, or both.

The key advice most police foundations offer to new or would-be police foundations and departments is to reach out to others and not re-invent the wheel. They point to police foundations across North America as exemplary models that learn from one another about how to expand their network and frame their activities. As the interviewee from a Northeast foundation related:

> The key thing is to reach out to some of the bigger folks which we've done as well. Places like New York and Philly and San Diego and jurisdictions around the country that have a police foundation… and always just keep that network going to see what different activities they're doing, what's working, what's not working. And through the International Association Chiefs of Police, the IACP, there is a police foundation track that's been gaining steam too so we're part of that track and participate in regular monthly conference calls with that group (Northeast Foundation 2).

Additionally, interviewees suggest it is important to keep the foundation mission clear, keep it focused on the police department, and find a solid board who see law enforcement organizations in a positive light. All this boosts the legitimacy of the police institution. As the interviewee from one of the Midwest foundations described it:

> That's a big thing ... the importance of being able to see their law enforcement in a positive light because usually when you're seeing the police, something's wrong. So if the foundations lift up and provide that the tool and mechanism to get that visibility, that positive interaction, I think that's really important (Midwest Foundation 3).

Discussion

What was common across foundations was an effort to implement new programs and funding initiatives. Foundation personnel report wanting to expand operations, recruit grassroots initiatives, and grow their board. Nonetheless, they all share one central aim: extending the mission of the police. Police foundations are not only trying to acquire more funding for police, although this is a main effect and which could be a situation where corporations influence policing practices, but the police foundation is also trying to attract as many partners and stakeholders as possible, even actors who cannot provide much funding. Attempts by police foundations to attract and retain partners exemplify the foundation as an extension of the greedy police institution. Charities are not without politics and influence, and rather than mitigating conflicts of influence, nepotism, and cronyism, they could equally play a part in breeding regressive social processes (Carman 2015; Barman 2006).

There is a sense in which it does not matter if police foundations bring in an extra 30 million dollars for police annually because police already receive ample public funding to engage in police work. Indeed, on this point one might ask about the adequacy of one foundation representative's earlier rationale of wanting funding for equipment and technology to "stay current with our peers" in the first instance since the effectiveness of police work with the community is apparently not the main goal. Put differently, the equipment and technology being purchased tends to be the kind purchased by Houston Police Foundation – horses, SWAT technologies and vehicles and others – that equate to the militarization of police and not to aid community policing programs as those are traditionally understood. What is as or more significant is aligning the interests of the community and its leaders with the policing mission, which reproduces the police institution. As one foundation member from a Northeast Foundation quoted earlier remarked:

> one thing we're looking at a lot more is bringing in grassroots initiatives rather than just corporate sponsorships. We want to work with individual citizens, even if it's smaller donations to get them involved (Northeast Foundation 2).

That is the crux of the matter here.

As noted in Chapter One, using gift theory to describe dubious, ambiguous exchanges does a disservice to gift theory. In some ways, the gift and gift theory need to be contorted to apply to such disreputable exchanges (Rossman 2014). Gifts are only one form of exchange, and it stretches the idea of a gift too far to refer to *quid pro quos*, bribery, nepotism, cronyism, and other phenomena as a gift. We also explained that while there is much evidence of corporatization, including in what foundation personnel say as outlined in this chapter, there is more going on with foundations and other forms of funding than corporatization. This is why we turn to greedy institution theory to conceptualize corporate donations to and sponsorship of police as well as other police activities such as paid detail policing. Greed is too alien to be in the same ballpark as gifts or generosity. While greed is familiar if not central to corporations and thus corporatization, here it goes beyond economic capital to include social capital too. The greedy institution wants people involved. Doing so without coercion is more agreeable, which is why police foundations have become so prominent. It wants people to conform to its mission and validate it and reproduce it by bringing in more small donors, stakeholders, and partners. The police foundation can get everyone from corporations to community involved in this greedy institution's mission. Foundations can get community stakeholders to value policing as an institution and as a response to transgression. This is the ultimate achievement for police and the police foundation. In these ways, police foundations are working to align diverse community and neighbourhood interests with one mission, the police mission. Some people working for police foundations and no doubt some board members who may be wealthy, affluent people are well-meaning and have philanthropic intentions. However, good intentions do not displace the goals and objectives of greedy institutions and may be manipulated by police foundations. As an extension of police, foundations are an example of this greedy institution in action. The money going into police foundations from corporations or other donors represents the translation of economic and social capital into resources for police. More than the resources, it is the aligning of interests that matters since such alignment will reproduce the police institution over time.

Police foundation personnel are careful what they say about policing and their foundation's practices too. They do the work of selling the police worldview and attract corporate funds, but they seek to do so in a risk averse manner. This is clear in the simple fact they do not publicize all information about the funds they receive and where the funds go. They do so only strategically (see Chapter Six). They also convey a seemingly neutral, professional narrative about all facets of the foundation. The board members of police foundations may be business oriented in greedy and financial terms, but by virtue of being there, they have already aligned themselves with the police mission and seek to bring others into the police fold. Attracting social capital is part of attracting economic capital and is crucial for the police foundation's mission and the police as an institution overall, hence the composition of foundation boards include members who can attract both forms of capital. As police foundations rapidly spread further and attract more stakeholders, despite the donations being smaller, this extends to reach in the power of the police institution even further. This is because every donor and stakeholder that aligns themselves with the police foundation is also aligning themselves with the police mission, which ultimately reproduces policing as an institution. While corporate boards tend to compete against one another (Burt 1983; Pennings 1980), police foundation boards are friendly towards and try to learn from one another. This means police foundations constitute a major and rapid mutation in organizational form, one blending the legal status of charities with the corporate board structure of corporations to reproduce and replicate the greedy police institution overall.

Conclusion

In this chapter, we have drawn from interviews with police foundation staff and board members to assess their views and police foundation operations. These interviews were sometimes difficult to arrange due to lack of trust among respondents and sometimes the interviews were tricky to conduct, as many respondents provided brief answers and in some senses were cagey. This speaks to the nature of the police foundation and its interest in managing information as it manages funds flowing from the private sector to police. Managing information is a key dimension of what the police foundation does (also see Chapter Six), not only to prevent knowledge of the volumes of funds entering the police and its sources, creating a taint for police, but also to prevent disreputable associations or conflicts of interests being claimed as it regards police and corporate interests. Nevertheless, we have suggested there is more going on with police foundations than the transfer of economic resources from the private sector to the police. That would be enough to mount a serious criticism of these foundations as these transactions have encoded within them conflicts of interest and create resource imbalances in the public sector where police receive many more monies than needier community and social development organizations. Some interview responses reveal how police foundations operate as cash cows (Jancsics and Jávor 2012) while at the same time shielding disreputable exchanges (Rossman 2014) from public view. Beyond accumulating social and economic capital (not to mention political capital) on behalf of police in ways typifying the greedy institution, this legal cover leaves open the possibility that cronyism and nepotism thrive in these spaces (Jancsics 2015).

Accruing of social capital is a major crux of the matter for greedy institutions. It is the accruing of connections, partners, and stakeholders that matters in a material sense because those partners and stakeholders are likely to not only donate to the foundation over time, but to support the foundation, to support police, to speak in favour of police and social control, as well as speak in favour of sometimes militarized enforcement and control funded by foundations and the private monies they attract, as a way of remedying transgressions and distress in communities. Therefore, the police foundation has emerged as a powerful vehicle for reproducing the loyalty, the conformity, and the interest that police as a greedy institution require and demand.

Chapter 4

Corporate-Police Partnerships and the Extension of Greed

Introduction

Earlier in this book, we focused on the police foundation as a vehicle for attracting economic and social capital to policing capital from the private sector. This economic and social capital, when aligned with policing, reproduces public police as an institution. The process is what greedy institutions do to command loyalty and conformity. However, corporations are not being naively tricked into this process, as they have their own gluttonous interests. Donors to police foundations are not only willing givers of money to police, but they are also aware of how it is beneficial, and at times they may demand of police things in their self-interest as well. Corporations are another sort of greedy institution, perhaps not one as rigidly hierarchically organized as institutions like police and the military, but they are nonetheless greedy in seeking to maximize their profits and gaining exclusive customer loyalty to the brands and products they sell, and perhaps also greedy in the broader sociological sense of trying to align their interests with those of others, not the least the interests of police.

Aymaliev (2017) argues corporate motivations for donations to police are multifaceted and go beyond the instrumentalist or strategic perspective. There is undoubtedly some philanthropic intent, however, there is more to this economic exchange and charity than altruism. The same could be said for sponsorship. While this is also the case in North America, the instrumentalist or strategic perspective nonetheless remains central. But what exactly is the strategic goal? We have argued it is greed, though not purely economic greed. As we argue in this chapter and throughout this book, greedy institutions relentlessly seek to align the interests of others with their own. Aligned interests are worth more than an injection of cash. In this chapter, we explore some partnerships and sponsorships that exist between police and corporations that appear to be a direct transfer of funding or other kinds of tricky transactions beyond donations through intermediaries like the foundations discussed in earlier chapters. Once illuminated, these transfers also appear to constitute more direct conflicts of interest. Once again, police foundations

DOI: 10.4324/9781003167914-5

exist to mitigate those conflicts of interest and provide a buffer against them, but this has not stopped some corporations from donating directly to police. Nor has it halted police greed from accepting or encouraging such practices. Although in this book we are arguing police are a greedy institution and that the police foundation emulates this greediness, corporate sponsorship of and donations to police (whether through the foundation or not) take several forms. This chapter attempts to relay its variation and complexity. Part of this variation stems from the multifaceted motivations of corporations and other donors. These relationships take several forms we reflect on here.

We have developed this typology of eight forms of police partnerships and sponsorships in relation to corporations based on an inductive reading of data collected on this topic. We delve deeper into some issues in other chapters, but here we combine these insights from news media accounts and some controversies with interviews with sponsors and donors as well to provide an account of police-corporate partnerships and the greedy character of these exchanges. Drawing from news accounts as well as some interviews with sponsors and donors helps substantiate our thematic analysis of news reporting and provide insights from within the mindset of the corporate donor and sponsor. Moreover, in this chapter the focus is corporate motivations, which provides a different perspective and view than offered in other chapters. First, sometimes corporations donate to police agencies in ways that seem strategic. Second, given their public prominence and visibility, police departments are at times treated as advertising spaces. Third, sometimes there is direct funding of police activity by corporate entities through a form of paid detail policing that seems to selfishly promote only a private interest. Fourth, there are examples where openly received donations seem to be an alternative income or revenue source for police departments. Fifth, there are examples of exchange between corporations and police that pertain to technology where companies seem to be brokering relations between police and military vendors in the US. Sixth, often donations to police appear to be bids for long term contracts that are lucrative. These tricky transactions might be a stealthy form of rigging future contracts and other economic relationships. Seventh, these corporate policing partnerships are sometimes mediated or brokered by past or present police executives. Finally, some small donations appear to be signs of altruism, although we speculate these also signal that these entities believe in the police worldview and donate as a gesture of support for it.

Some examples in this chapter are international, revealing these patterns are appearing in networks beyond North America. All the examples reveal how corporations, too, are acting greedily in these exchanges and these relations at the same time as police, as a greedy institution seeking to replicate and attract more economic and social capital. Corporations are trying to attract protection and loyalty that reproduces their brand. These examples show some dark money flowing between corporations and police and reveal some practices that depart from the rule of law, but more generally these examples demonstrate how entwined police are with private capital in the 21st century.

Eight Channels for Greed and Corporate-Police Partnerships

Donations and Strategic Investments

First, sometimes donations are made to police agencies by corporate entities in ways that appear to be strategic investments. These donations would stand to benefit the corporate donor in some way that would protect their assets. One of the most notorious of these in Canada was the Enbridge pipeline company donations in 2013 to Hamilton police to purchase all terrain vehicles and safety equipment, as well as GPS equipment to monitor and regulate spaces where a proposed Enbridge pipeline would be placed. Enbridge referred to this as a "Safe Community Program" and attempted to directly donate to police in other municipalities too. In this example, there is a direct link between police and Enbridge. Enbridge provides surveillance and other equipment to Hamilton police strategically to not only protect their pipeline, but also align the police with Enbridge interests and perhaps quell resistance to the pipeline. Thus, in this respect Kinder Morgan's funding of police departments in Texas via a different network, described in the book's introduction, apparently has a Canadian counterpart. Hamilton climate activists lodged a complaint against the Hamilton police for accepting $31,910 from Enbridge Pipelines, Inc. to purchase two all-terrain vehicles and related safety equipment as well as $9,500 for mapping and GPS equipment citing concerns that such influence may persuade police to quell opposition to the Line 9 pipeline from Sarnia to Montreal. The funding project dubbed Enbridge's "Safe Community Program" invites around 50 organizations to apply for funding after which there is a selection process (Carter 2013). The climate activist group claimed the Enbridge proposal included increasing the flow of crude oil by 25 per cent and shipping tar sands in a reckless manner that would threaten the pipeline's integrity. Given Enbridge's controversial history of oil spills and environmental destruction – including what environmentalist groups have since regularly claimed was the biggest inland oil spill in US history on the Kalamazoo River in Michigan (Matheny 2016) – these activists seemed to lodge the complaint as a precautionary measure to bring attention to the possibility of favouritism by police in which there may be an obligation to disperse protests. The supposed collusion between police and energy companies has garnered fear of unrestrained corporate exploitation of communities along the pipeline, considering strategic donations made to police in Gananoque, Napanee, Belleville, and other municipalities in Canada (Stone 2013). This collusion concern was recently revealed to be fully justified when it was reported that Enbridge had "reimbursed US police $2.4 million for arresting and surveilling hundreds of demonstrators who oppose construction of its Line 3 pipeline" in Minnesota too (Beaumont 2021).

Also in this vein, the convenience store chain 7-Eleven donated several electric stand-up vehicles (ESV) to the Dallas police in 2014. The ESV were to be used by police to prevent theft and trespassing. 7-Eleven donated these in the hopes they may receive greater police presence in the vicinity of 7-Eleven convenience stores. These are examples of strategic investments made by corporations in policing to have police provide a kind of tailored or curated policing response and protect the assets of the companies making the investment. The convenience store chain announced it would be doubling the Dallas police department's fleet of the T3 series ESV to "help increase safety and reduce crime in downtown Dallas" (Seven-Eleven 2012) given that the convenience store chain is a frequent target of theft and robbery.

This theme also emerged in interviews with sponsors. An Eastern Canadian sponsor, representing a telecommunications firm, intimates that they aim to sponsor events that involve their customers, suggesting these sponsorships are meant to strategically strengthen relationships with those customers:

> [I]n these kinds of cases, we have a large number of customers in the policing arena and the, you know, one of them is the * police service... They were kind of the hosting organization for [the police department]... that year. We've, you know, we have an office in * so, you know, they ticked the boxes of: Are our customers involved? Absolutely. They're in fact one of our, you know, good customers, was a sponsor (Eastern Canadian Sponsor 1).

They continued:

> it was going to help to put our brand out in front of a bunch of current *and potential* customers that, you know, we thought would help us drive the business, so, that's what caused us to entertain that sponsorship (our emphasis) (Eastern Canadian Sponsor 1).

Police as Billboards for Sponsors

Second, occasionally police agencies, given their public prominence and visibility, are treated as advertising spaces. In some instances, the highly visible police become advertising spaces for corporations. As Fleury-Steiner and Wiles (2003) note, police at points become spaces for advertising for commercial actors. In a city north of Boston, police recruited advertisements from local companies. Several police departments chose to follow suit by allowing advertisements on police cars. Melrose, the small city north of Boston planned to allow up to three advertisements per vehicle at a rate of $15,000 annually, equivalent to the leasing cost of a cruiser (Lazar 2007). Another scheme would have automakers arrange a sale of a new police car for $1 to the city in exchange for advertisement placement facilitated entirely through Government Acquisitions LLC (Wood 2002). The company said they would modify the vehicles' paint jobs to suit the sponsor's desires (Druley 2002). The advertisers would be affixed to the police vehicles. The police offered to modify vehicles and paint jobs as needed to accommodate the advertising. Similar proposals in the UK that entail sponsorship deals for multiple police departments sponsored by the same company would allow logos to be plastered across police vehicles and stations (Duffin 2013). This, again, is a direct form of private sponsorship of police, one in which police and corporations become mirror images of one another.

In another example, a local police station in Chennai in India can be seen with billboards over their entrances, despite a prohibition order from the Chennai police Commissionerate, advertising the names of police donors and sponsors. These billboards have sparked controversy regarding the image of police that such an advertisement projects. Police stations are not allowed to use or associate the names of private firms and/or donors with the names of police stations and high offices of the police department, although there was some ambiguity about the rule and desire on the part of police and the company (Raghu 2018). This theme also appeared in interviews with sponsors. The sponsor quoted earlier, a telecommunications firm, noted their sponsorship of fire and police conferences was to advertise their services to potential clients in those sectors. They noted that they usually get their logo present on conference materials. They explained:

> it was going to help to put our brand out in front of a bunch of current and potential customers that, you know, we thought would help us drive the business, so, that's what caused us to entertain that sponsorship (Eastern Canadian Sponsor 1).

Paid Detail Policing as Direct Corporate Pay

Third, another element of direct funding of police by corporate entities is paid detail policing, which we examine in Chapter Five. In Detroit, paid detail patrols were organized in a relationship among Detroit Police, the Michigan Department of Transportation and Marathon Petroleum. Marathon Petroleum paid for officers and patrol cars to be present in the vicinity of the corporation's infrastructure. In this joint venture, the refinery sponsored two patrol cars and funds for officer pay (Marathon Michigan Refining Division 2014). The refinery is in Oakwood Heights, which some have called a ghost town since relocation offers were begun by the company. The community is claimed to have its fair share of criminal activity, which includes several crack houses, gunfire, and arson cited by residents (Canadian Press 2014). Another example is the Ontario Lottery and Gaming Corporation (OLGC) having seconded officers running security at its casinos. The seconded officers on paid detail were caught in a scandal where a large number of insider wins by lottery retailers was discovered. The Ontario Provincial Police (OPP) is reviewing the assignment of OPP chief superintendent in his secondary role as vice-president of corporate security at the OLGC since 2004. Michael Sharland was the second highest-paid officer in the province and became head of security in 2004 when the OLGC began to investigate a disproportionate number of "insider" wins by lottery retailers. The investigation found no evidence of officer interference or obstruction (CTV News 2007). This case brings attention to the practice of secondment by police departments (Jolowicz 1994) and some conflicts of interest that such postings entail.

There are also privately funded fraud investigation units, a kind of paid detail not explored in Chapter Five. Investigation units are supposed to investigate fraud in the same corporate sector sponsoring it. An increasing trend for banks, insurers, automakers, and credit card companies is to hire police for criminal inquiries organized into specialized units entirely paid for by private sector financiers. The Dedicated Cheque and Plastic Crime Unit (DCPCU) consists of officers from London and the Metropolitan Police working alongside industry fraud investigators (Financial Fraud Action UK, n.d.). The Association of Payment Clearing Services, later known as UK Payments Administration Limited, representing members of the financial industry, spent nearly 12 million Euro on the DCPCU, which already receives nearly five million Euro annually from banking institutions. The donation is part of a larger sum of nearly 23 million Euro donated from several corporate sponsors including Land Rover, BMW, and Nestle (BBC News UK 2012). In addition, a New Insurance Fraud Enforcement Department is being funded by a 9 million Euro donation from the Association of British Insurers over three years. The National Vehicle Fraud Unit now entirely funded by the Finance and Leasing Association was once partially funded by taxpayers. Finance companies are not the only organizations that hire police to investigate fraud. Media reports revealed that Virgin Media secretly paid MET to investigate a case of fraud that cost Sir Richard Benson's company 144 million Euro annually (Barrett and Mendick 2012). These deals are legitimized under the 1996 Police Act and apparently do not count as donations which are capped at one per cent of the annual MET outcome. As we note in Chapter Five, this is a paid detail funding model whereby these funds are paid directly to police from the corporate sector. What kinds of *quid pro quos* or conflicts of interest are generated?

This theme also emerges in our interviews with sponsors. All interviewees stated their concern for public safety motivated their donations and thus did not seem to solely promote a private interest. One donor from a Western Canadian city specifically stated their funding does not and should not fund day-to-day policing:

> The truth is in...the Police Foundation, the first thing you've got to establish is we are not raising five cents for operations. Nothing. And we won't. Because the more successful we are, the mayors will keep trying to come in, take your money. No operations (Western Canadian Sponsor 1).

However, the individual mentioned that he and other members of the foundation were able to leverage police contacts gained through foundation work to resolve personal public safety issues. He tells the following anecdote:

> I have a friend who's a... very big donor [undecipherable] the police department, and he lives in a very, very wealthy neighbourhood and there's this crazy person across the street, a woman who's insane, right? And every time somebody parked a car in front of his house, she would vandalize the car. She didn't like people parking on the street even though it was perfectly legal. They couldn't stop her. The people were afraid to go visit this guy because this crazy woman would come out of her house, screaming and yelling. And he couldn't get any satisfaction. So we went right to the chief and said, Jim, you've got to do something about this. *laughs* You've got to protect this guy. And so they dealt with it. Got restraining orders and all the sort of stuff in place, right? (Western Canadian Sponsor 1).

He also anecdotally recalls a conversation with a police officer who operated a charity. After the sponsor donated to the charity, the officer gave him a window sticker commemorating the donation and, apparently jokingly, suggested he could show it to traffic police to avoid tickets.

The notion of displaying a sticker showing police loyalty influencing police conduct is not outlandish as it might first seem. In Toronto in 2000, "Operation True Blue" became a public controversy when the police union sold stickers in exchange for donations from private citizens in connection with a fundraising campaign (Canadian Broadcasting Corporation 2000). It is difficult to think of a phrase more indicative of loyalty to the police institution than "true blue." Significant aspects of this campaign entailed collecting funds to help the police union challenge any politicians who did not support the union and to help elect those who did (also see Duncan and Walby 2022). The union created a list of individuals who did or did not donate money and distributed vehicle decals and wallet cards to those who had. While the Police Board then passed a by-law to prohibit it, there was an understanding that police would treat those with decals or wallet cards more leniently, entirely contrary to the rule of law. Then the union refused to fully comply, leading the Board to commence action in the courts, citing Ontario's Police Services Act. There, the Board showed "the campaign brought discredit upon the reputation of the Toronto Police Service" and that "[h]arm of such a nature could not be compensated for in damages" (Toronto (Metropolitan) Police Force v. Bromell 2000). This practice ended in 2000 but it shows the willingness of the greedy institution to change its enforcement practices using this little mechanism of a sticker based on donations has happened before and the special influence of police unions within the institution consistent with greed we noted earlier. It also raises the question of whether 20 years later police boards and administrators, permitting corporate donations across North America, would still seek to halt such a greedy practice in its more corporatized form here or elsewhere due to its reputational damage to the rule of law ideal established previously in the courts and rhetorically touted by police themselves.

Donations as Alternative Funding for Police

A fourth approach is donations as an alternative funding for police departments. It is almost as if the police agencies became envious of paid detail arrangements and have sought to get their piece of the pie by creating arrangements where more of the corporate funds are funnelled into the police service itself instead of the pockets of individual officers. For example, in 2012, the Metropolitan Police in London received 22 million Euro worth of donations directly. The department then funded specific activities such as designated constables to reduce crime at petrol stations, an anti-fraud group, and more. The move was criticized for allowing private influence into public policing. Figures disclosed from the FOI request revealed that Metropolitan police received at least 833 donations to fund police operations. Some were to fund specific activities such as specific units that operate collaborative crime reduction projects in communities, the placement of designated constables to reduce crime at petrol stations, and a dedicated fraud investigation team called the "Dedicated Cheque and Plastic Crime Unit." The Association of Chief Police Officers has endorsed supplementary incomes from donations and suggests this type of income generation "help forces counter the effects of declining budgets and increasing pressure on resources." The association claims donations account for no more than one per cent of the department's total annual income, a cap instated by policy makers (BBC News UK 2012). In Chicago, a member of the City Council proposed police officers off duty to work in full uniform in the community, representing private interests who would fund the officers. A Council member proposed that this would entail off-duty Chicago police officers being present in full uniform at sites and events but funded by local businesses, civic groups, and churches. He argues that given declining budgets and increasing crime, other sources of funds are required. He suggested his plan would not merely apply to affluent neighbourhoods (Ponce and Bonafiglia 2013).

Many activities of police foundations appear to be alternative funding streams for police, as we examined in Chapters Two and Three. Focusing on the NYPD Police Foundation, the first foundation established in the US, the evolution of police funding in New York demonstrates this alternative funding clearly. Like many foundations, the NYPD Foundation is supported through private funding which is comprised of several city elites, corporations, and real estate developers helping to provide resources for departments that might be difficult to get through state and government funding (Trujillo 2019). Funding from donors has provided the NYPD with things like horses, bulletproof vests, bomb-detonating robots, crime-mapping systems, and body cameras. However, this sponsorship does not come without criticism. In addition to the foundation lacking accountability measures, the NYPD Foundation accepts gifts and donations from overwhelmingly white and wealthy hedge-funders and real estate firms, who also benefit from foundation programs such the "Commanding Officer for an Evening" which takes celebrities and well-to-do New Yorkers on police ride-alongs. As noted in Chapter Two, the NYC police Foundation is associated with a growing number of large corporations. In addition to those already mentioned these include Loews Corporation, CBS, the New York Giants, Blackrock Financial Management, New York Daily News, Mutual of America, New England Patriots, AT&T, Goldman Sachs, Bank of America, Verizon, Morgan Stanley, the New York Yankees, the New York Mets, and other big name New York real estate developers and other New York elites. From inception, the foundation has been pivotal innovation within the history of the NYPD and its expansion. The NYPD has the foundation to thank for much of its equipment and programs and the foundation continues to satisfy the needs of the NYPD (Smith 2018). While the article does not discuss the private sponsorship or funding of the foundation, the article outlines the complexity and sophistication of some programs and equipment, even noting their hefty price tags. Although the article focuses on NYPD, there is a discussion of some key programs launched in other states by police foundations.

While the NYPD Foundation was the innovator, there is no shortage of followers. Sometimes the police foundation is the conduit, yet other times companies seem to sidestep even the foundation shell corporation. For example, also reflecting this alternative income approach, though bordering on direct funding, Longboat Key Police Department aspired to use a private donation of $234,216 to upgrade technology in the department. The donation, made by a New York native who owns his own record label and manages talent and locations for MTV's "Siesta Key" program, will fund upgrades including laptops, software for patrol vehicles, and an enhanced license plate recognition surveillance system (Hauff 2018).

An analysis of the International Union of Police Associations (IUPA) shows, despite its mission "[to] help families of fallen or injured officers," only a fraction of donations is given to the Law Enforcement Officers Relief Fund. Rather, donations, which donees are made to believe will benefit the Relief Fund, wind up with telemarketers who are then paid to solicit donors. Bolstering itself as a non-profit union for law enforcement officers, investigations have revealed only a small number of families received a couple thousand dollars whereas top employees of the union received more than $100,000, and tens of millions went to telemarketers. Moreover, the article discusses the involvement of the Better Business Bureau, highlighting the IUPA's "D-minus" rating, warning donors about one union's affiliated organization's use of aggressive "high-pressure tactics" to solicit funds and repeated calls to people who had requested removal from call lists (Tampa Bay Times 2019).

This idea also came up in interviews with sponsors. A Cape Breton sponsor was solicited directly by police for funding for the conferences they sponsored. A Detroit sponsor mentioned their funding was used to train officers in first aid and pay for AEDs as well as first aid kits. Police projects funded by the Vancouver foundation and related businessmen included: repairs to a horse paddock; purchase of armoured cars; purchases of riot gear; and initiation of a cadet program. The sponsorship of conferences and the creation of a cadet program are ancillary policing activities, however training, facility maintenance, and the purchase of equipment are directly related to policing. Police departments seem to have made up for shortfalls with alternative sources of income through charitable organizations. Therefore, police departments appear to rely upon donations as alternative sources of income. One Western Canada sponsor we interviewed was recorded as saying: "if you want the level of policing that the public wants it's going to have to be a public-private partnership. All these municipalities are out of money" (Western Canadian Sponsor 2).

Corporate Funding as Network Expansion

Fifth, sometimes police are involved in networks with other government agencies and other corporate entities that create similar sorts of economic ties that bind. The funding relationship spans boundaries between public and private, corporate, and state (Giacomantonio 2014). For example, in Oakland, police departments met with military vendors in a meeting brokered by local government and private players in an urban security initiative. The sponsors of the event and the vendors then had unmitigated access to police and sidestepped typical procurement policies. The seventh annual Urban Shield in Oakland, CA invites police to attend training seminars and weapon technology exposition. In addition to federal funding, several sponsors have chipped in, including Lockheed Martin, Colt, Safariland (tear gas, stun grenades), and ATK (depleted uranium ammo). Participants included drone-makers, crowd-control experts, DNA-gathering device makers, tear-gas exporters, and armoured-vehicle manufacturers. It was hosted by the Bay Area Urban Security Initiative, which includes a few police departments in the Bay Area and is overseen by Cytel Inc (Lazare 2013). Critics claim the line between police and military is becoming blurred and increasingly intensified to repress protest and dissent (Before It's News 2013).

Some companies take up special centrality in these networks, facilitating greater capital flows. For example, thanks to a Massachusetts non-profit called Vested Interest in K9s (http://www.vik9s.org), police departments across the US are receiving donations of K9 protective gear such as bullet and stab protective vests and lifesaving body armor. Since its inception in 2009, Vested Interest in K9s, Inc. has provided over 3,500 U.S. made, custom fitted, NIJ certified protective vests, to various police departments. Vested Interest in K9s can provide departments with such equipment because of its generous private and corporate donations, an estimated value of $6.9 million (England 2019). The double entendre of the corporation's name could not more clearly reflect our focus on greediness in these funding networks.

There are other network formations that seem somewhat nebulous but nonetheless also appear to show expanding networks of capital exchange. In the UK, police appear to have arranged security contracts with large supermarkets and airline companies. These are not one-off paid detail arrangements but instead reflect much broader, deeper links between police and corporations. This case is not about private sponsorship, but rather deals with private contracting of police in the UK like paid detail policing. However, private contracts between police departments and corporations and businesses help fund millions of pounds of income. Unlike officers being provided for events like concerts and sporting events via paid detail, private contracts allow departments to derive an income from tailoring services to individual organizations (Milmo and Kirby 2019). In another case, insurance and utility corporations provide funding for police vehicle fleets through a grant program. Such funding requires departments to get creative when thinking about their funding needs and matching the purposes of the grant agency (Matthews 2018). Grants are made available by corporations, which enable police departments to upgrade their vehicle fleet. According to a captioned photograph, many departments are turning to green alternatives such as electric or alternative fuel vehicles with these corporate grants (Matthews 2019). Sometimes these networks are large and might have transformative implications for the relationship between corporations and police. However, other exchanges seem based more on lower-level brokerage or patronage. For example, Exotic Motor World in Staten Island donated a 2017 Dodge Durango GT to Blue Lives Matter-NYC as well as hosting an appreciation event at the dealership. The vehicle was donated to show support for police, including neighbours across Hylan Blvd. The vehicle is to be used to transport families of fallen officers between boroughs or to Blue Lives Matter events, as well as transporting the Blue Lives Matter Team to families of fallen officers. We saw in the book's introduction that a *Black* Lives Matter supporter was trampled at a protest by a horse made possible by private police funding; here *Blue* Lives Matter gets free rides from similar funding.

This theme also appeared in interviews with sponsors. A Canadian sponsor indicated they brokered meetings between police officials and the current Canadian Minister of Defense, Harjit Sajjan.

> And it has spin-off benefits like one of the senior police officers that I got to know quite well through my association. He was best friends with the guy that just became our national minister of defense, Harjit Sajjan, and when Harjit came back to * about 6 or 8 weeks ago, we set up a dinner, we brought a whole bunch of our clients together in a private dining room and we had a very open session with Harj. Which, our clients loved it 'cause it gave them a chance to get to know way more about the Canadian armed forces and the Canadian military and Canada's role globally, in peace-keeping right (Western Canadian Sponsor 1).

He does not suggest, however, that this meeting extended to discussion of funding or acquisition of material by police departments.

Corporate Contributions as Bids for Bigger Contracts

Often donations are bids for longer-term contracts. If the corporation is about maximizing profit, it follows their funding of police in various guises will be partially about maximizing profit too. The bigger contracts are more lucrative revenue streams for corporations, draining the public purse more efficiently and permanently. The big contract is the big ticket for corporations and they will even offer technologies on a trial basis to broker the deal. For example, Taser International has funded many Association of Chiefs of Police events and has funded the Association of Chiefs of Police Foundation. The Taser stun gun and body worn camera manufacturer clearly wants to fund these events to ensure more weapon and camera contracts are signed in the future by those police departments. In some cases, after the contracts are signed, police members will then go on to have careers with the corporation, suggesting there is a high level of nepotism and cronyism involved. Taser International (now Axon), the largest supplier of stun guns to police, made a $300,000 contribution to the Association of Chiefs of Police (IACP). Cited as publishing guidelines for acquisition and use of stun guns, the IACP claimed the funds would go to the families of fallen officers and would not involve endorsement of the products produced by the donor. Furthermore, a *USA Today* review claims to have discovered a network of hundreds of police officers on the payrolls of companies and receiving funding in a way not dissimilar to paid detail arrangements, including Taser, Armour Holdings (protective equipment),

ASP (baton manufacturer), and PepperBall Technologies (non-lethal weapons supplier) (Johnson 2012) mostly to train police to use their products (Johnson 2011). Internal Audit, one agency investigating the procurement process for the Albuquerque police department of lapel cameras, revealed there were no other bidders on the contract awarded to Taser International. Chief Ray Shultz retired shortly after the contract was awarded to consult for Taser (Boetel 2014).

Police museums may also become a site where corporate monies make the difference for bigger contracts for technologies signed later. The National Law Enforcement Museum in Washington, D.C., also received many corporate sponsors, as have many other police museums. Though it may seem to be a curious donee to fund, the corporate sponsors are likely trying to associate their brands with law enforcement. However, this high-level sponsorship could also be seen as an attempt to compel police to monitor closely the premises in vicinities near their corporate headquarters and other assets. There are many associations and policing entities that hold annual events and corporations are very often major sponsors of these events, such as Lockheed Martin, Motorola, Verizon Wireless, Digital Ally, Dupont, and Ericsson. Many of these large corporations sell technologies to police departments. Any sponsorship of galas or balls or annual events should be seen as an attempt to broker long term contracts. A funding network of 93 corporate sponsors have contributed millions of dollars to the planned National Law Enforcement Museum. Motorola and DuPont have each donated over three million dollars. In return, the companies received the right to display the company names throughout the building as well as securing millions of dollars in contracts. Although members of the museum board claim donations do not result in an obligation to do business with donors, Vice President of the DuPont Protection Technologies says, “Anybody trying to promote their brand is looking for a way to promote goodwill.” Additionally, a portion of the 19-member board are executives from DuPont, Target, and Motorola (Johnson 2011). Motorola is a major player in these networks, often sitting on police foundation boards (Luscombe et al. 2018) while recruiting police and intelligence officials to sit on its board (Mulvany and Gordon 2014). Between 2005 and 2011, Motorola donated more than $26 million to police foundations and related first responder non-profits (Mulvany and Gordon 2014). Motorola also donated millions to help create the National Law Enforcement Museum in Washington D.C. in 2016. In turn, many police have selected Motorola for radio and other technology contracts and purchases. Similarly, the Encana Corporation supports YouthLink, a Police Interpretive Centre which achieves its goals by allowing youth to view and interact with police equipment such as firing a replica sniper rifle and riding in a virtual helicopter as well as learning about police work such as K-9 units and forensic work.

Police conferences and galas and banquets also figure centrally here. The annual International Conference for Police Law Enforcement Executives

(ICPLEE) recently held in Montreal provided an opportunity for networking, training, product exhibition, and acquisition of sponsorship monies. Donations were organized in several brackets where higher amounts of donations enabled certain benefits (ICPLEE 2014a). The conference expected vendors from several areas related to law enforcement to attend every year including tactical and protective gear, identification technologies, surveillance, transportation, uniforms, and weapons (ICPLEE 2014b). However, several controversies surrounding sponsorship have been documented including the donation of concert tickets to members of the CACP which consists of police chiefs and senior executives from across Canada. The cost of tickets to a Celine Dion concert was covered in part by Bell Mobility and CGI Group Techna (a long-term firearms registry contractor) (Blatchford 2009). Taser International was rumoured to have donated $200,000 (platinum sponsor) on top of annual donations to the conferences hosted in various cities. Despite claiming to neither purchase nor endorse any products of conference sponsors, the CACP produced a document and a press release detailing their position on Conducted Energy Weapons (Tasers) (Marshall 2009). Their reports have acknowledged that despite scientifically tested safety parameters, they consider CEDs or Tasers to be "safe in the vast majority of cases" (Ward 2005). Taser (now Axon) has had to work hard to "sell" the criminal justice sector and politicians on their technologies. In the end, criminal justice professionals and politicians end up selling the idea (the efficacy) of Axon technologies to the public. But the only "benefit" of these moves and claims is to the owners and stakeholders of Axon when long-term contracts for electrical weapons or body-worn cameras are tendered.

Police Executives Mobilizing Institutional Greed

At times, corporate partnerships with police are mediated by policing executives. Policing executives have already accumulated enough cultural capital to know how to convey and funnel social and economic capital in these networks from the above activities. They are well trained to further advance these partnerships when they go on to work in another sector or for another organization. They are well positioned to work as "boundary spanners" (Williams 2002) who can bring together previously disparate fields and agencies. For example, in Oakland, the former police chief helped the police create a deal for Motorola and several cities in California. The former chief was a board member and shareholder of Motorola at the time when the deals and contracts were negotiated. Motorola has had a healthy relationship with police agencies across the US, providing high-tech weaponry, software, and surveillance equipment. William Bratton, who is a board member and shareholder of Motorola, was a critical participant of overseeing the approval of multi-million-dollar deals between Motorola and his police department during his time as LA's police chief. In 2011, Motorola paid Bratton $100,000 and another $160,000 in stock options for his services. On top of the $8.45 million purchase of the Integrated Public Safety System, the city approved a $5.25–million maintenance contract and a $3 million non-recurring budget for the communication system (Pueblo Lands 2013). In Detroit, Penske donated $8 million worth of vehicles and maintenance costs to Detroit police and police executives were involved in brokering the deal. A group of prominent businesspeople donated $8 million worth of 100 police and 23 EMS [emergency medical services] vehicles including automotive retailer Roger Penske. Penske says the partnerships with Detroit's three automakers will also cover maintenance costs (Cwiek 2013).

The theme also appears in interviews. This again speaks to the pivotal role of social capital in these exchanges, which here are shown to have an amplifying and multiplying effect. A Midwest police sponsor states their funding of police has resulted in close ties with police departments, and they remain in contact outside of funding requests:

> I: Has it created a closer connection with the police and your organization? P: Yes it has absolutely. Yes, I have gotten more of a relationship, I talk with them frequently because as they do their work, they update me, and we talk about next steps and things that happen (Midwest Sponsor 1).

They further state their local police foundation facilitates relationships between the police department and the sponsor's foundation: "The * Foundation cause they're kind of the intermediary between the police department and us, along with other foundations." The extent of these conversations and relative ranks of the police officials involved is unclear. Relationships between police and sponsors are much closer in a Canadian case. The foundation representative had a personal relationship with the former and current Chief. He also agrees with a statement made by the interviewer that foundation members broker relationships between police and equipment manufacturers. We asked:

> Is it ever the case that if they needed something like face shields or other specific kind of equipment, and then say one of the trustees had a connection with someone in that industry, could they then reach out…?
>
> Foundation representative: Sure. Happens all the time. Yeah, you know because we're… 18 trustees, and we're all in many, many different businesses. And we all have contacts in many different businesses, so… you can often make things happen. But the police department itself would have no ability to do that, right? They're busy policing, we have all these contacts with people (Canadian Foundation 3).

Therefore, the police institution's executive has close relationships with the foundation, but the extent of their involvement in furthering the corporate policing partnerships is undefined. Based on other statements, it seems police approach the foundation with projects to fund and then, either formally through a presentation to the foundation, or informally through an agreement with an individual foundation associate, a decision is made, and they receive the funding. In informal arrangements, the foundation members use their own personal assets or leverage their business connections to fulfil the funding.

Altruism or Shoring Up the Police Worldview?

Some donations do show how the police worldview has captured the corporate imagination. A few small companies have made manifold small donations to police too. These are difficult to interpret, so we would say they remain ambiguous. We speculate these entities believe in the police worldview and see the donation as a gesture for reinforcing it. For example, management and staff at Hugh Munro Construction donated $10,000 generated through a Halloween fund-raiser, private donations, and company donations. These funds are devoted to the K9 Unit Dog Vest and Retirement Funds. Pappas Restaurants supports the Houston Police Foundation, remarked upon in the book's introduction, through their Adopt-a-Horse program with a horse in the Houston Mounted Patrol being named Lil'Pappas after the business. Pappas Restaurant also sponsors a Barbecue lunch at the Mounted Police Facility which includes activities for both children and adults. The West Coast German Shepherd Schutzhund Club donated $2,500 for items such as canine medical kits, scent boxes and bite sleeves to the Victoria Police Department. The Victoria Police Department emphasizes the importance of their K9 unit for finding bombs and narcotics, stating the unit is used both operationally and at community events. These funds also assist dogs injured on the job and to prevent future injury. Petland held a fundraiser at their Regent location for the Winnipeg Police Service's K-9 unit. This fundraiser had the public interact with Winnipeg Police officers and dogs and was a part of an international fundraiser set up by Petland. A calendar sale supported by Petland, Esdale Printing, Bayview Construction, Horizon Hearing Centres, Canad Inns, Setcan, Urban Tactical, Pita Pit, Birchwood Animal Hospital, Urban Canine, and Barks n Bubbles Pet Spa raised $20,000 in donations to the Winnipeg Police Service Endowment Fund. WPS emphasizes dogs are trained in tracking, criminal apprehension, obedience, evidence recovery, narcotics and explosive detection and are responsible for hundreds of arrests each year. The Optimist Club of Aurora, a service organization focused on assisting youth, donated $5,000 to the ECO-TRIP program hosted by the York Regional Police Community Services. ECO-TRIP gives at-risk youth (age 14–17) identified by police, school or social agencies mentoring, wilderness training and personal skill development from York Regional Police Officers as well as workshops geared toward character attributes (respect, responsibility, courage, empathy, initiative, integrity, and perseverance). York Regional Police received a total of $75,836 in cash and non-cash donations. Donations came from Optimist Club of Aurora Inc ($5,000), GO transit ($20,000), Flato Management Inc. ($5,000), Allstate Canada Group ($4,400), Economical Mutual Insurance ($3,600), Sharon and Bob Virtue ($1,000), Scotia Bank ($3,000), Versaterm Inc ($2,000), Trivision Broadband and Telecom Inc. ($2,000), Saint Joan of Arc Catholic High School ($1,500), Musharaf Anwat ($1,000), Fundraising Dinner Gala ($24,086), among others. All the entities are attracted to and aligned with the police mission through these exchanges, transactions, and endeavours.

We include this final category to acknowledge corporate and private donations to police may reflect some ambiguous, even sometimes altruistic motivations. However, they may also be indicators of police greed, as more local, community, and grassroots groups are enrolled in these funding networks and aligned with the police vision.

Conclusion

These eight kinds of police partnerships and sponsorships in relation to corporations show the extent of private influence in policing and the attempts by corporations to shape policing. To return to our conceptual framework, we suggest these transactions are about economic exchange and power, but they are also greedy forms of exchange insofar as they are attempts to align the interests of some groups and agencies with others. They are attempts to align the networks and social capital of police and corporations together. The energy industry has long undertaken efforts to align government and social control agencies with its interests. Information and communication technology corporations do much the same as they stand to benefit greatly from lucrative contracts. Earlier, we argued police are a greedy institution and they attempt to align the interests, as well as economic and social capital of donors with the police mission to replicate this institution. This chapter has shown some ways this process unfolds.

However, it is not simply a one-way process. Other greedy entities are similarly trying to align police interests with corporate interests. Given the number of examples, it is apparently not a difficult task. When taken together, the examples show that the interests of police and corporations become entwined in these networks and exchanges. The tricky transactions extend greed, both financial greed as well as the police worldview, entrenching it in corporate spheres and community relations, precisely as it does its own members when they work paid detail. We hope to have shown these tricky transactions go well beyond gift giving and receiving. The political, social, and cultural stakes demand a conceptual framework that can account more clearly for power, conflicts of interest, nepotism, cronyism, and the nefarious outcomes of exchanges of dark money.

Chapter 5

Shadow Figures

Paid Detail Policing as Private Funding and the New Brokers

In the acclaimed 2010 Hollywood film, *The Town*, four Boston robbers led by Ben Affleck's character and dressed in elderly nun outfits and masks rob an armoured car. Following the robbery, a shootout with alerted Boston Police, a harrowing high-speed chase and evasion, the robbers' getaway van screeches to a halt in Boston's North End. The robbers exit the van clutching duffel bags of stolen cash and rifles to enter their waiting switch car. Suddenly they stop cold, realizing they have unexpectedly halted mere feet from a parked Boston Police cruiser. The officer inside sits with his window down adjacent his paid detail assignment, a street construction site devoid of workers (Boston has a longstanding city ordinance that requires a police presence "at every project requiring a street work permit" (Boston Municipal Research Bureau 2008)). The stationary officer is apparently oblivious to his police colleagues' frantic activity only a few blocks away. The officer's and robbers' eyes momentarily meet. Despite the robbers being perceptibly fresh from a crime scene, without flinching or speaking the officer deliberately turns his head to lock his gaze on the construction site in the opposite direction, literally looking the other way. The foursome then piles into the switch car and escapes.

This scene in *The Town* is a rare Hollywood depiction of paid detail policing. The officer's dull, non-cerebral, sedentary, and easy assignment sharply contrasts with Boston Police hotly and dangerously pursuing and firing on the robbers, and FBI sleuths expertly uncovering the foursome's next heist plan before a dramatic shootout and arrest at film's end. The officer in the parked Boston Police car is at best comic relief. Disengaged from pursuing colleagues and heroic demands, here he is literally left to freely look the other way upon noticing a crime in progress. He is what we call in this chapter a "shadow figure" – unnamed and seemingly unimportant to this film's plot but also real life. The presence of such a shadow figure in real life is due to a greedy institution's demand for dark money framed and exchanged through obscured funding networks. Such dark funding would have placed the Boston officer there at that day and time, as it does for uniformed police officers at similar assignments every day and night across urban and rural North America. In

DOI: 10.4324/9781003167914-6

such funded assignments, officers are usually positioned as little more than human totems, temporarily erected to seek patron or client compliance, rather than acting as professionals using superior knowledge and technology to detect, pursue, and bravely arrest perpetrators. Hollywood bank heist films like *The Town* attract a large viewership, but paid detail's shadow figures are unbefitting film formats and foci, since viewers would find them inherently uninteresting and unsympathetic subjects on the surface. Police know this and prefer to keep paid detail funders and officers' identities obscure and, as we show, they frame paid detail policing accordingly. The framing of paid detail is subtler, more targeted and limited, and qualitatively different from other police framing seeking to coax private funding exchanges. Ironically, had the fictional *The Town* or a documentary film illuminated the underlying dark funding that places these shadow figures at construction and other sites, consistent with police as a greedy institution, it may well have revealed more politically contentious, higher monetary values, vaster networks, greater criminal potential, and farther-reaching implications for the rule of law than any robber foursome's heist planning and duffel bag booty. For this reason, we return to controversies associated with paid detail funding and the holes in these and other funding policies in Chapter Seven.

Chapter Two mapped the police private funding terrain and documented the size, pervasiveness, and a brief history of paid detail funding. It revealed paid detail policing is found not only adjacent to construction sites but also at major sporting venues, retail malls, parking lots, film shoots, financial institutions, schools, casinos, hospitals, overload transports, bridges, pipelines, festivals, weddings, funerals, nightclubs, bars, and far beyond. This chapter further illuminates and explores these long-standing, widespread, and mutating funding arrangements consistent with police as a greedy institution. The chapter's subtitle, shadow figures, is apt for three reasons. First, shadow figure connotes the mostly undocumented, unreported, and sometimes fully concealed source and volume of capital in paid detail policing that flows into police pockets through networks. In these practices, named sources of this funding tend to remain in the shadows for observers and the public. Second, shadow figure invokes the notion of police officers adopting a role that is a mere shadow or shell of their self-imagined or promoted ideals, operating outside the framing of police both as professional, knowledgeable, heroic crime fighters, and as sincerely devoted community policing practitioners. In paid detail, the many standard rituals of policing (Manning 2008) become empty imprints and are replaced by muffled and muted greed. Finally, the term shadow figure alludes to the lack of transparency and oversight in paid detail policing that allows for "looking the other way."

The organization of paid detail funding and the shadow figures it produces varies by jurisdiction, including between and even within Canada and the US. We examine this variation and several aspects of these shadowy and mutating practices, including models of assignment selection, and brokering. We discuss how police departments engage in moral regulation of officers and how they prevent officers from obtaining employee status with funders while on assignment consistent with a greedy institution that seeks to control its members even while being funded by external organizations in these networks. We then explore paid detail framing, showing it is more subtle and narrower compared to other private funding forms, although in confidential interviews with police it is sometimes dubiously claimed to serve "the community." Next, we discuss how paid detail has been mutating towards greater regulation over time. A major related development we assess is the rise of newer corporate paid detail brokers like Athos Group and Frizell Group noted in the book's introduction. These fast-growing and aggressive corporate entities taking root in the paid detail field are expected to funnel funding into police pockets. Thus, in this chapter we document key aspects of paid detail practices, consistent with police as a greedy institution. We return to paid detail policing in Chapter Seven.

Paid Detail Practices

Uniformed police lean against a brick wall outside a nightclub in Cleveland's entertainment district; sit on a chair in the Detroit Tigers' bullpen during a major league baseball contest; direct traffic on a busy roadway into an Evangelical church lot in Toronto's suburbs; position next to an automated teller inside a TD bank in Manhattan; stand next to a diamond ring display in a jewellery store in Windsor, Ontario; sip coffee in the emergency waiting room of an Ottawa hospital; or in countless situations similar to *The Town*, sit in a patrol car adjacent road construction work. Paid detail policing is often in plain sight like this; it is remarkable for how utterly unremarkable it is. But since there is little to distinguish these uniformed officers from those on regular patrol or assignment, where its funding is concerned, the public is typically none the wiser. Paid detail funding rents a physical security presence for specific places or for specific events such as these through exchanges with nominally[1] external organizations. In paid detail, there is little to no criminal intelligence gathering beyond the private venue or event and remarkably little activity beyond rudimentary checks of venue entrants' identification or filling a log or waving to traffic. Even though officers usually carry a radio, our research revealed that completing occurrence reports or radioing into police dispatch during an assignment is exceedingly rare. Instead, these assignments are widely assumed in police circles to be safe, barely monitored, lucrative, and "easy money" gigs. It is a rare gig that leads to confrontation, in which case with their various non-legal weaponry such as pepper spray and rubber bullets and surveillance technologies, police power typically grossly outmatches those they confront, such as peaceful, unarmed oil pipeline demonstrators (see Beaumont 2021), and do not place individual officers in much risk of any harm. As we discuss later, paid detail almost never involves direct orders from the external funders either. Officers on paid detail rarely use acquired expertise related to investigations. Police taking an assignment with an external funder is not really about reducing crime, not even within a specific venue. Notwithstanding pre-emptive moral regulation or NYPD's higher-ranking officers or new corporate brokers occasionally visiting officers on paid detail assignments, or where higher ranks are along for the paid detail funding ride at higher pay rates – discussed below – actual assignments are usually without any close or regular oversight.[2] What is perhaps most interesting where a greedy institution is concerned therefore is what it *does not* require of police. It seems designed as an easy transfer of considerable funding from distant external organizations that are expected to be loyal, to the police institution's nearer and dearer members.

How Police Get Paid Detail Funding: Assignment Selection and Brokering Exchanges

In the US especially there is much variation in paid detail arrangements across jurisdictions, in Canada less so. Systems are in place for paid detail assignment selection involving slightly differing exchanges and network access points. Reiss (1988) surveyed 13 police services in US cities and found paid detail had grown immensely since the 1950s partially due to police officers' increased demands for greater income. He identified three forms of brokering assignments. The first "officer contract" model involves individual officers arranging assignments and requesting approval by police administrators. The officer locates a potential funder, then approaches the department with details of the potential assignment (e.g., who the funder is, whether there is alcohol sold at the venue in relation to the department's policy, which vary considerably as we note later) to seek approval. This model is still used in Detroit. Once approved, the same officer regularly works this paid detail assignment when requested by the funder from then on with no additional approvals needed. This arrangement is slowly being replaced by other formulations as we note later in the chapter. The second "union brokerage" model entails a police association or union brokering officer-funder contracts whereby the union does the same as the department, in the next model. Finally, the "department contract" model involves the police department brokering funder assignments for officers and overseeing payment of officers after funders transfer the required funds (Reiss 1991, 229). The third model is still the most common form of paid detail brokering and is still used by large US police departments, such as the NYPD and Boston Police, as well as by most large Canadian police departments like Toronto and York Regional Police (Ontario). We also discovered a hybrid model operating in Seattle for a time which entailed a private paid detail broker corporation that was an extension of Seattle's police union, one which has since been forced to shut down amidst controversy (see Chapter Seven) and transfer its assignments to another commercial, but still police-affiliated firm called Seattle's Finest. In Figure 5.1, we show these models by combining two and three and introduce another which we discuss towards the end of this chapter.

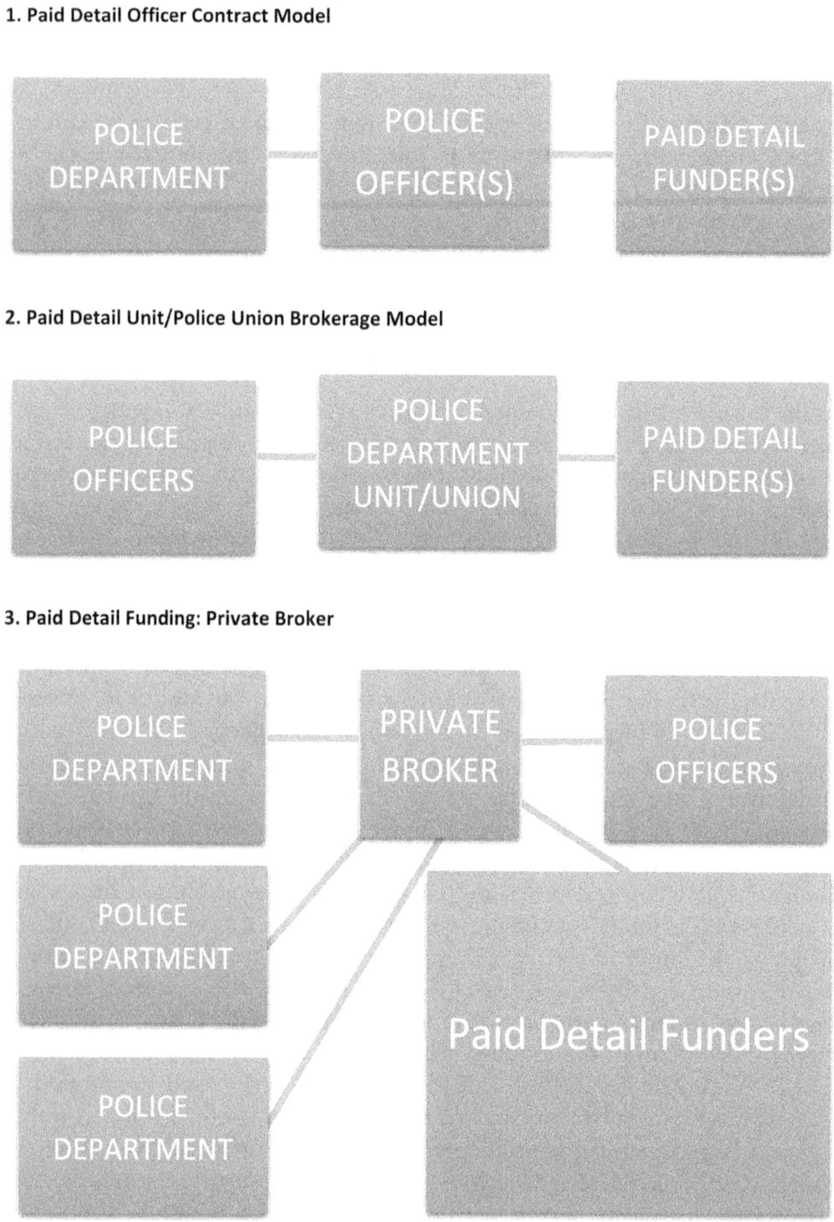

Figure 5.1 Three Paid Detail Network Models

These systems depend on a department paid detail unit comprising several clerks and in most cases one or more coordinators, who are typically sworn officers, to administer these exchanges. At a large Canadian regional police department we visited, this unit was housed in a closed room in Headquarters. In it, we observed four clerks with headphones and microphones taking assignments and seeking outstanding funds from funders, all managed by a coordinator. In a smaller, municipal police department in Canada we were familiar with, there was only one officer designated as the paid detail coordinator. These paid detail units and their personnel are part of the police department and can be understood as brokering exchanges between officers and those who are expected to fund them. Where there is paid detail coordination, departments typically charge an administrative fee, which we found was between 10 and 15 per cent of the value of exchanges to broker and administer the deal with external organizations. The San Francisco Police Department had a 15 per cent administrative fee (Matier 2019). Ottawa Police Service had a 20 per cent administrative fee and in 2018 planned to increase it to 35 per cent so that "background checks" of funders would be included (Ottawa Police 2018). To our knowledge, this is the highest such fee in Canada.

Separately or in conjunction with the third model is "first come, first served," whereby an assignment is posted in some manner in the police department and the first interested officer to respond via email, in person, or otherwise, takes the assignment. In unionized departments where officers have first refusal of each paid detail assignment based on seniority, the union sometimes acted as the paid detail broker. One system is based on assignment of points gained from working paid detail, whereby those with fewer points are given the opportunity to adopt the next assignment before those with more points. A more recent model relative to these assigns officers to paid detail by randomly drawing from a list of interested officers. A similar system involves rotation of the opportunity for assignments where seniority does not matter. Each interested officer rotates to the top and is offered a paid detail job upon its arrival. If an officer refuses, they return to the bottom of the list of those seeking funded assignments. In a large Western US city, for example, a police representative explained:

> These jobs are available… They get them almost on a daily basis, as jobs come in, it'll be put out and officers will say 'hey, yeah I'll work it' and send a request back and say 'yeah, I can work this shift, this shift and this shift.' And the coordinator then would have to look and match that… Someone who's working all these hours and is a high earner would be at the bottom of that list of people that were offering to work an assignment… the person that maybe hadn't worked that often would get first crack at the assignment (Western US Police 1).

In most departments we studied, paid detail policies regarding events reserved the right for administrators to decide how many officers are required for a given assignment requested by an organization, and then expected the organizations to loyally fund it based on what police decide. For example, the lone NYPD paid detail advertising pamphlet reads:

> Depending on the size of the detail, type of event and location covered, multiple officers may be necessary. In these situations, the NYPD will determine the minimum amount of coverage necessary, along amount [sic.] with supervisory coverage, based on safety and security considerations" (NYPD 2016, 2).

As shown in Chapter Two, the paid detail funding rates for officers are almost always set by the hour. These vary (e.g., $68.50 US in Miami-Dade and $112 US in Regina, Canada), but are generally high relative to officers' regular pay and higher for Sergeants and Captains.

Many departments had requirements to limit the amount of paid detail that officers could work in a period such as a week or a month. For example, Ottawa Police paid detail policy specifies in one section: "17. There must be a minimum of one hour between a regular duty and a paid duty and or between any paid duties" and in another section "18. The total amount of time a member may work in a 24-hour period is 15.5 hours" (Ottawa Police 2016). These stipulations do not matter if the department does not monitor them. Policies usually indicate when funding for a higher paid sergeant or higher rank will also be required based on how many regular officers are required (one higher rank for every five officers etc.), with the latter determined by the police. As a funder explained: "If there's a certain number, if you have over a certain number of officers that you need a sergeant, which jumps on the pay scale as well" (Ottawa Funder 1). In some jurisdictions a police department will indicate that one officer is necessary per X number of people attending an event. If there is an additional formula behind these arrangements in this or other departments, it is often kept hidden from the public and prospective funders. In one instance, an officer explained how they would offer some regular patrols but "we would discuss with the event coordinators ... we will provide this many officers but we want you to provide an equal number and they would pay for the... off-duty officers." He noted for a large street festival, "staffing is made available but with the understanding that ... the event organizer is going to you know, chip in and hire some extra officers" (Western US Police 1). To loyal funders, police do not deem it necessary to explain greedy demands for paid detail funding. Unlike garage mechanics, police do not point to a manual describing why a job requires a given number of paid detail officers and hours of labour. For example, the NYPD

> evaluates each requested detail and based on its assessment of safety and security concerns, determines the minimum number of officers necessary for the assignment, as well as the number of Officers required to supervise (Pierre v. City of New York et al. 2020).

Under such arrangements, uniformed police typically adopt a potential assignment for four, eight, and less often for 12 hours in duration. As a paid detail broker explained: "almost all of them have a four-hour minimum because it's not worth them suiting up otherwise. They don't want to get all dressed up… for 45 minutes" (Southern Broker 1). Because of varied duration but more so because of the varied venue and conditions, we found officers do not consider all paid detail assignments equally. For example, there are assignments that require:

> going into the less desirable parts of town. Officers don't want to do that…There are certain events where it's known that officers are provided the opportunity to… get breaks either to use the restroom or to get a meal…They're just dumped [there] and not really monitored. Or like… the ones that they are treated a little bit better on, and then obviously the less hassle the better… We call it cherry picking assignments (Western US Police 1).

No officers are explicitly required or forced to *initially* take a given assignment in all the models above, which means there is much self-selection from within the approved possibilities:

> [C]ertain officers will want to work at certain locations with… certain construction companies that you get to know, know the individuals and the work habits… there's a natural tendency for the officer to select those things (Western US Police 1).

This self-selection is consistent with the easy receipt of funds from external organizations for any given officer but it also raises key questions about the rule of law we will discuss in Chapter Seven.

Mutating Paid Detail Policies

The history of paid detail funding suggests it has been in place for many decades in some jurisdictions, as discussed in Chapter Two. It also has been changing in specific directions over time. A funeral home business owner who has used paid detail escorts in Central Canada since the 1970s explained:

> [T]he cost has gone up significantly over time. It used to be...you paid for three officers off duty and it just went to them, and they got paid time and a half for their four hour minimum... and you just wrote the cheque directly to the officers involved. Now it's much more formalized. There's a specific form you fill out and it has to be in so many hours before and the forces have said that... it isn't just the officer's time, but... they have a paid detail office that organizes it and they have to cover the cost of that, and they have cars and the maintenance and the gas and, so there's an administration fee and a vehicle feel...And you know, currently it's around $1800 for three officers to provide service for a funeral, and...it is four hours, and after that you're paying even more (York Funder 1).

A former officer described a change in his large Western US police department:

> I had worked secondary employment in a number of capacities... anywhere from clothing manufacturers, sporting goods, trade shows... Where you were paid directly by the company itself. Then I also [later] had the opportunity to work with the police department that the contractors would go through... to hire police officers that would show up in full detail gear... (Western US Police 1).

Another officer described changes in his mid-sized Canadian police department. Presently

> [t]here is an administrative fee...There wasn't in the old system where you... and the businessperson agreed to a new work form on a regular basis. But now with this off-duty coordinator and the tracking of it and the paying of the officer, there is an administration fee... Back then an agency or businessman would contact the police officer directly...[T] hey come to the front door and ask and they would just post it on... a paid detail board. A clipboard. It would say: 'Are you interested in working this job? Contact the owner directly yourself and make your own arrangements.' That was then...It would be posted, and first come, first serve and you make your own arrangement... Now ... a coordinator manages it... With this new system... you just get picked for your work, you have not got a choice... you get what they give you (Central Canadian Police 1).

A newer corporate paid deal broker in the US similarly explained how older paid detail arrangements worked:

> Typically the way that's worked in the past is... you want a police officer to patrol the parking lot in the evenings you would find... a friend who is a policeman and you would ask them about it and they would generally

> volunteer to do it and they would be the coordinator and they would fill all the shifts and you would usually pay them an extra couple of dollars for them to make sure that all the shifts that you wanted were covered by friends of theirs...and you would typically pay those officers either with cheques or with cash... A lot of it is...under the table and they pay them with cash, which creates a lot of issues (Southern Broker 1).

The installation of paid detail offices plainly reflects police as a greedy institution in that the administration takes something off the top of exchanges. There is a sense in which this arrangement funds not only an officer, but in larger departments, also civilian positions, and other department desires. No precise calculus was provided by any department regarding how the 15 per cent administration fee (the fee we most often encountered) was determined or spent or whether there had been a cost assessment to arrive at this figure. We discuss corporate brokers later in this chapter and they represent perhaps the most significant mutation in paid detail funding in recent years.

Moral Regulation of Paid Detail Funding by a Greedy Institution

Examining police paid detail policies plainly reveal that police administrators who design policies think their officers may acquire other loyalties in some assignment environments. This sentiment exemplifies a greedy institution. Police executives must be concerned about the public reputation of police but also manage the allegiances of individual officers, which becomes more difficult in paid detail settings. The moral regulation of officers on paid detail assignments coheres with police as a greedy institution. Coser's (1974) work predates the moral regulation literature and subsequent research has not made the link, but some of what Coser deemed to be greedy institutional practices equate to moral regulation. Coser (1974, 15–16) suggests greedy institutions often attend to sexual attachments of its members, although, as we show below, neither celibacy nor promiscuity of officers on paid detail is the goal.

Hunt (1999) provides a framework for the study of moral regulation. For Hunt (1997, 280), the "'moral' dimension is not a distinctive characteristic of the regulatory target but rather is found in the linkage posited among subject, object, practices and their projected social consequences." He writes

> moral discourse links a moralized subject with some moralized object or practice in such a way as to impute some wider socially harmful consequences unless... subjected to appropriate regulation. Moral regulation... is relational (Hunt, 1997, 280).

We suggest below, however, that if police officers are "subjects," then "object" or "practice" includes persons (as objects) and spatializing practices (or spaces) as well, and these become factored into police administrators' regulation of police officers on paid detail. In moral regulation of officers consistent with a greedy institution, administrators seek to regulate the kinds of private sites and events that are accepted for assignments, including location, what objects are involved, and for whom. This is accomplished, depending on the department, through paid detail assessments, at least until a permit is received by an officer or a specific funder is regularized. Police superiors assess the risk level and moral status of the proposed user, workspace, or object with which officers are deemed likely to come in contact. For paid detail funding, the moralizing agent is the police chief, coordinator, or other administrator and some officers themselves; the moralized object or target is an officer's assignment site and funder, a set of practices, and a feared social consequence (degeneration of the police image in the public eye). Below we lend understanding to moral regulation of paid detail consistent with a greedy institution. We suggest that any perceived immorality of police can detract from police legitimacy.

Risk stemming from paid detail from the police department's perspective is tied to risk management of officers. This management is sometimes preempted by a department's moral regulation of paid detail officers which entails linkages of moralized elements: objects, spaces, and funders. The NYPD (2016, 2) pamphlet, for example, reads: "[L]icensed premises, government and quasi-governmental entities, security companies, and personal protection/bodyguard situations are specifically excluded." Other than government entities, this is consistent with many jurisdictions across North America, as shown in Table 5.1.

While there is much moral regulation, Table 5.1 shows wide variation across North American police departments; what is deemed immoral for officers in one is sometimes not in another. Some policies identify marijuana or cannabis by name, others address sex-related practices, others are more concerned about cash or bodies spoiling the imagined pristine loyalty of officers, and so on. Nonetheless, we discerned consistent attention to certain elements. We identified many moral restrictions on spaces, objects, and funders with which or whom police are not permitted to associate, but which are not necessarily physically dangerous. There was no cost–benefit calculation or knowledge gathered about their circumstances, and in this sense, these are not about risk management (Haggerty 2003), they constitute moral concern. The categories discussed below become linked in ways that render assignments morally risky. These linkages constitute the immoral of paid detail exchanges and networks. As will be seen below, these can leak into one another, since an object must be used in a space, an officer's presence presumes a space, and a funder usually requests of police what spaces, even public ones during some events, could allow their presence. In most policies regulating paid detail, police departments seek to ensure this funding leads to these practices only at sites consistent with what they deem to be positive morality and optics for the

Table 5.1 Paid Detail Prohibitions in 16 North American Police Departments

North American Police Department ↓	*Labour Dispute*	*Conflict of Interest*	*Security/ Bodyguard*	*Discredits Department Reputation/Dignity*	*Cash/ Valuable*	*Checking Baggage/I.D./ Screening*	*Criminal Organization*	*Liquor Served/ Clubs/Bars/ Cannabis/ Gambling*	*Sergeant/ Chief's Approval Required*
Boston (PD)									Yes
San Francisco (SE)	X	X		X	X			X	Yes
Chicago (SE)	X	X		X	X			X + Medical Cannabis Centre	Yes
Jacksonville (SE)		X	X	X	X			X + Services of Sexual Nature	Yes
Miami (PD)		X	X	X		X		X	Yes
Tampa Bay (PD)	Limited	X		X					Yes
Austin (SE)	X	X	X	X	X	X	X	X + Strip Centres/Sexually Oriented Business	Yes
Seattle (SE)		X	X	X	X			X	Yes
York Regional (PD)	X		X	X	X	X		X	Yes
Winnipeg (PD)	X	X			X		X	X	
Edmonton (PD)									Yes
Hamilton (PD)	X		X ("Bouncer")		X			X	
Halifax Regional (PD)		X	X	X				X	Yes
London (PD)	X	X	X	X	X	X			Yes
Ottawa (PD)	X	X	X	X	X			X	Yes
Calgary (PD)	X	X	X	X			X		Yes

X = Prohibited, PD = Paid Detail, SE = Secondary Employment

police institution and its closest members. The attention to regulating these elements and the exchanges and networks they presume show, perhaps more than any other aspect, how there is more to private sponsorship and funding where paid detail is concerned than corporatization, as discussed in Chapter One. Rather, it befits a greedy police institution demanding its members retain a certain morality, even in far flung and diverse external spaces outside of regular duty to receive funds provided by external actors also expected to be loyal to police.

Moralized Spaces

Moral regulation literature has shown how particular spaces, such as "adult businesses," are moralized through law. For example, zoning regulations in the US require these businesses to operate at a defined distance from "innocent" uses of space, such as churches and schools (Valverde 2003, 48). This is due to the adult businesses' assumed capacity to morally damage the latter through a murky osmosis. Five kinds of spaces were deemed by police departments to be morally risky, inherently having the capacity to morally corrupt officers working within them: adult entertainment clubs with or without alcohol service; bars, nightclubs or events where alcohol was served; sites of gambling (now called the less morally objectionable "gaming"); sites where sexualized services or goods were sold; and places that dispensed marijuana or sold marijuana-related products. A Southern US police department representative underscored one such pre-emptive relation when asserting there are "certain locations that are completely not within the realm of ever being approved and that includes strip clubs... a City police officer could never work a job like that" (Southern US Police 1). We could find no evidence in policies or other documents why these kinds of spaces were singled out, and no evidence to show greater risk of physical harm to officers. These excluded funders may well have wanted to support police with paid detail funding and have officers present as many other private businesses would, arguably even more so. But the police institution prefers to control where its members go, even while technically off duty.

Moralized Objects

Objects from private realms are deemed to morally corrupt officers too. These objects are thought to be problematic depending on whether officers handle them or are in proximity. These include nude or elite bodies, alcohol, sexual aids, cash, and valuables. One Eastern Canadian police department representative explained: "[W]ith the bars, if a liquor establishment hires us, we are on the outside, we do not go inside. We are not to be inside security... even though they're hiring us, and our job is to not go inside." Something morally problematic for the greedy institution's members was thought to happen "inside." For many departments whether alcohol sales are the main source of profit for a paid detail funder determines which funders will be permitted to have paid detail officers. York (Ontario) Regional Police's paid detail policy prohibits officers from "[a]cting as the only or primary security for an event or location where the primary purpose of the premises is the sale of alcohol" (York Regional Police 2015). This is echoed by Winnipeg Police Service's policy, which stipulates paid detail is not to be granted where a potential user has a "liquor license [establishment] where alcohol is the predominant source of income" (Winnipeg Police 2015). Seattle Police's policy prohibits paid detail at a business "that sells, produces, or dispenses marijuana, marijuana-infused products, marijuana extracts or marijuana concentrates" (Seattle Police 2015). Seattle Police also restricts officers from establishments "that sell or dispense intoxicating beverages" (Seattle Police 2015), peculiarly not specifying "alcohol." Nor are drugs other than cannabis – a widely touted "corruptor" in policing literature (Bayley and Perito 2011, 4) – commonly remarked upon in this and other policies. In other departments, valuables or cash can apparently corrupt officers. According to one police chief, these became corruptible if "handled" by an officer:

> There's some duties we just don't do. We don't guard money, we don't do cash security. We tell them just to hire Brinks or a private contractor... We would never handle cash. We would never handle tickets. It's not something that we would do as police officers. As far as guarding cash... at a marathon sporting event or something... there's nothing legislated around it, we just have that in our own internal policy (Western Canadian Police Chief 1).

Many departments also prohibit police from serving as a personal bodyguard. One police chief explained their department

> was asked to be a personal bodyguard for a performer and [the request] was denied. We do not do bodyguard security. They were recommended to explore other avenues such as a private security firm (Western Canadian Police Chief 2).

Apparently, the closeness of the vulnerable elite body brought with it moral risk that could rub off on police and cause their loyalty to potentially spread elsewhere. Touching cash or valuables, being close to forbidden bodies, or being in a space where this could happen was enough to be deemed immoral. While accounts of police corruption such as Bayley and Perito (2011, 4) suggest its catalysts include "gambling, prostitution, and alcohol," little attention is paid to that fact that objects, spaces, or suspects are sometimes deemed to cause this corruption. We discuss corruption in Chapter Seven, but the point here is that mere proximity to alcohol, marijuana, cash, valuables, and certain bodies is deemed enough to risk morally tainting an officer. While some policies focus on space, objects were deemed to have a morally spoiling potential on their own, irrespective of space, by splashing the officer with immorality. This suggests the greedy institution assigns mysterious luring powers, regardless of where they are located or what officers do with them. Rather than actuarial calculations reflective of standard risk management (Haggerty 2003), these policies are those of a greedy institution, imagining "worst-case" moral scenarios (Ericson 2007).

Moralized Funders

Some kinds of funders – seemingly irrespective of space or certain objects' presence or proximity – were deemed morally risky as well. A common practice for almost all paid detail policies was a background check or at least need for prior approval of funders by police administrators or the chief, respectively. Some funders associated with criminal organizations could not privately fund officers: "Anything that we think is related to some nefarious purpose… like an organized crime group… we don't do those sorts of events either" (Western Canadian Police 1). In regular policing, these groups might be considered criminal suspects and ripe for face-to-face investigation or undercover operations; in paid detail funding networks, they are deemed sources of moral risk and pre-empted from paid detail provision. Police administrators almost never conceive of paid detail as a strategy of infiltrating suspect funders, or a means of gathering criminal intelligence about drug or other operations at paid detail sites and events that later lead to arrests and charges following assignments. We encountered not a single instance of this strategy in our research. Rather, without the department means of avoiding moral risk linked to suspect funders while gaining information by, for example, going undercover, departments prefer to simply pre-empt officer contact with suspect funders or halt a specific "easy money" arrangement if criminal acts occurring there come to public attention.

Paid Detail Officers: Greedy Extensions or External Organization Employees?

One of the most interesting questions about paid detail funding is whether officers taking up temporary assignments become employees of external paid detail funders. If officers are not employees of funders, it strongly suggests these external organizations or individuals are merely providing funding and sponsoring the greedy police institution rather than hiring the occupiers of these roles as their own temporary employees. We found much evidence to support the former. This is consistent with the variable, but extensive moral regulation of officers discussed above. As well, as outlined in their policy, NYPD officers on paid detail and their uniforms are "inspected" by sergeants (Pierre v. City of New York et al. 2020). The requirement to wear the full or nearly full uniform at these assignments suggests officers on paid detail are not employees of external funders of this service. The greedy police institution seeks to exercise much control over its officers, even while assigning them to external event holders, businesses, and others who fund them as paid detail. A paid detail funder from the Eastern US, remarked:

> They are in uniform and wherever they are assigned to be they will check in and they will say: 'What's going on at this event?' ...We have got an exit and an entrance point here ... with our Ice Cream festival they would be like, 'okay, so you have got money here. I see you are selling t-shirts over there.' Points where people might try to sneak in or sneak out, like I'll go over there and have this one wander around, so *they would come up with a plan with me together* (Eastern US Funder 1; emphasis added).

Funders devise a security plan "with" paid detail officers here, rather than the funder dictating what they wanted as though police were subservient employees. Similarly, a funder from Ontario explained that rather than police obviously being employees for his event, instead "they're *kind of almost* part of our team for that night" (Halton Funder 2; emphasis added).

Our research nonetheless revealed paid detail policing sometimes shows tensions between what funders expect from officers during assignments and what officers do. In a few instances, funders of paid detail were unsatisfied with limited control over officers they were funding. For example, regarding a large Central Canadian regional department:

> [T]hese two actually... patrolled the grounds, they went around, they took walks, they'd go into... check the bathroom every once in a while... but the ones I had last year when I asked if they could split up, I was just told rather snottily that 'No we're not. We're not supposed to split up.' And... that was the end of the discussion...(Central Canadian Funder 1).

Similarly, at a music event held on a public waterfront in a smaller Canadian city that required the event promoter to fund paid detail police, the funder complained the mostly male officers lounged under a tent drinking coffee and spent far too much time talking to the event's younger women patrons rather than being more visible and vigilant, in this case for liquor infractions. However, unlike the funder above, this one was reluctant to confront the officers directly to encourage them to change their conduct.

Significantly, the NYPD's rules for paid detail provided to NYPD officers and paid detail funders indicate officers are *not* to be employees of funders:

> v. Control Over Officers' Work During PDP Details
>
> 113. *The NYPD maintains direction, control, and supervision of the work performed by Officers during PDP details.*

> 114. Upon arrival at a participating business, the NYPD commands Officers to report to the business's representative or to the ranking Officer supervising the detail.
> 115. Additionally, the NYPD directs Officers to sign in on a Paid Detail Attendance Sheet when they arrive.
> 116. The NYPD cautions Officers that they are subject at all times to NYPD rules and regulations while working on PDP details.
> 117. The NYPD assigns high-ranking officials, such as Sergeants, Lieutenants, and Captains, to perform daily rounds of PDP details to monitor Officers' work.
> 118. The NYPD mandates that Officers report to the NYPD any arrests or Officer injuries that occur on PDP details.
> 119. At the conclusion of a PDP detail, the NYPD directs Officers to sign out on a Paid Detail Attendance Sheet and present a Paid Detail Card to the participating business's representative or the ranking Officer for signature.
> *120. The NYPD instructs participating businesses to report any Officer who breaches NYPD standards.*
> *121. The NYPD also instructs participating businesses to report any Officer who breaches the business's own internal policies.*
> Case 1:20-cv-05116 Document 1 Filed 07/03/20 Page 14 of 4315 (Pierre v. City of New York et al. 2020; emphasis added).

Note sections 120 and 121 that encourage complaints from funders, "responsibilizing" funders to police paid detail conduct if necessary but not be placed in a position to act on misconduct consistent with an employee. It is revealing that funders are encouraged to complain about paid detail rule violations to police administrators in these arrangements, but nowhere are they encouraged to report criminal activity on their premises during these assignments, something which one might expect would be of interest to the police. Though not explicitly encouraged, there is nothing in these rules that addresses officers "looking the other way" either.

The single webpage for Regina Police (2021) paid detail information reads:

> The Regina Police Service shall entertain requests for the Special Duty use of its members... Regina Police Service members remain under the exclusive control of the Regina Police Service... Officers will perform policing duties only and will not assist in matters not ordinarily within an officer's duties.

Ottawa Police's (2021) paid detail program webpage similarly reads:

> The Paid Duty Program will allow clients to hire off-duty officers on a contract basis to provide a police presence at their events. Officers will

> not be assigned to any function that requires that they act outside the normal scope of police duties.

Note the department requirement that officers are not to "act outside the normal scope of police duties." It does not state they will fulfil all duties while at the external event, only that they are not to be controlled by the event sponsor.

Another noteworthy aspect of the webpage is that police "shall entertain" persons' requests to fund and "will allow" clients to fund paid detail. This peculiar framing suggests an expectation of funding and that the greedy police institution will decide who will have the privilege of providing it. The notion that police "will allow" and "shall entertain" private funding contrasts sharply with corporate marketing or framing of products, as well as with the notion of graciously receiving a gift. Imagine if Apple (the technology company) announced they "will allow" or "shall entertain" allowing consumers to purchase the latest iPhone, or if a friend on her birthday announced she "will allow" or "shall entertain" receipt of your gift! This seems neither like private corporation marketing nor gracious gift solicitation, consistent with Chapter One. This framing shows even when externally funded, it is not enough for the police institution to relinquish greedy control of the morality of its members.

The greedy police institution's dream is to obtain funds from external sources by encouraging acceptance of the value of a police presence (as opposed to numerous other measures that could be used instead, ranging from flaggers or signs to volunteer security providers to video surveillance, depending on the assignment). Avoiding conflict with other efforts to obtain external funds is consistent with the traditional police view of detecting and arresting perpetrators (such as in foundations and Crime Stoppers), while retaining full control of its members' loyalties.

In the US, civil law specifies paid detail funders are to avoid supervising police as employees or manage the risk they pose by others for the new brokers as discussed later in the chapter. One broker explained one reason is due to liability:

> There is a component of civil law called co-employment and companies who don't follow the tenants of co-employment could be sued by a subcontractor or a vendor. Even though they didn't meet the IRS [Internal Revenue Service] requirements they could be sued as an employee giving them a greater leg up in terms of the civil tort they might have against the user… which means supervising and treating them like employees, and in other words you're my "employee" until it's convenient for you not to be my employee anymore [and] then you're not. The law says if it was convenient for them to be your employee for so long then guess what? Now they're your employee…[O]ur clients, who are savvy enough

> like big corporations, know not to allow co-employment issues to occur and we do our best to ensure that as well (Southern Broker 1).

This broker therefore was able to maintain this distinction between service provider and employee for corporate funders and was part of their framing discussed later.

One funeral home funder of paid detail for traffic control articulated this distinction consistent with loyalty to police, loyally agreeing with the police claim that paid detail equates to public safety and with not being "in control of the police":

> While we are… paying the police department, there's no assumption that somehow, we're in control of the police. There's a dangerous line there to be crossed if I happen to think 'I know that police officer and therefore I want him or her and therefore maybe I can tell them what to do' [when] my relationship gets cozy enough with them… I think there's an important independence that the police have to maintain… to do their job professionally and do it well. And while… that independence is being slightly compromised by them being paid by the customer as opposed to the taxpayer, there's still an expectation they will perform in accordance with the Police Act and with the independence required to be able to ensure public safety and that they're not favouring the person who's paying them over the person who's crossing the street… and needs to not be hit by a car. So I think that independence is probably important and we have no objection to that. I think it's a better system that way (Central Canadian Funder 2).

Complaints from at least a small minority of community-based funders have been a constant for decades, as these groups have argued they cannot or should not have to fund paid detail (LaFleche 2009). Due to local by-laws that police unions and departments have advocated for, some community groups with few resources are coerced into funding it nonetheless. This is the exact opposite of the community-based rhetoric and framing we see in police and police foundation communications (see Chapter Six). This retention of control by the police department over the officers' work exemplifies the police as a greedy institution.

Framing Paid Detail

It is widely assumed policing today is becoming more technologically oriented and reliant on expert knowledge. Knowledge-centric police work has been, for two decades, suggested as the emergent stock and trade of police (see Ratcliffe 2008; Ericson and Haggerty 1997). As the saying goes, policing has become "intelligence-led" (Sanders et al. 2015; Cope 2004). Police are presumed to gather, analyze, as well as arrest and charge suspects based upon acquired knowledge about transgressions. Such self-representation occurs when police knowledge and expertise culminate in, for example, a major drug and firearm seizure (see, for example, CBC 2020a) or mass arrest of gang members following an investigation or surveillance sting. Such an accomplishment is then – with the impressive list of arrests and haul of seized drugs, firearms, and cash on display – communicated via that long-standing communication format – the public press conference – and now through Twitter and other social media platforms (O'Connor 2017). The public sees this activity through such representations. Ironically, unlike paid detail, this work occurs at distant crime scenes, in department offices, and in surveillance vehicles and patrol cars often far from public scrutiny. In contrast, regardless of the shifting models of exchanges and networks, paid detail is framed for a narrower, mostly private audience, and is both subtler and far less publicly visible than framing for sponsorship and donations. Paid detail practice itself does not become represented in the latter framing of funding (e.g., foundations and Crime Stoppers) either; it is conspicuous by its absence. Paid detail policing and its attendant issues are difficult to reconcile with the image of the professional, active, virtuous, heroic officer or one committed to community policing. Police departments and foundations do not call for more sponsorship and donations by depicting an officer passively watching a film shoot in Vancouver, opening a gate on the Kinder Morgan pipeline site in Blanco, Texas, or looking the other way as in *The Town*. Paid detail practices are everywhere, but officers' paid detail funding and the arrangements underlying it are not to be framed for public consumption.

Although they were permitted in the past, and still are in a few US jurisdictions, such as Detroit, individual officers are typically not permitted to promote paid detail and seek funding for it. For example, Boston Police rules indicate: "Sworn officers may only accept details processed through the Department's established system. Under no circumstances shall an officer seek, solicit, or promote paid details outside the approved system of detail distribution" (Boston Police 2004). Individual officers are prohibited in this jurisdiction from promoting paid detail and framing it themselves. Similar prohibitions are found in many North American jurisdictions.

This lack of public framing of paid detail funding is less true of the police institution itself, however subtle it might be. The public framing of paid detail is typically through the procedures for a limited and subtle web presence. A police administrator from a Western Canadian city concisely described their paid detail promotional efforts:

> Do we promote or actively advertise? We do not but if you do go to our website… you will see that we do have the prices for special duty officers clearly laid out, but we don't have a big huge [sic.] advertisement for special duty officers (Western Canadian Police 3).

Departments usually devoted only a page to explain procedures and then a form and sometimes a contract that would make these arrangements possible. Several examples follow. Peel Regional Police in Ontario have a page devoted to paid detail called "Paid Duty Officer." It is neither elaborate nor especially persuasive. It merely states paid detail's existence in a humdrum manner along with non-exhaustive reasons to fund it:

> **Scheduling a Paid Duty Service**
> Off-duty police officers are available for hire to provide police presence for a range of functions including: Community events. Weddings/Banquets. Funerals. Traffic control. School events. Concerts. Sporting events. Wide load/high value escorts. Film shoots (Peel Police 2021).

This could not be less promotional. The Miami-Dade Police Department similarly includes only three sentences on their webpage devoted to framing paid detail:

> **Off-Duty Police Services**
> Let us provide security for your home, business, or event. Request off-duty police services, apply for off-duty police permits, submit credit card payments and view permit activity. An Off-Duty Coordinator will contact you within two business days to finalize the arrangements of your request (Miami-Dade Police Department 2021).

A coordinator from a department in a smaller city in Western Canada indicated since taking over paid detail responsibilities that "what I've done I've put an application form on our… website, so anyone inquiring is directed there to make the initial request" (Western Canadian Police 5). The first page of a pithy NYPD paid detail pamphlet available online in large font followed by the police commissioner's name reads: "The FINEST in uniformed security for your organization." Capitalization of "finest" invokes the notion of "New York's finest" traditionally used as a positive moniker promoting police to outsiders (and appropriated by the commercial broker Seattle's Finest (2020)) and it makes the point that paid detail is about being "uniformed" security provision rather than any other kind of service, which speaks to potential rivals from the private security industry who are also uniformed. As with the Seattle police chief's 1971 response to a complaint by a private security firm about paid detail services in that city, mentioned in Chapter Two, the NYPD seems cognizant, but is neither public nor explicit about the existence of private sector competition.

To the extent police uniforms communicate meaning to observers at paid detail sites, they also frame. Usually there is no difference between regular and paid detail uniforms. Uniforms with badges and insignias traditionally communicate authority and power and demarcate the blue line. This is precisely why private security guards have usually donned facsimile uniforms and driven police-like vehicles as part of their "toolkit" (Mopas and Stenning 2001), and which often skirt the laws prohibiting police impersonation. However, in rare instances when there is a difference permitted in the paid detail police uniform, it is subtle too. For example, in Yankee Stadium in New York, uniformed NYPD officers can be found wearing an additional, but discreet lanyard with "paid detail" imprinted upon it. Similarly, for some Texas police departments,

> sometimes they'll approve a modified uniform... instead of your full patrol uniform. It might be... a different kind of pants and maybe a polo shirt that says 'police' prominently displayed on the back and maybe a facsimile of your badge on your front chest area (Southern Broker 1).

Few casual observers would notice such differences, much less what they mean, but a uniform is required of officers on paid detail regardless. As with any uniform, it communicates to its wearers, in this case the officers themselves, to remind them to whom they have pledged loyalty. As the military institution has known for centuries, and Sir Robert Peel knew too, the very notion of wearing a police *uni-form* is about pledging loyalty to a single greedy institution, in this case the police.

The tension in framing paid detail is between making potential funders aware of police expectations of loyal organizations, without damaging the traditional crime-fighter image of police or a genuine commitment to community policing ideals, promoted elsewhere and which we discuss in other chapters. Yet a different framing of paid detail funding emerges behind closed doors during interviews with police when they are pressed. As with foundations and other sponsorship we discuss in other chapters, there is use of community but also public safety rhetoric to legitimize these practices. One police representative in Western Canada somewhat incredulously explained:

> Has the hiring of police officers by organizations benefitted the service? I would say that the benefit is to the community not necessarily to the organization because we're not going there for the organization. We're going there sort of for the public safety, the risk management end of it (Western Canadian Police 3).

Responding to criticisms of paid detail, some police administrators claim having more visible officers working – regardless of where or who funds them – deters crime or better readies these officers for emergencies should they occur elsewhere while on paid detail assignment. The validity of this claim has never been empirically tested using an experimental design or otherwise; moreover, many paid detail assignments occur indoors away from full public view or feature a paid detail officer in open view but standing, lounging, or sitting rather than actively patrolling and watching for crime other than what is of interest to the funder, suggesting that any effective deterrent effect is questionable at best, especially since it would be known on site that they are unlikely to arrest and lay charges for transgressions. We know this because of how rare it is to learn a paid detail officer has made a key arrest or even passed along intelligence leading to such an arrest due to observations on paid detail. In fact, the emphasis has been to place officers not where there has proven to be great risk for crime and thus where police might deter transgressions or where a presence would help other officers to act. Instead, the opposite is true, again consistent with the notion of "easy money" assignments. For example, in 2014, paid detail permits for twenty Buffalo, New York police officers providing a presence outside bars were suspended due to perceived risk to officers following a violent incident in Molly's Bar (Terreri 2014). In 2015, Toronto Police also stopped paid detail at the local "Muzik" nightclub for a time, following a fatal shooting during a paid detail shift (Powell 2015). No one wants any police or other persons to be placed at great risk unnecessarily. But what is interesting is that there was no evidence to suggest stepped up patrols by regular Buffalo or Toronto Police would be brought following discovery these were allegedly violent crime prone sites or events to deter these acts which, according to police themselves and their worldview as seen in their other framing, is their responsibility to do. Instead, paid detail was simply halted, full stop. This also supports the notion that paid detail is relatively "easy money" and could be halted *en masse* with little effect on or concern for the public about future transgressions occurring there. Regarding emergencies, a vague term where police are concerned, we did find a couple of instances where this happened. However, since in most jurisdictions police officers are "always on duty" anyway, it is unclear how being at a paid detail gig would make response faster or if they would be likely to be in closer proximity to an event than off-duty personnel. It also implies that what officers provide at these assignments is unimportant and easily abandoned in the case of an emergency.

Interviews with funders of paid detail revealed funders did not learn of the possibility and requirements of these arrangements from police department marketing. In interviews all said "no." Instead, they reported paid detail to be a tradition in their organization and the practice was merely passed along by other or previous staff or members and then followed, something which was consistent with a kind of blind loyalty among funders towards police. Many could not recall when they had first heard of paid detail arrangements. For those external organizations, police did not have to frame paid detail policing funding prior to receiving it. The organization had already bought the police rationale for it and were loyally fulfilling the funding requirements. The fact there is so little public promotion of paid detail and yet its use is widespread with little opposition or resistance suggests an unquestioned loyalty on behalf of most funders in some cities. A police administrator explained funding is due to repetition or word of mouth:

> Sometimes it's just repetition of events and they know the process so it's year after year, just repeat or because of other events and they're now putting on a similar event. They've talked to those groups and have heard what they need to do (Central Canadian Police 1).

The question of why some funders keep paying for paid detail also raises the question of legal compulsion.

Forcing Loyalty through Law

Law requires some paid detail funding. As with civil law, it is no surprise that a greedy institution has sought to arrange laws to support its desires and worldview. What sparked these laws demanding paid detail funding might have been an earlier loyalty towards police that was then enshrined sometimes decades ago. Thus, the police institution and supporters convinced state and provincial legislators and municipal or city councils to enshrine their demands for loyalty in laws. This legal backing symbolically encourages loyalty and generates funds for police officers. Thus, when a paid detail requirement is set in law it comes with an expectation of loyalty and deference that all law demands of its subjects who stand before it. Here law emerges as majestic (Silbey and Ewick 1998), something to which one must bow, not question. Some laws are labour contracts in the form of collective agreements. For example, the Toronto Police Service sets out rules for paid detail assignments, including number of paid detail hours allowed in a 24-hour period and in relation to regular duties. Other laws are city ordinances or municipal by-laws; still others passed at the state or provincial level. As noted at this chapter's outset, Boston's city ordinance requires police to be present for street construction (Boston Municipal Research Bureau 2008). Toronto and San Francisco similarly had city by-laws/ordinances requiring paid detail. One source is legal regulations concerning traffic and highways during construction or repair. Seattle's by-law (section f) states: "When existing traffic signals are to be countermanded, in which case only a Uniformed Police Officer shall be the flagger." Yet few funders we interviewed seemed to know or express concern about from where the legal requirement to have paid detail officers had stemmed. It was required, and that was it. They discussed these requirements as a done deal revealing a kind of loyalty to both police and law:

> [W]here there is regular traffic or traffic control lights...that is otherwise operated by something, by lights, they have to be there (Western Canadian Funder 1).
>
> MTO regulations... It's an automatic when you're changing the direction of the flow of traffic through an intersection... I have to have a paid detail (Central Canadian Funder 1).

> Georgetown, which is a little different than Austin, they have what they called a special event permit, and when you do a five km race, you have to fill out this permit and...you have to get police officers, just because you might have to close a street (Southern US Funder 1).
>
> [W]e put on a series of running events and paid detail policing is mandatory through the city... whenever we cross an intersection that's governed by a stop-light (Central Canadian Funder 2).
>
> No road can be closed without a police officer, so you can't just hire security to close a road off. It has to be a police officer. Any time you're redirecting, closing a road, there's sort of a temporary closure, then you have to have a police officer (Central Canadian Funder 3).

The other common legal requirement pertained to events where there was liquor consumption:

> Now the Manitoba Liquor Commission, it is on the permit that you have to have police there. So you have to have a policing presence nowadays... maybe four to five years ago, they put it in. It's roughly around the same time that we decided to go with the police presence (Western Canadian Funder 2).
>
> The municipal bylaws around events and events that sell liquor stipulate that there must be paid detail presence. It doesn't stipulate how many officers, however. That decision is sort of handed over to police services (Central Canadian Funder 4).

Significantly, as in the case above and noted earlier, in almost all instances where state, provincial or local laws demanded paid detail officers be in place, the amount of funding to be provided (the number of officers required), was left to the police department that would then instruct the funder how much funding was expected:

> It's just a local ordinance, basically anytime you have to submit for that special event, it's up to the police to determine... whether or not they are required in the first place, and then, if so, how many (Western US Funder 1).
>
> Perceived traffic flow in the area for construction works is determined by the police (Central Canadian Funder 5).

The few funders who questioned paid detail requirements typically failed to achieve clarity:

> I don't know where the origin is, where the policies are, who developed the policy, because we asked municipal councilors. They have no idea... one of my good friends who runs a fiddle festival... took them to task and went to the city and went to the police office and said "Can you

> give me the bylaw that demonstrates that I have to have paid security?" They couldn't find it. They said, "well let's go to the clerk's department" and they couldn't find it at the clerk's department. So who created this legislation? Where is it coming from? …So they've adopted it from, I don't know the police association… I don't know where it comes from (Central Canadian Funder 6).

Much paid detail is demanded by police when negotiating exchanges with organizations seeking to hold a public event, even where the requirement for paid detail is not enshrined in law *per se*. This possibility was not lost on the few critics of paid detail in media (Luscombe et al. 2017b, 756). In readers' comments surrounding news coverage of paid detail in Toronto: "What the cops are doing amounts to extortion, organized crime" (Casey and Loriggio 2015) and "Having the municipality tell an event or construction site it has to provide security or traffic direction is one thing, but forcing them to hire off-duty police officers for this is simple extortion" (Bell 2014). Strong-arming organizations and individuals to fund paid detail officers behind the scenes is a framing of a different kind which we remark upon in Chapter Seven. We did not uncover evidence in Canada and the US through our interviews and other document collection of such framing, but it can be glimpsed in serious controversies that have arisen in several US cities.

Paid Detail Over-Extension and Greedy Officers

While we noted earlier that to say police are a greedy institution does not necessarily refer to individual officers, there are instances of institutional greed filtering down to individuals and translating into monetary greed. One manifestation of this is corruption we discuss at length in Chapter Seven. In Chapter Two, we showed the levels of paid detail funding flowing into officers' pockets, the large sums officers acquired through paid detail funding. Recall some salary increases were not minor for some individuals. One Western US police representative related that for officers

> if you maxed out your 40 hours every pay period, which is 50 per cent more of what you would normally work, but that 50 per cent is paid at time and a half, so you're actually increasing your salary 75 per cent (Western US Police 1).

A police union representative from a big city in Texas explained "if a baseline police officer is making anywhere from $70,000 to $85,000 (US) a year, they can even… double that salary" (Southern Police Union 1). The Western US police representative quoted above explained:

> [F]inancially officers often extended themselves too much…There are officers… that will work every hour of overtime that they possibly can,

> and… that comes sometimes to the detriment of their family. They'll buy… things that they probably on their normal salary wouldn't be able to afford but they buy them, and then if the overtime does dry up on them, now they're stuck with… a large payment on a boat or a house or a car or something… They buy these extravagances and it's to their detriment (Western US Police 1).

Similarly, a union official of a big US city department of comparable size related "there are some officers that make an absolute living off of these things and live way beyond their means" (Houston union). However, it should be understood paid detail can compensate symbolically and in real terms police departments by reducing demands for higher salaries and rates for officers. By running it through paid detail unit offices, such as in Boston, New York, and Toronto, or by passing it to loyal corporate brokers, the department can use funds generated elsewhere on things they desire rather than having to spend more on officer salaries.

Corporate Paid Detail Brokers and Networks

Increased regulation and paid detail units is one change noted earlier but more recently corporate paid detail brokers and the creation of new networks have emerged. This reflects not only corporatization remarked upon in Chapter One, but also police as a greedy institution. These brokers include but are not limited to Frizell Group, Athos Group, Seattle's Finest, Blucadia, Off-Duty Services, and Extra Duty Solutions in the US. Thus far, no such brokers have emerged in Canada.

Our research showed Extra Duty Solutions has had especially remarkable growth. Thus, beginning in the first quarter of 2016, only a few years ago, this paid detail broker commenced with one police department in one US state and by the second quarter of 2021 had 110 departments. Figure 5.2 shows this stunning growth in police departments brokering for and capital flowing into police officers and this broker's pockets. Coverage has moved from one to 18 US states during this period and corporate revenue has jumped from 244 thousand to $16.1 million USD (Extra Duty Solutions 2021).

Based on its recent "client list" included in a bid to gain another client, most of these departments are small rather than large city departments (Extra Duty Solutions 2020a). Another corporate paid detail broker in Texas described its aggressive framing strategies, which are decidedly greater, more complex, and employing more communication formats than any single police department's limited promotion:

> We're trying as we speak to grow especially in other areas in Texas. We've had one or two assignments in Austin. We've had a few in Dallas. We've had a few in South Texas… we would love to get more permanent assignments in all of those areas as well as even more in

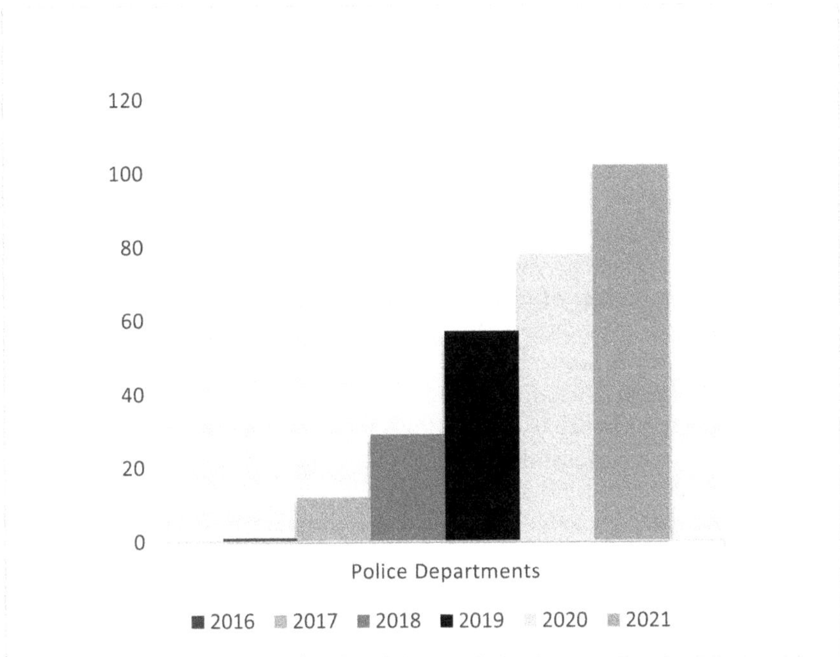

Figure 5.2 Growth of a Paid Detail Broker

Source: Extra Duty Solutions 2021.

> Houston... just like every other small to medium sized business to try and increase our search engine optimizing stuff. We're doing Linked-in ads. We're running blogs. All of a sudden we started that a few months ago and tried to get our rankings higher. We do a lot of mail outs. We just got into the trade show business last year... and we're looking into doing more trade shows. I speak whenever I can... Whatever it is, I'll volunteer for it. I've written a couple of articles about that sort of thing. So we're just trying to be in full sales mode at this point to try to build up in particular that side of the business... we've really been focusing on the police stuff... we have the capacity to handle a lot more business than we have now (Southern Broker 1).

This same broker promoted paid detail by demarcating a key "choice between off-duty police officers and security guards and... I've actually written blogs and articles about that and you can find that on my Linked In page and the pros and cons of each" (Southern Broker 1). This strategy is significant since it plainly seeks to pry apart any convergence of police and private security that criminologists have discussed at length and which police only hint at (e.g., the NYPD paid detail pamphlet). In previous work, we documented how public corporate security operatives made distinctions among police, contract security, and their superior standing as corporate security (Walby et al. 2014). Although police distance themselves from contract security providers in terms of professionalism, ability, and power, this is typically done informally, through police union framing, but certainly not by a chief of police. Thus, paid detail brokers framing the need for paid detail funders on behalf of police, as in this instance, is new and significant. As noted earlier in the book, through exchanges and this framing, these corporate paid detail brokers become an extension of the greedy police institution. The limited promotion of paid detail at the department level noted above when contracted with these third-party brokers is enhanced considerably. Framing for both, however, remains targeted and narrow, aimed mostly at private organizations including corporations to encourage them, sometimes strongly, to join, rather than framed for public consumption.

Corporate brokers transmit and amplify the claims of the police institution to suggest paid detail funders should provide public safety by funding paid detail. One broker provides for enhanced surveillance of officers while on paid detail. Yet this surveillance was linked to being able to react to emergencies elsewhere and not their conduct, as one broker owner explained in an article written for the police friendly *Police Chief* magazine:

> Using a smartphone app[lication] officers working off-duty assignments can be tracked in real time, allowing dispatchers to immediately identify the presence of off-duty sworn personnel in proximity to critical incidents (Sweeten 2021).

Brokers' loyalty to the police institution becomes clear when one describes monitoring officers. It is evident due to the broker being a former police officer and in how the broker's organization deals with "brethren" sleeping or otherwise violating paid detail rules or laws on assignment. One corporate broker explained:

> I am very pro law enforcement. I'm a former federal law enforcement agent…[T]he vice president of my company… is a 20 plus year municipal law enforcement officer from Texas who most recently when he retired was at the assistant chief level of the agency he worked for here in Houston. We're both very pro law enforcement and… sometimes we find people [i.e., officers] asleep or doing something they're not supposed to do but we try not to. There's two prongs to this. One is in marketing. *I try not to emphasize that some of our police or former brethren are less than scrupulous when it comes to following 100% of the rules and so we might mention it in passing but we certainly don't emphasize it.* We'll say we spot check and which we do and we… make sure that they're doing okay and doing what they're supposed to do. We usually let that stand for itself.

> If somebody specifically asked us: "Have you ever found anybody...?" "Well yes we have." [But] we typically don't report it to our clients when we have fired someone. For example, this very big energy sector client that hired us. It was our second biggest client... we just renewed the contract we have with them... because of the volume *we fired dozens of cops that have been assigned to their facilities. [But] we never tell them*" (Southern Broker 1; emphasis added).

Another key commercial paid detail broker, like Frizell, Extra Duty Solutions, and Athos, but operating in the US Northwest and covering Washington state, and noted earlier, is Seattle's Finest (2020). Like most other brokers of this kind, it was also founded by an ex-police officer back in 2002 and is currently run by this 20-year veteran of the Seattle police department (Miletich and Carter 2017). This commercial broker reports they engage in preemptive moral regulation of police officers like that discerned above and which is found in many police departments regarding funders and proximity to certain objects and spaces with which they are associated. For example, Seattle Finest's front webpage states boldly in large fonts: "What We Don't Do. We do not provide services for Liquor Establishments, Anything Cannabis, Adult Entertainment" with no further explanation or reference to any specific police department policy (Seattle's Finest 2020). The likely effects of such elements are deemed obvious.

In earlier work (e.g., Lippert and Walby 2019, 126–128) following preliminary research, we called these brokers "vampires" because they seemed to suck the lifeblood out of paid detail through profitable fees that might have otherwise gone to a police department or local government via their administrative fees for a paid detail unit or upkeep and training of officers themselves. However, considering more research findings above and conceptual advancement we contend these entities instead actually befit and are part of the broader greedy police institution and operate as a network. We now suggest the new paid detail brokers are more like police foundations, in that they serve as middlepersons in this model that rivals the police department paid detail units in New York, Boston, and much of Canada but which extend the views of the police institution. These brokers, along with paid detail units, police unions, and sometimes individuals (the various brokering models presented earlier), promote the police worldview to narrow audiences while monetarily benefiting from it in one way or another (administrative fees, union dues, handsome pay, corporate profit, etc.).

Paid detail arrangements in smaller US departments especially are being slowly replaced by corporate paid detail brokers. One such broker explained how it worked:

> What we do is say, 'don't hire the cops directly. Come to us and here's what we'll do. We use costs plus formatting...' It varies in different parts

> of the state depending on how many officers there are and the demand... [in] that area of Texas the going rate is typically most cops will work for about $35 an hour... We don't keep a penny of that, so we would charge our client $35 an hour plus a fee and out of that extra fee is give or take about 30-35%. We do a number of things. One, we do all the payroll so you don't have to write a 100 cheques next week if you had a 100 cops a week you only have to write one cheque a month or two cheques a month...We take care of the 1099 fees at the end of the year say we have one client that single-handedly uses 400 or more officers over the course of the year they don't have to do one 1099 per officer, we do it (Southern Broker 1).

In the US, these arrangements are being shifted *en masse* to corporate paid detail brokers who keep funding arrangements, including levels – but not the availability of officers themselves – and their framing to target funders of these services hidden. There is something of a corporate paid detail broker takeover occurring. One such broker explained how paid detail is framed for external funders, as opposed to the public and his "speech to clients":

> We go to businesses and say to them: 'Look you have been hiring off-duty police officers for years and years... and you have spent big bags of money on doing so but you have fooled yourself into thinking that you have no risk or potential liability'... So... a bank directly hires an off-duty police officer to sit in their lobby and a masked man wielding an assault rifle comes busting through the doors of the bank and there is a shootout. In... most states in the US, even though the officer is off-duty the very millisecond... in which he has to take law enforcement action even though he's off-duty he instantly is on duty by the color of the law so now he has all the rights, protection and coverage and you know force of his agency and his law enforcement training and experience and... the municipality's immunity from litigation... as if he was on duty. That instantly happens so now he's in a shootout with the bad guy. He kills the bad guy. He did so as a law enforcement officer. Let's say the officer is shot in the arm. He has a legitimate worker's comp[ensation] claim. A level of insurance would kick into effect because he was instantly on duty even though, only moments before he was not. Well, our speech to our clients is this: 'That's swell if you have an armed gunman coming into your bank but what if the chandelier in the lobby in the bank fell, the screws came loose and it fell and the glass broke and it took out that officer's eye? You would be sued up the Waazoo... because that guy or woman is not covered by worker's comp[ensation]. They're not covered by anything.' That's the reason why the bank has worker's comp insurance for their own employees. So that you have the protection against being sued (Southern Broker 1).

This concern over legal liability is more pronounced in the US than in Canada; the former being known to be much more litigious. Thus, it was no surprise Melissa Sanchez who was trampled by a police horse at a protest, as described in the book's introduction, decided to sue the police and others. However, this difference in litigiousness may well explain why the corporate paid detail brokers working on police behalf have not yet spread to Canada.

Brokers also pitch to obtain a contract city or municipal governments and police departments and why they should work on behalf of police, the other side of the paid detail arrangement: For example, the City of Orange Township in New Jersey following a request for proposals received two bids from corporate paid detail brokers, Extra Duty Solutions (EDS) and AMS, respectively (Extra Duty Solutions 2020b). The former was then selected for a two-year contract. In a cover letter, EDS framed it to the City and its police department as follows:

> [W]e are confident of our ability to provide a seamless and hassle-free solution for the administration of the law enforcement off duty program. Our solution will encompass client interaction, communicating and scheduling extra duty details among the officers, client invoicing and collections, and officer payment through the City. All aspects of our solution will be consistent with the rules and approach the City, and the Orange Police Department (OPD) require we take (Extra Duty Solutions 2020b).

One paid detail broker had no less than 110 different police departments in their network; and that was in only one US region. Each of these 110 departments had numerous funders. The introduction of the broker has expanded paid detail networks. These brokers are now key nodes within the larger police funding and sponsorship networks. Another effect of the rise of these brokers is that paid detail becomes standardized as it is corporatized, since one broker will now handle multiple police departments in a network. Previously, in the US, they were all separate, dealing with external organizations a bit differently on their own. The paid detail networks consequently grow in size but not in number. We return to these brokers in Chapter Seven.

Conclusion

Paid detail policing is a significant source of private funding of police and it too shows police as a greedy institution. Once these shadow figures – both the numbers and officers – are identified, they cannot any longer be ignored as a key component of the private funding of police. Any notion that paid detail policing is a marginal phenomenon – temporally, spatially, and quantitatively – is dubious. Attention to paid detail also reveals the complex, varied ways a greedy institution seeks to morally regulate its members as well as the external organizations – the numerous funders – which it demands and expects to adopt the police worldview and provide support through funding. In the meantime, paid detail policing continues unheeded in the shadows. How this funding is administered has been mutating towards greater regulation and corporatization. Attention to paid detail is important in an age of increasing exchange between private and public policing realms (Button and Wakefield 2018; White 2012). On the one hand, paid detail policing is public in that it is *public police* whose presence is being rented. The uniform officers wear to these assignments alone is a public symbol of power and potential deadly force. On the other hand, paid detail policing is usually private in typically involving private organizations renting this presence for private events. Paid detail arrangements are not necessarily exclusive of other networks, as discussed in Chapter Two. It may well be that private paid detail funders are also donors or sponsored and thus enrolled in those networks too. This overlap may be because paid detail funders are not necessarily approved by the police department and donating/sponsoring might help grease the paid detail approval wheels. Indeed, in other work we document an instance where a nightclub in Toronto had paid detail suspended following a violent incident but then following becoming a sponsor of a Toronto police, paid detail assignments were reinstated soon after (Luscombe et al. 2018).

When it is illuminated, paid detail shows a greedy police institution that has departed from its ostensive civic, public principles and scruples (Loader 2016) and, as we take up in Chapter Seven, sometimes even from the rule of law. Long-standing crime fighter images (Phillips 2016; Crank 1994) that have characterized police also fade under the light of paid detail funding research; it is hard to reconcile this image with the counter image of the Boston Police officer parked at the construction site and looking the other way. This fading may be a good thing, as we discuss in the book's conclusion, which lends itself to thinking about the prospects for what policing might look like in a generous society instead.

Notes

1 We use "nominally external" since there is a sense in which the external organizations that in part pledge loyalty to the police institution by funnelling paid detail funds are not "external."

2 While body worn cameras are proliferating across the US and to a lesser extent Canada, that police claim are for accountability purposes (Lippert and Newell 2016), we could locate but a tiny fraction of departments requiring these cameras to be used by officers during paid detail assignments.

Chapter 6

Framing Dark Money as Community Benefit

Introduction

In earlier chapters, we examined networks that emerge among various organizations, corporations, police foundations, paid detail brokers, and police. We focused on the network dimension of the greedy institution and how foundations, sponsorship, and donations extend those networks. One element of the greedy institution we have not yet fully explored is framing. Cox (2016) argues framing is a fundamental yet overlooked element of the greedy institution. This chapter assesses these communications on police foundation websites. We examine the visual culture and politics of foundation communications to show how they attract and recruit economic and social capital for police foundations and the broader police institution. Showing how this framing construes dark money and the networks it engenders as community benefit, we argue this framing is crucial to both the operations and growth of the greedy police institution as it aligns other groups, organizations, and interests (also see Cox 2016).

In documenting how crucial this framing is to the police, we connect our inquiry to the broader literature on police engagement with media as well as police use of social media. The character of these communications reveals something about the police foundation as part of the greedy police institution. Framing includes some information and excludes other information in a message, statement, image, or composite of words and images (VanGorp 2007; Creed et al. 2002). Framing is communication and is an attempt to convey ideas and persuade an audience into believing and conforming to those ideas (Kuypers 2005; Kuypers and Cooper 2005). Police foundations and police departments engage in framing to convey ideas and convince audiences of their veracity or truthfulness. We reveal police foundation communications focus on the community and diversity. Not unlike the communications of foundations and think tanks in the oil industry (Carroll et al. 2021), this framing must construe the positive community value of exchanges. These police foundation communications, we argue, are meant to mainly distract from the exchange of money from corporations to foundations and,

DOI: 10.4324/9781003167914-7

in turn, from foundations to police. Police foundations are aware of this image of police and they launder the reputation of police as well as social and economic capital emanating from the corporate realm and transferred to police.

To engage in this analysis, we draw from literature that details how to analyze visual data including the methodological writings of Altheide and Schneider (2012) on qualitative content analysis. Banks (2007) also lays out dimensions of visual research. We draw from his comments on content analysis of photographs and their manifest and latent content. Manifest content is akin to denotation, the literal or direct meaning of elements of a text or image. Equally important when examining visual politics is latent content. Latent content is similar to connotation (Valverde 2006) and entails a range of meanings and associations. Assessing those meanings requires some interpretation. Our interpretation of the manifest and latent content of these communications and images is in some ways directed by our greedy institution and corporatization framework. What follows is a combination of interpretation guided by our theoretical framework and an exploration of other themes that emerged from an inductive reading of these texts.

We are building on research that examines police communications (Ellis and McGovern 2016; Mawby 2013). Most literature on police communications has focused on police departments; we apply these insights to police foundations. We point to two of these works that we build on before elaborating on related literature and offering our analysis. Walby and Gumieny (2020) examined police claims about philanthropy on social media platforms, especially Twitter and Instagram and how police frame their own philanthropy by giving back to the community in some way. This work examined tweets that included textual information, images, as well as hashtags. By analyzing these facets of social media data, it is possible to look at how communications create a social network. In their analysis, Walby and Gumieny looked at how police departments sought to appear integrated with the community. The communications suggested police are warm, friendly, and benevolent. Part of the analysis contrasted such happy and welcoming police images with the reality of their criminalizing and often violent practices. In a related study, Duncan and Walby (2022) examined how police unions engage in social media and broader media communication. The police voice that emerges in police union communications is more aggressive and gruffer than police department social media communications. In police union communications, Duncan and Walby show unions and especially their presidents or directors are aggressive and belligerent towards police critics including local politicians and journalists. What is absent from this literature is an investigation of framing in police foundation communications. As we have argued throughout this book, police foundations have become a pivotal part of the police institution. Focusing on framing within a greedy institution conceptual framework allows exploration of how those ideas are assembled and their intended meanings, and how they seek to generate more and more funding and loyal members for such an institution.

Framing in Context

We now assess some literature on communications to provide context before offering our analysis. Police communications have moved online, requiring an understanding of online and digital culture. As Mau (2019) argues, the status competitions of today's society have moved online. More people are communicating online to augment status and build social networks. People also seek out online what Mau calls the power of nomination. People want to be notable. Police have moved online to achieve notoriety and they issue their communications accordingly. This dynamic is part of what Stalder (2018) calls the digital condition whereby people seek belonging by communicating with others online. They do so by drawing on what Stalder (2018) calls "referentiality" which is how people assemble, combine, or incorporate aspects of visual culture into their own communications. It is a reference that makes an association with some other meaning. An example is a meme where we take one kind of symbol or image and put a spin on it. It is effective because of its referentiality as it points to an accepted aspect of culture. That referentiality is used by large organizations today to increase their popularity. These organizations frame what the public knows about their operations. Police do this by posting communications that provide some nomination, but which also might be entertaining via references to popular culture. To do that, one needs a platform and a profile.

These aspects of digital culture are also sites where police departments participate and do the same. They use framing and referentiality to build profiles and expand their reach. Large organizations have more resources to hire people to curate more impressive profiles (Bollmer 2018). These workers in rhetoric become professional framers who polish and scrub the police image and represent the police institution in the best possible light. These communications are as important as face-to-face interactions and communication. We have adopted these methodological measures to study police foundation framing. We collected and systematically analyzed a sample of communications and observed these websites over a two-year span to discern how the funders communicate and interact (see Murthy 2008).

There is also important literature in policing studies on police communications. Bullock (2018a) has argued police use of social media is increasing. Most police departments have multiple social media platforms today. Bullock suggests this might be an attempt by police to normalize their existence. Bullock (2018b) goes further to argue that many communications on these platforms appear friendly and community-oriented. Crump (2011) has offered a typology of the various uses of police social media. Crump argues some police departments seek to build a network and expand their reach while others use social media for surveillance (see also Trottier 2012). Hu, Rodgers, and Lovrich (2018) find police departments in the US use social media to engage in message change. The message about police in news media and among community members might be one of violence, antagonism, fear, discriminatory based on race, gender, and class, and increasingly illegitimate. Police themselves use social media to soften their image, to persuade the public they are more than crime fighters. Therefore, they argue, police social media use attempts to humanize police officers, although there might be some variation from region to region, country to country, and even department to department. Meijer and Thaens (2013) as well as Meijer and Torenvlied (2016) similarly find police use social media in varied ways.

As Wood (2020) points out, police engage in communications that appear to be a distraction or camouflage. Wood shows police now use memes in social media communications. They curate social media platforms to be entertaining and engaging. Though not on social media itself – instead, on police websites – Sillince and Brown (2009) argue the police presence online is chameleon-like. They argue police websites can feature different pages and content for different audiences. Websites that are JavaScript based instead of HTML script-based are dynamic and may display different content depending on the page's visitor. This reveals police as crafty curators who engage in strategic framing. Police foundations do this as well. We examine police foundation communications from 2016 to the present in Canadian and US cities on both their websites and social media. As in other chapters, we pay attention to smaller and larger foundations with an aim to reveal variation and trends. Below, we examine the patterns in the textual information conveyed on these police foundation websites and communications as well as visual communications evident there.

Police Foundation Websites, Newsletters, and Communiqués

This section examines newsletters and news releases posted on police foundation websites from 2017 to 2021. Overall, we have discerned community and diversity as a prevalent master theme or frame. Undermining or contradicting the community and diversity frame is the second main form of framing, which focuses on funding for police and police operations.

Community and Diversity Framing

There are several communications in these newsletters and news releases that portray police and foundations as engaged in community building. These are interesting in relation to critiques of police as antagonistic violence workers. For example, one communication showcases the community safety and mental health initiatives operated by the Vancouver Police Department

(VPD) and Vancouver Police Foundation (VPF) that received a donation of $1 million from Wall Financial Corporation (VPF 2021a) (see also Chapter Seven). The support was considered timely by the VPF due to crime statistics and concerns expressed by Vancouver residents about limited resources to address mental health, and homelessness. The donation from Wall Financial Corporation was pledged to VPD mental health initiatives that provide additional resources to front-line VPD officers and individuals experiencing crisis in Vancouver. The communication frames this as a benefit to the community, however it is really funding for VPD initiatives and VPD members. Another communication elaborates the VPD Canine Unit calendar, a yearly project to raise funds for the British Columbia Cancer Foundation and British Columbia Children's Hospital (VPF 2020a). The project is described as "a very worthwhile fundraising initiative and an opportunity to take our furry partners to connect with the community" to underscore the humanity of police behind their "scary" uniforms and vehicles. The objective of this framing is to soften the image of police and portray police and the foundation as donating to health initiatives, but really it depends on taxpayers who are already paying for police to purchase a foundation K9 calendar. Other communications show VPD in the community. One article focuses on the Vancouver Police Soccer Club, a VPF funded program and its partnership with MoreSports to provide young players in the club without means to purchase their own football gear (VPF 2018a). A similar communication focuses on a 3-on-3 basketball tournament hosted by members of the Delta Police Department and supported by the Delta Police Foundation (Jacques 2019). The tournament included over 100 high school students. This focus on community in these communications belies the fact the police institution has been shown to disrupt formation of community (Clear 2009).

Although the framing by US police foundations tended to focus more on police than community, some newsletters and news releases reflected the community category. For example, one Seattle Police Foundation (SPF) news article spotlights the Precinct Picnics, a community outreach event to provide opportunities for each precinct's surrounding neighbourhoods to come together and enjoy an afternoon with Seattle Police officers (SPF 2020). The Seattle Police Department brought police horses and police vehicles to the picnic for the public to engage. Another article spotlights the annual Sergeant Santa event hosted by the Detroit Police Department and the Detroit Public Safety Foundation (DPSF), an event that aims to help families across Detroit during the holiday season (Pamplin 2020). The story reports that anonymous donors and corporations like Comcast ensure at least two police families from each Detroit precinct and additional families in the city will receive toys, clothes and other items purchased by the foundation. In other words, the foundation uses the funds to mainly buy toys for the children of police officers. A similar post announces the annual NYPD Holiday Sleigh Ride supported by the New York Police Foundation (NYCPF 2020a), an event aimed at bringing the police and community together. Activities include local sightings of Santa's sleigh and his police superheroes. Another initiative noted is the partnership between the NYCPF and the New York Giants for the National Football League team's #TogetherBlue campaign (NYCPF 2020b). The announcement states the Giants will support the Options Program that helps young people cultivate career opportunities, building bridges between the police and New York communities. These communications focus on police as contributing to community.

There are also several news releases focused on police and foundation attempts to foster diversity. These are interesting considering critiques of police as an institution dominated by straight, white males. For example, one article discusses the Healing Path Necklace Initiative, founded in 2020, and how important it is for the Vancouver Police and VPF to foster relationships with Indigenous communities (VPF 2021b). The article also discusses the importance of beading to Indigenous culture, and the significance of officers and community members wearing them. Another communication highlights the work of the Chair of the Vancouver Police Foundation Board, Dr. Sherri Magee, and her achievements for the VPF (VPF 2021c). Dr. Magee reflects on her experiences volunteering for the VPF and the positive impacts of VPF funded initiatives. Magee notes the impact of VPF programs on youths, women, and seniors, describing the VPD officers who undertake these programs as "dedicated, professional and very compassionate." One of such VPF program, the Women's Personal Safety Workshop, created by two women VPD officers using VPF funds, has trained approximately 30 women officers to deliver the safety workshops. Another communication introduces the VPF funded Out on Patrol program, a peer-support initiative for law enforcement personnel that focuses on sexuality, community engagement, and education (VPF 2020b). Out on Patrol is described as providing a safe space to address some of these concerns for officers. The program is alleged to be a bridge to the LGBTQ2S community. Another communication spotlights the VPD cadets program focusing on a diverse group of students from different ethnic backgrounds including: African Canadian, Chinese, Filipino, First Nations, South Asian, Middle Eastern, and other ethnicities (VPF 2019a). A newsletter entry describes the VPF sponsorship of the VPD Senior Health and Safety Fair (VPF 2018b). The purpose of the fair is to provide information on Seniors Centres and Networks, Elder Abuse, Safety, Health, and Diversity. Another story from the CPYF highlights the Calgary Police Cadet Corps, which is a foundation supported program that engages the city's youth offering opportunities to develop leadership skills, enhance physical fitness, and build skills such as camaraderie, positive social interaction, and personal achievement (CPYF n.d.). The program enrols children into the police mission at the earliest possible age. All these communications focus on diversity as a hallmark of police and the work of the police foundation. However, there is ample previous research showing police as an institution has long reproduced sexism, racism, and homophobia. This focus on diversity in communications belies the fact the police institution itself has been critiqued for reproducing racism and sexism for decades (Kringen and Novich 2018; Silvestri 2017; Palmater 2016; Miller et al. 2003).

Police-Centric Framing

The second form of framing in these communications focuses on police funding and operations. This seems at odds with the community and diversity frame found elsewhere in these police foundation newsletters and news releases. For example, one story entitled Project 529 Reduces Bike Theft in Vancouver starts by highlighting how a VPD officer became involved with addressing bike theft (VPF 2021d). The article discusses Project 529 – an online information-sharing platform and bike registration database system that reunites stolen bikes with their rightful owners and deters would-be thieves – and the positive impact this has had. This is an example of a VPF funded VPD operation. Another story elaborates the Project Landmark initiative funded by a VPF grant (VPF 2020c). The program allowed the VPD to hand out over 2,000 number plates to residents to post on their fences and garages in back alleys to increase visibility to police. Another item pertains to the Vancouver Chapter of Beyond the Blue – a community of support for police spouses and their families (VPF 2020d). Using a peer-support model to provide families with training to thrive in their roles as the support system for police officers, allowing police families to share their experiences and to support one another without taking the place of resources and programs that VPD provides its members. One more story details VPF award grants for projects and equipment (VPF 2019b). The VPF funded Project 529 above as well as youth programs like NewKids VPD Youth Police Academy that introduces kids to policing in Canada, new technology and special equipment, and the VPD Illicit Drug Presentation Kit maintained by the VPD and used by members when seeking to educate groups on drug topics. All these communications detail funds going to police, normalizing police involvement in these endeavours.

A video on the Edmonton Police Foundation (EPF) website (EPF 2018a) highlights the uses of donations and the difference foundation funding makes in community policing as well as its impact on the Edmonton residents' quality of life. The video introduces the launch of four new EPF-funded programs within the Edmonton Police Service, including police programs focusing on youths, police dogs, police research, and police mental health programming. Elaborating this mental health program, another video (see EPF 2018b) tells the story of Cst. Doug McLeod, an Edmonton officer traumatized by a shoot-out, to spotlight the mental toll of policing and introduces the re-integration program, an EPF supported peer driven program ran by the Edmonton Police Service to address mental health issues. Another EPF video (EPF 2018b) spotlights the True Blue Friends campaign, an EPF initiative that aims to raise $5 million dollars over five years to establish an Operations and Intelligence Command Centre, a 24/7 police unit that will work in conjunction with the EPS frontline members and investigators to provide intelligence to frontline members to respond to events and use data to identify high crime areas. The claim that police foundations exist to fund community slips away as more stories on their funding of core police operations appear.

A Boston Police Foundation (BPF) story highlights the foundation's support to local precincts, including a donation of over $1.4 million to help support officer wellness, community policing, new technology, and the equipment to keep Boston safe (BPF 2019a). Another story showcases the 7th Annual Honoring Our Heroes Celebration that entailed Boston businesses coming together to host a BPF benefit (BPF 2019b). The goal of the event, wholly consistent with the greedy institution's aims, is to bring local and loyal business owners and residents together to support Boston police and help the BPF ensure every police unit has the newest equipment. The Back Up Boston's Finest initiative is referenced, speaking to the Boston Police's and the BPF's work in ensuring every officer has support for fitness initiatives and suicide prevention. Another article features an infographic showcasing statistics on the mental health of officers in Boston (BPF 2019c). The statistics are: 25 percent of all police officers have high blood pressure; police officers are 30 times more likely to suffer a heart attack than the general population; 40 percent of police officers are obese compared to 32 percent of the general population; 176 police officers died by heart attack or suicide in 2018, and more officers die by their own gun than other type of line of duty deaths. The infographic noted the BPF approach to these issues including providing gym equipment and physical training to officers for stress relief.

The Seattle Police Foundation website similarly focused on benefits of the foundation for police. One article announces the SPF's 2021 Blue Tie Ball, an event to highlight the work of the officers of the SPD and raise funds to provide grants to improve employee development and assist in providing equipment and technology to ensure officer safety (SPF 2021). The February 2019 SPF newsletter features: the 2018 grants supported by the Seattle Police Foundation; the announcement of Cop-I-Con, an event to unite community members and officers to learn about policing from police; and the announcements of the Blue Tie Ball and the Seattle Police Awards Banquet. An NYCPF article announces the New York City Police Foundation's initiative would roll out 550 new light-weight bullet-resistant vests for NYPD detectives (NYCPF 2020c). The article notes the inadequateness of the current NYPD bullet-resistant vests and the benefits of the new vests. The initiative was made possible by public donations to the foundation, and the Police Commissioner expressed gratitude to the NYCPF donation. Another NYCPF article shares highlights of the NYCPF's annual gala including recognition of distinguished

NYPD members (NYCPF 2018). The event was attended by over 1000 of NYC's business, civic, and cultural leaders and over $4.5 million dollars was raised. Highlights included the speech by the NYCPF's president Susan Birnbaum who emphasized the shared responsibility of public safety and the importance of equipping the NYPD with tools to reduce crime.

A Los Angeles Police Foundation (LAPF) (n.d.) story references LAPF efforts to raise funds to purchase state-of-the-art equipment and technology that improves the effectiveness and efficiency of the Los Angeles Police Department (LAPD) in the prevention, identification, and investigation of crime. Some equipment includes body-worn cameras, enclosed canopies for field officers collecting vulnerable crime scene evidence, high-tech communications equipment for the LAPD's "Situation Room," and tactical vests. A Houston Police Foundation (HPF) story likewise focuses on the HPF's newest project, a campaign to fund the construction of a $10 million tactical village, a space to be used by the Houston Police Department for training (HPF 2021c). The goal is for the tactical village to provide a venue for tactical training. Perhaps the greediest initiative of a police foundation described in these communications, a 2019 New Orleans Police and Justice Foundation (NOPJF) article, describes the Mardi Gras parade and the role of the New Orleans Police Department during the event. It calls for public donations to sponsor a Mardi Gras meal or snack for officers attending the parades. The article highlights the Adopt-A-Cop program created by the NOPJF for citizens and businesses to donate food or money to feed officers while they patrol the Mardi Gras parade.

Overall, in these newsletters and news releases we observe more police-centric framing communicated by US police foundations. The community framing is over-emphasized by Canadian police foundations. These two frames (community/diversity, and police-centric) appear to be at odds. We interpret this as revealing the duplicitous nature of police foundations. The framing makes it appear foundations and police exist to benefit the community. But other communications in these newsletters and news releases make it clear greediness is at the core of what police foundations do as an extension of the greedy police institution.

Managing Police Images

In this section, we focus on images found on police foundation websites and within their newsletters. The NYCPF hosts numerous programs to bring the community together. The foundation has assembled a Community Affairs Rapid Response Team to engage community, in part using a new foundation-funded and totally ostentatious NYPD video game bus that draws kids onto the bus to play video games. They boast "this community is our community," seeking to ensure everyone feels heard. In addition to community, they focus on funding police, for example, with the "50 Grants for

50 Precincts" initiative during the fiftieth anniversary of the NYCPF that entailed multiple photo opportunities and a plethora of social media content featuring mainly officers of colour posing in front of police murals and other iconography. The message is that by giving to the precincts, the NYCPF is giving to community, an association we have questioned in this book (also see Little Sis 2021). On the Community Strength page of the website, they contend communities need to work together with law enforcement to create a safer city. Looking at the visuals, NYCPF portrays community through interacting with the public. There are multiple photos with officers at events and speaking engagements. A group photo with four women-presenting individuals shows a group of women of colour. This image displays the diversity within the force. By contrast, the BPF displays an array of photos that are most visibly represented as male. This has the effect of portraying Boston Police as principally composed of men or suggests men are the department's only visible members.

The HPF has a newsletter but provides limited access to these records online. The focus is on funds for officer training and equipment, asking the public to donate. For example, the HPF website banner and logo boldly states: "You Can Make a Difference," imploring viewers to transfer money to HPF and by extension the Houston Police Department. The slogan suggests that one of the only ways or best ways to make a difference is to increase monies for police, rather than to boost funding for grassroots community and social development. The images on the NOPJF are also limited. Looking at the website reveals there are current projects to install additional surveillance cameras in the city and other funds granted to police. The NOPJF banner and logo implores the viewership to "Invest in Safety, Invest in Community, Invest in New Orleans, Click to Donate to Adopt-a-Cop." This messaging conflates funding for police foundations with safety and community, which is a tenuous if not misleading association. Designed like an online shopping or gambling portal, the viewer can give money to NOPJF with just one click. The NOPJF-funded SafeCam Platinum program is marketed as an expansion of the NOPD's SafeCam program that would allow business owners and residents to install cameras that feed directly to the City's Real Time Crime Center. The images contain various police officers in blue garb. Their age, gender, and racial/ethnic identity is diverse. There is an image that depicts an officer embracing another of the same sex, to suggest a diverse sexuality too. Next to that is an image of a diverse group of individuals engaging with officers who supposedly represent the community of New Orleans.

The VPF website focuses on LGBTQ people, youth, Indigenous community members, and other vulnerable and marginalized groups. The images convey the idea that creating positive relationships with the police foundation solves community issues. Various images on the website depict community. In one, donors are masked while engaging with officers. Another is of a group of ethnically diverse children. Another image shows an officer and an

Indigenous artwork display. The EPF page has fewer images. However, all are filtered in a blue hue. This colouring is akin to Blue Lives Matter or Thin Blue Line thinking, which has been widely critiqued. In the banner image, the messaging implores viewers to become a True Blue Friend by sending money to the EPF, asking the viewer: Are you for #TrueBlueFriendYEG? Another image in blue shows young smiling people flanked by police officers, also asking for more foundation funds. In another image, a group of hands join in a circle representing unity and community. The text underneath the image conveys that the community should value the safety of the police. Another image shows the interactions between law enforcement and the public, visually communicating that both entities are one.

Examining the Delta Police Foundation website reveals their focus is to build better relationships between the police and the community. The foundation prides itself in its community-centred approach. There are photos presented showing police engaged with community. A picture of the 3-on-3 basketball tournament noted above represents a diverse group of individuals. Community is also visually communicated through the donations and the fundraiser events. The Calgary Youth Police Foundation webpage displays multiple photos of how the Calgary police engage with youth from their community. The multiple photos of youth depict the vast age range the police youth foundation encompasses. The community in Calgary is depicted visually through a diverse array of children and acknowledges the different genders present. Community and diversity are a focus of these images on police foundations websites. Otherwise, the third frame is focused on police as notable community figures.

Police Foundation Twitter Pages

To add to this analysis, we have examined the Twitter communications of police foundations in Canada and the US. We looked at posts from the first half of 2021 and the second half of 2020. We examined the average number of posts, the description of the foundation, the types of posts, the types of pictures and videos posted, the hashtags included, the types of re-tweets, the interactions with the members of the public, and the thematic orientation of the Twitter pages.

The mission statements of the foundations are displayed prominently on these Twitter pages. The NYCPF indicates it exists to promote excellence in the #NYPD and improved public safety in #NewYorkCity. The HPF describes itself as serving a vital role in connecting private investment dollars with effective public safety solutions. The NOPJF indicates it is a non-profit dedicated to supporting the people in criminal justice processes in New Orleans. The LAPF indicates it is the largest source of private financial support for the LAPD when funding is unavailable from the city budget. The BPF describes itself as supporting the brave men and women of the Boston

Police Department by funding vital programs, equipment, and technological capabilities. The DPSF argues its mission is to promote public safety and enhance the capabilities of the Detroit Police Department. Finally, the Seattle Police Foundation suggests its mission is to raise support for the Seattle Police Department.

In Canada, the Delta Police Foundation suggests its mission is to encourage excellence in policing by promoting support for the Delta Police Department. The VPF description indicates it helps the #VPDgobeyondthecall by funding projects and initiatives not covered under their operating budget. The Calgary Police Youth Foundation suggests it funds programs to reduce youth victimization and criminal activity by focusing on education, prevention, and early intervention. The EPF argues it offers a simple formula for a safe community, #EPS + #YEG = #TBFYEG. It argues Edmontonians should stand with the EPF "as a true-blue friend." All these police foundation mission statements indicate a clear connection to police departments and indicate the mechanism by which private funds are funnelled into them. In contrast to imagery on the websites or even elsewhere on Twitter, there is little indication in the mission statements of community connections or impact. This is interesting, as Twitter limits the number of characters that can be included in any communication. When forced to decide what information to include, foundations focus on funds and support for police. However, as we have shown earlier, much other framing rhetorically focuses on community, raising questions as to why.

Concerning the types of Twitter posts, the New York Police Foundation focused primarily on support and appreciation for former officers, event promotions for donations and fundraising, and raising awareness of foundation supported purchases. The NOPJF, likewise, expresses support and appreciation for officers and event promotions for donations and fundraising. The LAPF concentrates on requests for support and donations, major crimes in LA, and memorial posts for officers. The BPF focuses on requests for donations as well as events and memorial posts. The DPSF focuses on requests for donations, events and fundraising, memorial posts as well as awards to staff and police and many tweets about identity and community. The SPF emphasizes donations, memorials for fallen officers and police dogs, as well as re-tweets of citizens showing support. In Canada, the DPF concentrates on requests for support as well as re-tweets from Delta Police. The VPF emphasizes community events, foundation donation drives and events, youth and community programs funded by the foundation as well as partnerships with Indigenous communities. The Calgary Police Youth Foundation emphasizes donations and funding drives, and the Calgary Police Museum. The Edmonton Police Twitter page focuses on fundraising and donation drives as well as updates about the funds awarded.

Regarding the photos and videos posted on these Twitter pages, the NYCPF offers several images of officers winning awards, police on duty in the community, and pictures of police dogs. The pictures and videos of police are framed in a positive light, showing them at community events and volunteering, which portrays the police foundation as primarily community oriented. The NOPJF focuses on police on duty serving community as well as new police grants and the contribution they will make to community. The LAPF concentrates more on crime education and reduction infographics. The BPF focuses more on fallen officers with their images. The DPSF also emphasizes fallen officers and their families as well as women officers. The Seattle Police Foundation likewise focuses on fallen officers and images of police dogs. The Delta Police Foundation images depict police in the community, police with youth, and paint a picture of police as integrated with community. The VPF focuses on police within the community and police with youths. It shows many pictures of police dogs wishing children a happy birthday. The Calgary Police Youth Foundation concentrates on police programming with youth. The EPF also emphasizes police working with youths, and the community impact police have. Overall, the police foundation Twitter pages emphasize community and display many images of police warmly working with community members. The police foundation Twitter images also display diversity. These images are crafted to connote the police foundation facilitates the integration of policing into community. However, these images can be juxtaposed against the mission statements of police foundations on the very same Twitter pages which focus on supporting police rather than community.

There are also hashtags posted on these police foundation Twitter pages deserving attention. Drawing on qualitative content analysis, we note the associations made with these hashtags. The NYCPF uses #buildingasafercommunitytogether as well as #copscommunityandkids, and #NYPDconnecting. All these hashtags focus on community again rather than funding for police operations and technologies. The LAPF uses #supportLAPD and #LAsfinest which are more about police than community. The BPF used the #saferBoston and #lawenforcementappreciation often, while DPSF Twitter used #neverforget in relation to officer shootings. In Canada, the DPF used hashtags such as #communityfirst, #bestpoliceforce, #copsforcancer, while the Vancouver Police #K9hero, #dogswithjobs, #indigenoushistorymonth, and #soallkidscanplay. These hashtags focus on community connections. The use of these hashtags is a mechanism to recruit community connections and the funds and loyalty they image are located there. The CPYF used the #prideinservice, #weareCPS, and #indigenouspeoplesday while EPF used the #foreverwatchfulneverforgotten and #bikethievessuck. Overall, foundation use of hashtags either emphasizes support for police and is associated with themes like blue brotherhood or police solidarity or concentrates on community and attempts to portray the police foundation and police as working and integrated with the community. Further, as social media researchers (Bollmer 2018) have demonstrated, the use of a hashtag is also a mechanism to recruit new supporters including new funders of the police foundations and new community groups potentially (re-)aligned with the police mission.

Concerning additional themes, on the NYCPF Twitter page there are a few communications focused on youth-oriented programming, family and community-oriented programming. These are represented, for instance, in images of police playing basketball with youths. Such a communication attempts to portray police and the police foundation in a positive light and show police as supportive of the community. The LAPF, perhaps in contrast, was one police foundation page that concentrates more on crime and crime prevention itself. In this sense, there is some variation in these communications. Likewise, the DPSF was focused mostly on support for and donations provided to police. They did not depict as much engagement with community or youths as other pages. The situation in Canada also reveals variation. The Delta Police Foundation page re-tweeted the Delta Police Twitter communications more frequently than other pages. The VPD was much more positive. It featured many tweets with energetic and positive language. It used emojis and pictures in almost every post, and almost every post was about community. Most posts showed police working with community in a positive way. The Calgary Police Youth Foundation Twitter page featured calls for donations and fundraising and posts about outreach to youth groups, which is the focus of their foundation. The EPF Twitter page focused less on community and more on police dogs and police events. Though they did display community in some posts, they were more likely to show pictures of police dogs or even re-tweet posts from Edmonton Police on the history of policing.

There were additionally some messages about COVID-19, police dogs, condolences for fallen officers, recruitment of new officers, and other police charity work. However, overall, what this analysis reveals is that Twitter pages of police foundations either focus on support for police or more rhetorically show police working with community. The aim of the latter is to soften the image of the police and show police engaging with community in ways that perhaps counter news media framing showing police violence and racism. In these ways, the police foundation Twitter pages we have analyzed engage in framing, creating a vision of the essence of policing and police foundations. This framing is positive. It rarely weighs into the stormy waters of criticisms of police racism and violence raised by, for example, Melissa Sanchez in Houston, members of Black Lives Matter, and millions of others attending global public protests during 2020, or the economics or sordid history of policing in North America. These are major silences on the social media pages, especially given these posts are from 2021 and 2020, and that 2020 witnessed protests and movements raise their voice against the police institution's practices as never before. This silence speaks volumes about the political nature of these communications.

Framing is about including some information and excluding other information in a depiction of an organization or a process. These police foundations have decided to include information about policing that portrays police in a positive light or about police connections to community, which portrays police as benevolent. However, silences in communication are important to note. The silences regarding the politics and economics of policing and controversies police have been involved in from corruption to racism are significant. Future research must dig deeper into these communications to quantify and compare the entire corpus of these Twitter communications and to assess their latent content. Nonetheless, we have shown that Twitter is a site for police foundation framing of the greedy police institution and this framing has a tendency. The tendency is either to focus on police as in need of support and in need of positive valuation or to focus on community, depicting police as a part of the community at a time when many communities are calling for police defunding. This also reflects findings in police communications literature (Wood 2020; Bullock 2018a; Sillince and Brown 2009), which suggests this attention to community in police communications (in this case, police foundation communications) is strategically constructed to achieve an effect. The effect of painting police, their activities, and their financial operations, in a positive light and as beneficial to community, we contend, is to launder the reputation of the greedy police institution.

Discussion

In this chapter, we have shown police foundation communications are oriented towards drawing people into the police foundation and the police mission consistent with a greedy institution. To achieve this, the communications are curated toward framing police foundations and police activity itself as oriented toward the community. The community is the master signifier (Jagodzinski 1998) in these communications. The way the communications are arranged visually points to the community as the focus of police foundation activities. However, as we have shown earlier and as we show in the next chapter, police foundation activities are not simply, solely, or even largely concerned with the community, as only a fraction of the funds that police foundations funnel into the shell corporation from the private sector end up in community hands. Much funding ends up in police department coffers. Using community as the master signifier in these foundation communications enables the police foundation to appear mainly philanthropic instead of existing to launder the reputation of the police and launder funds mostly from the corporate sphere. It is a form of framing that allows the police foundation to appear to have community needs on the minds of police foundation board members. When police occupy the frame, these communications position police variously as heroes or victims. Either way, police are at the centre of these communications and endeavours just as they are at the centre of various funding networks we have identified and examined in this book. The communications also further reveal the sheer number of militarized and surveillance-related police projects these foundations have fuelled. Every story of tactical gear or a new video surveillance system or video game bus undermines the rhetoric that these police foundations exist for community development.

Police foundation framing disproportionately emphasizes the community compared to the reality of how police foundations distribute the private monies they acquire and control. Given we know police and police foundation communications are strategic, why would police foundations choose to focus so much on community in these communications when it is clear from other records that they are much greedier? Communications in the greedy institution must persuade members of the institution to continue with their role. The institution and its members may begin to believe the strategic and dominant frames communicated even if they are, in some ways, outlandish. Recall most literature using the greedy institution framework focuses on the military. Military framing is focused on the good military interventions do. It must be effective framing to convince military members and their families to continue signing up. We have argued along with Cox (2016) that greedy institutions also use outward communication to attract other parties to align themselves with the greedy institutions. Framing is a way of enrolling others into the police project and mission. We assert framing is a core aspect of the greedy institution because framing allows audiences to understand what that institution is about (Cox 2016). These police foundations' press releases, newsletters, images, and Twitter communications do that. Police foundations websites and social media display these tendencies of the greedy institution too. It is almost as if police organizers have offloaded their work of being a greedy institution to the police foundation. The foundation can undertake the networking, fundraising and communications necessary to attract mostly corporate funds for police and sell the police worldview to potential funders and members. While the greedy police institution is not as large as the military or the family, it functions similarly. This framing makes people feel good about what they are doing as it aligns their interests with the mission of this greedy institution and enrols more loyal members. For these reasons we argue framing is a crucial part of what greedy institutions do (also see Cox 2016).

The focus on community in their communications is a perfect attractor of social and economic capital for the police foundation. The master signifier of community (Jagodzinski 1998) attracts people to become loyal and conform to the police mission. It attracts corporate players to sit on the board of the foundation. It attracts corporations to become donors and paid detail funders as well. It might attract communities themselves, in some cases, who may have concerns about safety and well-being, and are not sure whom to turn other than police. Who would balk at such perfect images of community, diversity, heroism, and safety? However, as we show in the next chapter, these dark money exchanges are full of corrupting tendencies, and the policies that allow this dark money to flow are full of holes.

Chapter 7

Controversies and Holes in Private Police Funding Policy

Introduction

Prior chapters have hinted at holes in private funding policies and related controversies concerning corruption and rule of law violations to which they can lead. Greedy institutions find holes in policy and dig deeper and wider for riches they desperately desire rather than being satisfied with already plentiful resources and personnel they need. Small holes have become a vast mine of donations, sponsorships, foundations, and paid detail from which institutional gold – more and more monies and loyal members – is greedily extracted. In Chapter Two, by analyzing police department policies acquired through FOI requests we assessed how these gratuities, gifts, donations, sponsorships, and foundations were supposed to be governed in eight police departments. While there were often department rules regarding individual officers seeking funding from private and external sources, we showed there were fewer about the department itself, including little about foundations and sponsorship, even where these forms and networks were in place. There was a lack of standardization and continuity across departments too. In Chapter Five, we discussed models of paid detail and policies across North America and a similar lack of standardization. Chapters Two and Five also showed the stunning, unprecedented growth in the US of police specific foundations and corporate paid detail brokers respectively. Here we discuss policy holes and possible responses. In doing so, we focus on sponsorships, foundations, and paid detail consistent with the emphasis of earlier chapters, including controversies, and the need for reform across jurisdictions. We contend these holes demand greater attention, regulation, and enforcement to ensure adherence to the rule of law and to avoid corruption and ensure not merely community input, but community control. Without this, we suggest these private funding forms further entrench or pave the way for new private influence of the public police institution and ripe conditions for corruption, rule of law violations, and further militarization. However, anti-corruption agencies and entities, outside the US Department of Justice and US Federal Bureau of Investigations (FBI), have not shown much official interest in police

DOI: 10.4324/9781003167914-8

sponsorship or donations or even paid detail policing. We further document some efforts at reform, following controversy, have stalled, or failed, implying that reform will be difficult and due to the power of existing funding networks and their framing apparatus, perhaps impossible.

We first return to several controversies and reforms. The aim is to show corruption and rule of law violations are not hypothetical and farfetched, but instead have led to documented complaints including criminal cases that were ironically – in the self-referential fashion that perhaps only a greedy institution could shamelessly accomplish – investigated by the FBI (i.e., the police institution). We then discuss how there are no formal limits on private funding, either in absolute terms or relative to public funding levels, which is the largest hole in policy and fulfilment of the greedy institution's dream. Finally, we explore policy implications of the rise and spread of commercial paid detail brokers and police foundations, something we have seen almost no recognition of much less policy options discussed. One major policy response is to seal off the expanding private funding mine fully and forever.

Controversies and Policy Holes

Foundation Controversies in Los Angeles, Baltimore, and Vancouver

In 2007, the LAPD became interested in new software designed with CIA funds by a company called Palantir and used its foundation to arrange its purchase (Winston and Graham 2014). The LAP Foundation approached giant retail corporation Target to help fund the purchase with $200,000 USD. This allowed the LAPD to avoid the public scrutiny that came with its competitive procurement process, using a "quicker, quieter way to get the software" instead (Winston and Graham 2014). This circumvented public accountability for the purchase of technology potentially not approved by City Council and the Police Commission. Palantir then donated $10,000 USD to the LAPD Foundation in 2008 for the "Above and Beyond" police gala and has done similarly in other US jurisdictions.

Winston and Graham (2014) note the LAP Foundation donated a horse to the LAPD purchased for $6,000 from the LAPD chief's daughter. When the *Los Angeles Times* showed the Chief and police commissioner had approved the foundation's horse purchase, they incredulously related they had not seen the conflict implications (Parker 2014). Winston and Graham (2014) also reported on two massive telecommunications corporations – Motorola[1] and Raytheon – that donated to the LAP Foundation while competing for a $600 million LAPD contract to provide emergency communications. Motorola was awarded the contract and donated more than $164,000 USD to the Foundation via its own foundation, the Motorola Solutions Foundation. In 2010, Motorola appointed ex-LAPD Chief of the LAPD, William Bratton, to its board with an annual salary of $240,000 USD (US Securities and Exchange Commission 2010). For their part, Raytheon donated $311,000 USD to the LAP Foundation to upgrade the LAPD's radio system while competing for the large contract. The LAPD denied a conflict of interest, asserting consistent with foundation framing and expectation of loyalty to the police institution, that donations were fuelled by "'an insatiable appetite to help'… not self-interest" (Winston and Graham 2014).

In the early 2000s in Baltimore, another police foundation controversy commenced when former police commissioner Edward Norris was convicted of misusing private donations held in the Department's charity account. The funds had been donated to the police for disadvantaged groups (Donovan 2016a). The Baltimore Police Foundation, which Norris had initiated in 2000, was deeply affected by this and was dissolved shortly thereafter. As with other police foundations described in earlier chapters, it had operated as a non-profit extension of the Baltimore Police. After the controversy centred on Norris, the legitimacy of the non-profit organization dissolved too (Donovan 2016a).

After his arrival, Norris quickly became the Baltimore Police Commissioner (Kilborn 2003). In August 2002, *The Baltimore Sun* began reporting on Norris's use of the charity account for personal expenditures (Gibson and Wilber 2004; Wilber 2003). An independent audit identified $7,663 US in misspent funds. Norris then left the Baltimore Police for the Maryland State Police (Wilber 2003). Federal investigators later found Norris had misused roughly $30,000 USD in charitable donations on personal gifts, private travel and accommodations, visits with women, and similar things (Rich 2004; Kilborn 2003). Norris was sentenced to six months in prison (Rich 2004).

This was only the first donation-related controversy in the City of Baltimore. Despite closing the Baltimore Police Foundation, private donations continued to flow through two Baltimore Community Foundation accounts created to channel funds to the police department: the "Baltimore Police Endowment Fund" and the "Baltimore Police Special Grants Fund" (Fenton and Donovan 2016). Between 2011 and 2013, Baltimore Police, through the Baltimore Community Foundation, had received roughly $900,000 USD in donations. In 2011, for example, Under Armour donated $300,000 USD for computers, Tasers, and other items (Fenton and Donovan 2016).

Billionaires John and Laura Arnold made a more controversial donation in 2015. In true domestic shell corporation fashion, the donation to the Baltimore Police Special Grants Fund was not publicly advertised by the Baltimore Community Foundation (Fenton and Donovan 2016). In November 2015, the Arnolds donated $120,000 USD to this Foundation's police fund for aerial surveillance for the Baltimore Police Department. John Arnold, after learning about aerial surveillance technologies, contacted Ross McNutt, owner of Persistent Surveillance Systems, to develop it further (Dart 2016). McNutt, who had created the surveillance program while in the US

Air Force for use in Iraq, had been seeking to sell his surveillance program to US police departments (Reel 2016). This program had been previously used in 2012 secretly for nine days by the Los Angeles Sheriff's Department in Compton, a predominantly African American and Hispanic Los Angeles suburb, which decided not to proceed due to image quality (Reel 2016). The Arnolds asserted they would fund this aerial surveillance technology if McNutt found a police department with which to partner (Donovan 2016a, 2016b). McNutt decided on the Baltimore Police Department (Reel 2016).

McNutt's surveillance camera-equipped Cessna airplane flying for five to six hours a day collected over one million aerial images of Baltimore (Dart 2016). McNutt and his staff then used the images to aid many Baltimore police investigations for months (Reel 2016). The Arnolds then contacted the Baltimore Community Foundation to donate another $240,000 USD to review the program's crime reduction effectiveness. This Foundation declined, but the National Police Foundation took up this offer to review it (Donovan 2016a). However, when a business periodical (Reel 2016) reported on the aerial surveillance program in August 2016, the City Council and Baltimore's citizens became aware of the program. It had been operating without a public bidding process, City approval, or even a Baltimore Police Department press release (Reel 2016). When these privately funded, extensive and invasive surveillance activities on behalf of the Baltimore Police Department were reported on, controversy arose over in addition to its secrecy, its possible effects on Baltimore's racialized communities and on citizen privacy (Rector and Broadwater 2016; Dart 2016; Broadwater and Donovan 2016). In their privately funded review, the Police Foundation (2017) concluded: "Unfortunately, it was not possible for the Police Foundation to quantify the value of the persistent surveillance used in the BCSP to improve violent crime clearance rates or reduce investigative time." The empirical evidence to support its use to reduce crime is missing, consistent with most other private funding endeavours we discussed earlier. Also consistent with the previously discussed analysis of foundation framing, was the Police Department and Community Foundation's use of a glossed over and completely obfuscating label for this secret mass surveillance program. It was simply called the "Baltimore Community Support Program."

As noted in a previous chapter, in early 2021 the Vancouver Police Foundation announced receipt of an "Amazing $1 Million Gift to Support Public Safety" (VPF 2021a) from a major real estate developer in Vancouver, the "Wall Financial" corporation. These foundation funds were earmarked for Vancouver Police (VPD) in the Downtown Eastside. Consistent with the foregoing analysis, regarding this "amazing" donation, the Vancouver Police Foundation representative related to media:

> 'I'd say that the VPD and its officers are essential partners in our community and the police foundation's mandate is to help support them

> and their efforts to build bridges with the community and to support those who are most vulnerable and at risk' (MacMahon and Wong 2021).

In earlier decades called "skid row" (Huey 2007), the Downtown Eastside has a long complex history of community activism (Blomley 2004). The notorious area of Vancouver, Sylvestre et al. (2019, 5) explain in their recent extensive study, is already "highly policed" and is "a concentration of marginalized and criminalized individuals, many of them Indigenous, struggling with addiction, mental illness, poverty and homelessness." We contend this donation is partially the gloss foundations are fond of, and here it is inseparable from gentrification efforts. In Vancouver's obscenely over-priced real estate market, "the most unaffordable in Canada" (Sylvestre et al. 2019, 5), this area is now ground zero for intensive gentrification.

This donation became controversial, having been instantly criticized by the Pivot Legal Society that focuses on poverty issues in the area and a Vancouver city councillor, among others (MacMahon and Wong 2021), although to no avail. Peculiarly absent from criticisms, media coverage, and police foundation framing of this "amazing" donation, both locally and in a major national newspaper, the *Globe and Mail*, is that the Wall Financial corporation is perhaps best known for its condominium real estate development in Vancouver. It is especially renowned for the immense "Wall Centre" condominium built in 2001, which towers over this city's downtown. More interesting is the absence of mention of two multi-million-dollar for-profit developments built by this Vancouver Police Foundation donor, one in the heart of and the other immediately adjacent to Vancouver's Downtown Eastside. One is the massive 15 story, 283-unit condominium development called Strathcona Village at 983 East Hastings in the Strathcona neighbourhood in East Vancouver built in 2018 (Vancouver Newcondos 2021). The other is Wall Financial's 83-unit condominium development under construction a few blocks away at 288 East Hastings. It is possible even more condominium developments are planned for the near future.

Gallaher (2016, 2) and other urban scholars (see Kern 2010) argue condominium development is intimately linked to gentrification and in her study of condominium conversion in Washington, DC she notes "because condos are often built for, and marketed to, well-paid professionals, they are seen as a harbinger of displacement to come." Although privately governed, condominium developments often rely on public police to confront those whom their boards or property managers deem to be nuisances and where private security is lacking or if ill-equipped (Lippert 2019). It is apt to suggest building large condominiums in this area is linked to profit-seeking of corporate developers that earmark private funds for police intervention there. We contend these properties' value and attractiveness to buyers would increase significantly if it could be communicated to potential residents or investors that this area was now or would soon become safer through more intensive policing by Vancouver Police.

A recent article in a local newspaper, aptly titled "Developers hope to Reclaim Vancouver's Downtown Eastside," about real estate market conditions in this area, shows why a condominium developer like Wall Financial might want to fund police efforts that may well help sustain property values and generate profit from better condominium unit sales:

> Real estate agents working the DTES zone say that conditions, already bad, have become remarkably worse since COVID-19 began. The spread of graffiti, garbage, discarded needles and the homeless "is bleeding" from Main and Hastings... east to Strathcona – where a large and apparently permanent tent encampment has been set up – and north to the Railtown area on the waterfront... Saul and partner Robert Tham [of a commercial real estate firm] say the DTES is attracting both large real estate developers and altruistic buyers, all aiming to fix Vancouver's most broken neighbourhood, despite getting little help from the City of Vancouver. "It is the worse down here now than it has ever been," Tham said, noting that, since COVID began, he often has to bribe itinerants to leave doorsteps when trying to show a listing. Police, he said, apparently turn a blind eye to drug deals and property crime that would not be tolerated anywhere else (O'Brien 2020).

Armed with a new $1 million influx perhaps Vancouver Police will no longer turn a blind eye to minor transgressions and the funding will allow for arrests, charges and "red zone" assignment and enforcement instead. We contend such policing would likely include "red zone" policing that excludes marginalized people from key public spaces (Sylvestre et al. 2019). In extensive research on "red zones," these spaces are imposed by police or the courts through various means on marginalized people in Canada, and undoubtedly also in the US. In relation to Vancouver's Downtown Eastside it was discovered criminal prosecutors used a "boilerplate Downtown Eastside area restriction" (Sylvestre et al. 2019, 154), one which Vancouver Police enforce. These "red zone" designations are found to have devastating mental, financial, and other effects on vulnerable people residing in or reliant on the Downtown Eastside, preventing them from accessing friends, informal, and formal resources that help them survive a harsh urban existence. Sylvestre et al. (2019, 170–171) write:

> The effects of red zoning are particularly aggravated for residents of highly stigmatized neighbourhoods, such as Vancouver's Downtown Eastside. Exclusion from such places not only cuts off access to the vital

resources, such as safe injection sites and low-cost housing, but also drugs that are concentrated there.

The fact some funds are to be used for community initiatives in the area does not preclude this possibility since police could re-direct any public funding for "hard" policing instead. Is it a stretch to think that Vancouver Police might target drug deals and property crime to a greater extent in this long-standing, extremely low income (often called Canada's "poorest postal code") area to aid gentrification and related displacement of unsheltered and Indigenous residents of this historical area, people who tend to have few other viable places in which to reside and frequent in ways that ensure their mental and financial survival? Also, the "amazing" thing about this donation may well be less its high value and more how comfortable Vancouver Police are receiving it. The press release comes with a photograph of a Vancouver Police administrator publicly posing with the head of this real estate development corporation and director of the Vancouver Police Foundation atop the exclusive "Wall Centre" condominium. Indeed, unlike some foundation framing discussed in the previous chapter, this instance allows visualization of the unabashed tight convergence of three key nodal types – police – foundation – private corporation – in this funding network, suggesting they are making policing decisions about the Downtown Eastside community far removed and distant from its streets and residents. What is perhaps most "amazing" is that Vancouver Police, already fourth among police departments on the list of largest public funding proportions of municipal budgets received in Canada, as noted earlier, through their policies are permitted to shamelessly enter such arrangements.

Sponsorship Controversy in Hamilton

In Chapter Four, we discussed the donations from Enbridge to Hamilton Police Service (HPS). Concerned citizens in Hamilton had discovered that Enbridge, a massive oil and gas corporation, had transferred private funding to Hamilton Police. The department received $44,410 from Enbridge and then purchased all-terrain vehicles as well as technology for navigation (Dreschel 2015). Police suggested this equipment was to aid off-road searches, especially for "wandering Alzheimer's patients" (Hamilton Spectator 2013). An environmental group called Hamilton 350 Committee then filed a formal complaint arguing the equipment will be used to patrol Enbridge property. The complaint letter, quoted in local media, and first sent to the police board that then referred it to the Office of the Independent Police Review Director (OIPRD) reads: "If there were a standoff between, on the one side, protesters and/or native people, and, on the other side, Enbridge Inc., would officers of the HPS be able to be truly neutral and impartial?" The complaint focused on violation of the rule of law. The Department was given 60 days to respond to complaints of preferential policing and violations of the right to equal treatment under the law consistent with Canada's Charter of Rights and Freedoms (Hamilton Spectator 2020). Ultimately, the OIPRD did not order the police department to return this donation or future donations. This example shows the failure of an existing and independent police oversight body in this jurisdiction to confront the problem and failure of oversight provided by Hamilton's police board. The Enbridge corporation eventually claimed to stop providing funding to police departments (Dreschel 2015), but not because it was ordered to do so or because departments refused to accept the monies. As noted in a previous chapter, remarkably similar arrangements but involving much greater flows of capital have been recently documented in Minnesota involving this same corporation and various police departments (Beaumont 2021). More is likely in the future.

Paid Detail Controversy in Toronto

In Toronto from the 2000s onwards, there has been controversy over the appropriate use of Toronto Police Service (TPS) resources for traffic matters, including construction on or near roadways and film production on streets. A question raised was why a much less costly civilian flagger or flag person – or even digital signage – could not fill the same role as a paid detail officer on assignment. The same controversy has raged in Boston and Seattle among other cities. Regarding Boston, for example, "the whole debate has been around construction flagging and whether you have to use a policeman or woman or you can use... a flagger" (Boston Funder 2).

By 2009, the annual amount of paid detail funding in Toronto was more than $24 million CDN. The rapid increase in the pay rate and number of hours worked between 2004 and 2007 was deemed a financial concern. Paid detail officers were required at all traffic obstructions for a minimum of three hours – sites that could deploy a flag person at one-third the cost (Taylor 2011). But dependence on paid detail for construction was deemed inefficient:

> [T]he paid detail officer would... sit in the squad car and keep warm ... it was really quite silly... police officers weren't guarding anything other than the holes [in the street] that they were standing over. Then that's an erosion of our people's view of what police officers do. If all they see is [sic] police officers in uniform standing on corners looking down holes drinking Tim Horton's coffee and eating donuts, it's not a good public message... It erodes the public confidence (Councillor 2).

Paid detail was also thought to undermine police legitimacy. Following a report by Toronto's Auditor General (2010), a city councillor explained policy changes and that paid detail had

> required for work on utility hole covers... on construction sites within certain metres of an intersection, and crane over swings over the street. All of these things seemed to require some sort of paid detail officer and it turns out we didn't need them... so we've stripped those requirements and saved hopefully not only the city a lot of money on contracts, but the private sector as well (Councillor 3).

Frequent funder nodes in this funding network had been other City departments, resulting in transfer of $7.8 million from these departments for TPS paid detail in 2009 alone. TPS administrators and the Chief responded to the Toronto Police Service Board (TPSB) and media by arguing paid detail's presence on the street prevented crime. A TPSB member explained that "the position that the chief has taken is that... it provides for increased police visibility in the community" (Police Board 1). Several revisions to Toronto's paid detail program were then suggested. First, the TPS Board Chair recommended much less costly auxiliary volunteers be used instead of TPS officers, an idea we return to in the next chapter, the conclusion. But this recommendation was deleted from the final version of the report to the Chief as were recommendations to fund Traffic Control Officers who would receive much less funding compared to paid detail officers. The Toronto Film Board recommended eliminating the requirement to fund paid detail officers for relevant activities, which was partially implemented after 2009. This resulted in decreased paid detail funding after 2009 and elimination of requirement to use paid detail services by many municipal units. Despite reforms, the controversy over paid detail continues to be "Toronto's perennial scandal," with the amount reaching $24 million CDN in 2014 (Kupferman 2014). In 2019 there was yet another recommendation made in a City of Toronto regarding street festivals to "overhaul paid duty" (Toronto 2019) but with little indication this reform happened. Instead, the volume of capital exchanged through paid detail arrangements in Toronto since it was first problematized remains extremely high.

Paid Detail Controversies in New Orleans, Seattle, and Jersey City

Perhaps most infamously exposed by the Knapp Commission's report on the NYPD in the 1970s (New York 1972), there are well-documented instances of rampant corruption in police departments. It remains unclear if similar strong-arming of potential paid detail funders is rampant in current dark funding networks. Extortion of potential funders of paid detail would include demands to hide that it is happening. In some instances, involving legal and illegal coercion to provide paid detail funding, it becomes difficult to distinguish between such arrangements and the "protection" offered by NYPD officers leading up to the investigations decades ago. Below we take up several serious cases stemming from paid detail arrangements that gained the attention of the Department of Justice or the FBI in New Orleans, Seattle, and Jersey City.

The Department of Justice investigated the New Orleans Police Department (NOPD) regarding an array of criminal activities and issued a major public report in 2011:

> There are few aspects of NOPD more broadly troubling than its Paid Detail system.
>
> NOPD's Detail system, as currently structured: 1) drastically undermines the quality of NOPD policing; 2) facilitates abuse and corruption by NOPD officers; 3) contributes to compromising officer fatigue; 4) contributes to inequitable policing by NOPD (Department of Justice 2011, xv).

The report goes on to state "few if any large police departments have a system of Details as entrenched and unregulated as in NOPD" and "[i]t is widely acknowledged that NOPD's Detail system is corrupting; as stated by one close observer of the Department, the paid Detail system may be the 'aorta of corruption' within NOPD" and that the "Detail system was a significant contributing factor to both the perception and reality of NOPD as a dysfunctional organization" (FBI Department of Justice, xvi) (see also O'Hara and Sainato 2015). New Orleans signed an agreement with the federal government, a federal consent decree, to among other things create a new centralized paid detail office (or unit) similar to those found in New York and Toronto and it now operates out of the City of New Orleans (see OPSE 2021).

In Seattle in 2017 media reported:

> The FBI is investigating allegations that Seattle police officers, with the help of the Seattle police union, may have engaged in intimidation and price-fixing while working lucrative off-duty jobs directing traffic at parking garages and construction sites (Miletich and Carter 2017).

The intimidation is alleged to have involved suggestions that regular calls for service would not be responded to if the company refused to be a paid detail funder. Unlike Canadian and other large US police departments including later in the NOPD above, the Seattle Police Department (SPD) was not administering and authorizing paid detail funding. Leading up to the FBI-led investigation of SPD paid detail (Seattle Times 2017), two companies, both of which were external to SPD, had been coordinating most paid detail assignments. Seattle's Finest was created in 2002 by a now-retired police officer (Carter and Miletich 2017), while the second corporation, Seattle Security, was an extension of Seattle's police union. As a result, former officers and union leaders oversaw SPD's paid detail prior to the 2017 investigation (Carter and Miletich 2017). The focus of the investigation included claims of police strong-arm tactics. This intensified when details of a conversation between a SPD officer and commercial paid detail broker were disclosed to the FBI. During this conversation, the SPD officer described how if officers wanted a funding increase from parking garage companies, they would threaten to ensure no officers would be assigned there until this raise transpired (Lewis 2017). Details also included the SPD officer outlining how certain traffic assignments were called "cake jobs" because officers would typically be required for 30 minutes, while being funded for four hours. These were even easier than most "easy money" paid detail assignments. The officer explained these jobs were protected and would proceed without interference because they knew employers would "end up with broken kneecaps" (Miletich and Carter 2017). One Seattle officer allegedly boasted "we would really break some bones if those (jobs) were messed with" (Lewis 2017a). In Seattle, paid detail policing had become associated with full blown corruption. The FBI investigation was due to complaints from funders to the police Chief about price-fixing and over-charging and to a police department audit (Lewis 2017b).

The investigation uncovered several issues (Lewis 2017a), including Seattle-based companies being pressured to fund paid detail officers or face unspecified repercussions; police using strong-arm tactics to secure off-duty work contracts; overcharging; requiring "management fees" paid to senior police officers to ensure staffing; having no system to adequately track and oversee officers' off-duty hours; pressuring building and construction site managers to fund police to ensure a police response in case of emergency. Allegations of corruption were not new. A report by journalists almost two decades earlier discussed such practices and earlier FBI interest: "FBI agents are believed to be asking officers whether they were paid for work they never performed at Staples office supply stores" (Lewis 2017a).

One officer admitted to overcharging by Seattle's Finest, a commercial paid detail broker and "squeezing" building owners since "no one in town has the power to stop any of it" (Lewis 2017a). According to this officer, other officers earned $1,200 to $1,500 USD a month without working a single paid detail shift, an arrangement remarkably like the regular payouts to officers uncovered by the Knapp Commission in the NYPD. Such suggestions of "squeezing" is a kind of framing that should not be overlooked as vital to private funding of police and expansion of related networks. It takes place with an exceedingly small audience but the exchanges that result comprise perhaps even darker networks involving police and funders than those discussed in earlier chapters. Since this is purposely kept off the record, it is difficult to locate first-hand examples of this framing except in criminal court documents.

> Seattle's Mayor issued an Order in September 2017, stating Seattle's Police Department does not directly regulate any secondary employers

> and has insufficient access to secondary employment schedules of off-duty officers, creating significant potential for mismanagement, conflicts of interest, inequities between officers… and… lack [of] transparency.

By 2018 the broker corporation that had been linked to the Seattle police union declared it would be transferring paid detail assignments to "Seattle's Finest." The Mayor ordered city administration to create a paid detail unit like in NOPD:

> We will not let the private interests of a few police officers tarnish our entire police department […] It is clear that we need total overhaul of how this city handles the practice of police officers taking secondary jobs […] Bringing the management of SPD secondary employment in-house is both in line with national best practices and consistent with recommendations from City Auditor, the Director of the Office of Police Accountability, and the federal monitor (Jaywork 2017).

As such, the Mayor called for a task force to restructure how the police department oversees paid detail. In Seattle the police administrators and City failed to make the changes they promised to make, leaving paid detail arrangements largely the same. Despite FBI investigations and announcements of reform by the City, by 2021 the City of Seattle and the Seattle Police Department had failed to reform the paid detail arrangements despite these deeply troubling happenings and exceedingly embarrassing criminal investigations (Gilbert 2021).

A similar FBI-led investigation into Jersey City Police Department's (JCPD) paid detail program commenced in 2017. Prior to the investigation, JCPD paid detail operated through a voucher system to keep track of hours and paid detail assignments. Under this system, the officer, the organization hiring the officer, and the job coordinator were each required to submit a voucher to the City for approval of funding (McDonald 2017b; Mota 2017). The most commonly-identified issues relate to conspiracy to commit fraud and to "accept corrupt payments" (McDonald 2017b). Several officers were identified. The previous assignment coordinator (see McDonald 2017a) for one precinct reportedly started his scheme in 2009 involved telling private companies and individuals to contact him rather than the City to arrange paid detail funding. As such, he became the broker. He then authorized other officers in the scheme. Sometimes officers received full funding for assignments. Other times he offered discounts to funders for future events. He collected over $230,000 from funders. The Assistant Job Coordinator from 2008 to 2016 of another district was involved too. One reporter explained he "assigned police officers … [and] provided fraudulent off-duty employment vouchers to another police officer" (McDonald 2017b). The officer reportedly accepted money from the City for assignments for which he was not present

(Department of Justice, US Attorney's Office 2018). He admitted submitting time sheets representing certain shifts even though he was not present and was paid $31,713 USD. Between 2010 and 2014, one funder had hired officers to provide security at some housing sites. The former Chief pleaded guilty to embezzling, stealing, obtaining by fraud, misapplying, and without authority converting money belonging to the JCHA. He is facing a maximum penalty of 10 years (others facing up to five years) in prison and a $250,000 fine. Three other officers participated in a bribery scheme through which they had performed but still tallied on his hours sheet. He aided another officer to do similar acts. The officer pleaded guilty to a bribery conspiracy related to the off-duty jobs program and admitted to one count of conspiracy to commit fraud and accept corrupt payments. The former Jersey City Chief also admitted to defrauding the Jersey City Housing Authority (JCHA) by obtaining compensation for off-duty work he did not perform and all face imprisonment and a 250,000 USD fine (McDonald 2018c).

The Mayor then announced the City was dismantling the paid detail program (McDonald 2018b):

> We thought this program was corrupt in so many different facets that the only outcome that was acceptable to us and, we think, responsible for the Jersey City taxpayers, residents and for the future of the Jersey City Police Department is to end the program in its entirety (McDonald 2018b).

The Mayor's tweet about all this immediately followed sentencing of officers charged in the FBI investigation. Apparently 10 minutes after the Mayor's tweet, over 40 "angry cops" called City officials to express concern, implying that reform of these arrangements would be difficult. A retired NYPD Deputy Chief of Police commented on the situation suggesting JCPD should "mimic how these jobs are handled in New York City" (McDonald 2017c). In 2017, 800 JCPD officers had received $16 million USD in paid detail funding, exceeding the volume of economic capital exchanged via paid detail networks in larger police departments. The Mayor stated "When you have $16 million... per year running through this program... It's clearly hard to keep people honest" (News12 Staff 2018).

The FBI revealed a criminal scheme that involved multiple ranks within the department. Federal prosecutors also revealed that leading up to his appointment, the JCPD Chief accepted $31,700 from a federally funded public housing association for paid detail for which he was not present (McDonald 2018a). After arrests, suspensions, and indictments, 11 JCPD officers from multiple ranks admitted involvement in the criminal scheme (McDonald 2019). Among these officers, four have already been sentenced: two received probation and house arrest, while the other two received 18-month federal prison sentences (Villanova 2018).

Reflecting on these three cases that resulted in major controversy, one is struck by the large size of the departments where this rampant corruption was discovered or investigated and, sometimes, criminally prosecuted. Two are among the largest urban US police departments and even Jersey City, the smallest of the three locations, serves more than a quarter of a million people. These are not miscues involving "rotten apples" at the bottom of the institutional ladder in small or obscure police departments with limited scope or consequences. They are decidedly more significant and troubling. They have also involved administrators and in one case, the Chief of Police. So it is with the greedy police institution; its greedy focus knows no barriers by rank upward or outward. Despite total banning of the paid detail system in 2018 in Jersey City, it has since started up again (Daurio 2020). One major change has been to prohibit officers from arranging assignments for themselves or other officers.

Policy Reforms

Illumination of Funders and Dark Funding Arrangements

The controversies discussed in this, and earlier chapters, arose only when entities outside the police institution cast light on these dark networks. This illumination happened not as a matter of course or because of adequate governmental or departmental oversight. Instead, it was typically due to media outlets and individual journalists becoming aware and then temporarily devoting resources to uncovering more dark money or savvy social movement activists and other citizens more concerned about the environment or anti-corporatization than police improprieties and greed encountering the effects of this funding, and then asking uncomfortable questions. Sometimes this type of pressure then forced federal authorities and the FBI to act to try to re-establish legitimacy. So how can one ensure these dark networks become known and undergo public scrutiny? Earlier we likened the private funding of police departments to a dark mine full of riches brought to the surface by masked miners and for whom we are mostly unaware what they received in return for loyally digging up riches for the police institution. We first consider unmasking the miners and obtaining a sense of what they did or might have received in exchange. Revealing funders' full identities would seem a necessary but not sufficient step to prevent corruption and rule of law violations but is no guarantee.

Only a handful of departments, like Vancouver's, had sponsorship and foundation policies. One exception is sponsors who have arranged to use police-owned (i.e., publicly owned) spaces to advertise, where there is a clear *quid pro quo*. The details of sponsorships were not required to be made public. A police board or administration and sometimes municipal or city governments may have been aware, although that was often unclear too, but the public was not. Even for sponsorships to which we became aware through controversies, the funding levels, duration, and precisely what was received in exchange from police was rarely specified. Such arrangements led to glimpses of sponsor identities. Most remained hidden in the dark mine.

Foundations are shell corporations designed to shield funder identities as well as the details of the exchanges between the foundation and the funder, and the foundation and the police department. They hide the identity and number of funders. We can only glimpse these networks through occasional mention in media or when the framing by police or the donor is advantageously revealed as marketing and promotion. For example, in Vancouver it was deemed an advantage to place a visual of a police administrator, a police foundation executive and a corporate developer representative high atop a condominium tower and release the fact of the large donation to media outlets. This announced arrangement permitted us to conduct further research into possible gentrification as above. However, these glimpses are happenstance and rare. Foundations are subject to the public reporting requirements of tax laws for charities and non-profits. These reporting requirements are not detailed and instead involve broad categories of amounts only. Even though many foundations have as either their major or only recipient of funding a *public* police department, they are still not required to reveal, other than providing an annual total, the details of funds transferred to the department including for what they were used. The reporting requirements of tax laws shed little light on dark money and networks.

Helping to keep the reality of police foundations and other private funding in the dark are the sophisticated and extensive communications strategies and practices outlined in detail mostly in Chapter Six, including the efforts of police unions. Any effort to reform or halt private police funding discussed in this book must also seek to analyze and counter those relentless communications. In large part, this has been happening through public protests and sustained efforts of groups like Black Lives Matter as well as others, albeit ones we humbly suggest might benefit from more research and understanding of the private funding that may soon be used to counter any effects of de-funding initiatives and announcements.

We also found police foundations are not subject to FOI laws in any jurisdiction from which we required information directly from police departments (Luscombe et al. 2017a). If their main or only recipient of funds is a public police department it is essential that they be made subject to such legislation to fill this gaping hole. The shell should be removed to lay bare to anyone interested in private funding the networks and nodal identities scurrying around underneath. If identities of all donors to these foundations were required to be posted on receiving police departments' websites in public view, it would be equivalent to shifting the entrance/exit to this dark funding mine to the city square or commons in full view of whomever wishes to view the miners exiting and inspect the riches they are transporting to the police.

As noted in Chapter Two, framing of paid detail arrangements is pithy. Consistent with this, no police department website revealed funders or officers' identities. Paid detail funding, as well as donations and sponsorships, was accessible only through FOI requests. Yet this was, to say the least, not a straightforward "ask and you shall receive" arrangement either. We have detailed multiple problems with obtaining data via FOI requests of police departments elsewhere (Luscombe et al. 2017a; Lippert et al. 2016) and one of us has addressed these aspects of FOI or equivalent regarding various public domains, including the police (Walby and Luscombe 2019). Even when we received disclosures from departments, and as will be evident in our tables and figures, it came in numerous formats, most using differing categories, with only some overlapping to allow comparison. Most often the disclosures required calculations or projections to find common figures to compare. Many were redacted such that the nodal funder's identity was removed; in other cases, names or other identifiers of officers were stripped from the disclosure; and in still other cases both funder and officers' names were removed. Some departments, such as St. Thomas (Ontario) Police, and Charlottetown (Prince Edward Island), for example, simply refused to provide requested information. Several other departments dubiously indicated revealing officers' identities would jeopardize officers' security. In the latter, they claimed police departments, revealing a massive hole in legislation relative to other provinces and states, were exempt from FOI altogether rather than fitting an exemption. One or two departments stood out as responding with timely, full disclosures of this information. Some police departments, somewhat incredulously, indicated they did not record paid detail, donation, and sponsorship information, meaning they may have had a paid detail arrangement but did not record it. Requiring all paid detail logs to be posted pro-actively for public viewing online could fill this hole. This would not necessarily prevent corruption or rule of law violations (knowing the officer's name sitting in this cruiser adjacent the construction site would not prevent him from looking the other way), but it would be a first step. Given the "easy money" nature of paid detail assignments, and that they are far less risky than regular duty and a range of other occupations such as farming and taxi or Uber driving, this is hardly unreasonable. It does not jeopardize officers' security for the public to know which paid detail funders were part of this funding network, and which officers received sometimes thousands of dollars for merely being present at sites or events. The public should know who funds their police department and what the police do after the fact.

Finally, gratuities are invisible private funding, as noted in Chapter Two. These are low value, but their pervasiveness may be vital for rule of law violations. Few departments required officers to refuse gratuities, instead leaving them to the "reasonable person" test and even for those departments that required reporting, we received no reports about the little gifts or donations that most people would deem to be "tips" received by officers while at work or otherwise. If anything, these were expected from the conforming and loyal public rather than something to regulate or prohibit. Requiring officers to refuse all such gratuities and minor gifts and donations could fill this hole. Policies and rules are in place for the latter, but there is almost no means to discern the extent and effects of gratuities, although as we noted there is some previous research on this aspect.

Random Assignments and Reducing Officer Choice

It is unclear why funders – especially if they wish to merely show loyalty to the police institution – would not want details of these arrangements known. For paid detail an alternative to unmasking the funders is to help reduce the choice of officers to provide a security presence for one funder rather than another. In Windsor, Ontario paid detail was problematized in the early 2000s. The Windsor Police Service was permitting its uniformed paid detail officers to stand inside downtown bars and receive cash from bar owners at shift's end. Other local businesspersons and media (e.g., Henderson 2000) raised concern that police were "turning a blind eye to alcohol and fire infractions" (Wolfson 2006), ensuring these acts or omissions would remain unknown. Moreover, officers could "own" assignments, a practice that continues in some US police departments, such as in Minneapolis and Detroit. As one long-time funder explained:

> A lot of police officers were getting too friendly with some of the people they were working with, especially some of the bars and some of those places that were utilizing a lot of off-duties (Windsor Funder 1).

In Windsor, this resulted in a commissioned report that recommended purchase of scheduling software that randomly assigned officers and arranged for officers' pay through the police department (McKaig 2006). This centralized assignment system made officers regularly assigned to the same funder unlikely, disabling claims about corruption (Wolfson 2006). Police officers could no longer "own" gigs.

Regarding selection or assignment to these positions we identified three models in Chapter Five, some had no system of selection; officers themselves coordinated it. For those with a system consisting of a "list" officers interested in assignments generally would enter their information and as each job came up they could take or leave it. For example, in one Western Canadian department, a police representative explained:

> When a special duty spot comes up members on this distribution list are sent they [have an] option to sign up or not… Assignments are based on a first come first served type of sign up (Western Canadian Police 4).

Only a handful of Canadian departments have implemented random assignment by drawing on an assembled list of eligible officers, but sometimes this is inadequate too. One police administrator explained that "if there are more people interested then there are spots available then we do a random draw to select the members" (Western Canadian Police 5). A police unit devoted to paid detail is needed to conduct this random assignment. One problem with random assignment, however, is that in any given period, sometimes less than half percent of officers "volunteer" for these "easy money" assignments. Officers can still in principle choose funded sites at which they want to be present rather than being randomly assigned. If there are many more than 25 per cent of the department on the list (i.e., a long list) this would be more conducive to preventing corruption. This is because officers, even if they wanted to, would rarely have an opportunity to select a return gig where they might be enticed to look the other way regarding transgressions due to knowing the site or event operator either through previous assignments or otherwise (repeat paid detail assignments are not the only way officers know business operators after all).

However, recall from Chapter Five there were several models of paid detail, whereby regular assignments are governed by individuals (once the funder is approved by the department), police unions, and newer commercial brokers we also want to discuss. For individuals and police unions there is little incentive to report daily logs of paid detail assignments to the public and it is more difficult to require in the absence of centralizing paid detail into a separate police department unit or office. Individuals are supposed to report their income from these assignments on their own income tax forms, but this tax information is not open to public scrutiny. Moreover, there is some evidence this is not always reported, perhaps most infamously by former officer Derek Chauvin when he was charged with multiple felonies related to failing to pay taxes on paid detail income of $95,000 over six years in Minneapolis (CBC 2020b). Given police unions' drive for more private funding and as a key node in funding networks we noted earlier, we contend this model would yield less likelihood of full public disclosure. Expecting random assignment to be conducted by individuals or unions is unlikely to be effective in this regard.

Selection was also affected by the need to avoid being labelled an employee, as with one commercial broker:

> We vet them and make sure they meet the criteria and then we put them into a pool. You could say a computerized shift system and then when we have an opening… Say we know next week we need an officer from noon until eight pm at this assignment then we put that out and broadcast to everybody that's in that pool and perhaps you know right now we have over 500 officers in that pool active… but we put that out there and say a 100 officers put in for it and then we would randomly pick the

> officer to work that so one of the IRS rules is that if you direct somebody's work by telling them where to be and what time to be there and you direct them to be there as a condition of their pay then that makes them an employee so if we went to officer smith and said you will be at this location at this time on this day to get this money then they would be an employee, but this way we say: 'Hey we need an officer at this time and this date and this place. Who wants to do it and we get 100 volunteers and we go, how about you?' And they don't have to go if they don't want to. If they don't then we pick somebody else so, yes in our case we do pick from a pool (Southern Broker 1).

This arrangement would not prevent officers from relatively regularly attending the same funded sites or events that might lead to corruption either.

Community Control and Effectiveness

In reforming policy and filling holes it should be noted there is little evidence much of the private funding arrangements benefits the community as police officials often claim. For all the discourse about "evidence-based" policing (Police Foundation 2021) that is part of police framing in recent years it is remarkable how little evidence, and few efforts to produce it through research, supports the private funding outcomes and initiatives discussed in this book. For example, the fact that the privately funded and foundation arranged surveillance program in Baltimore was reviewed at all is rare and even after this expensive review there was not credible evidence provided of its effectiveness in crime reduction and increasing efficiency. We earlier mentioned serious questions about whether Crime Stoppers and forfeiture reduce transgressions they claim to target on behalf of specific communities or the broader public and about whether such a narrow range they focus on merely detracts attention from more harmful transgressions by corporations, elites, or police themselves. If both are directed at the illicit drug industry, one wonders whether they are or even could be determined to be effective. Thus far the evidence is not there either. For foundations, sponsorship, and paid detail a similar picture emerges. To the extent most monies are used to further the police institution's political, economic, and social capital and little to address community priorities, they serve no community purpose and are not needed. If paid detail is effective in reducing transgressions, why are there so few examples of this kind of policing – despite its wide prevalence, extensive size and power of its networks, and high volumes of its exchanges – leading to arrests and charges? These are required to reduce the transgressions they claim to reduce beneath the community gloss we described earlier. Evidence of effectiveness would be a necessary but not sufficient factor that could support this private funding but without it, such funding should be halted.

A Central Canadian police administrator reiterated this idea about advantages of paid detail:

> [T]hey are still a public police officer... performing a paid detail function so there is some public safety issue. The expectation is that an officer would act as a public police officer... a visible police officer is actually deterring crime as I'm sure you know (Central Canadian Police Union 1).

Through this unproven claim, paid detail is alleged to retain "some" public value. But problematizing police and corporation claims of the neutral sounding "public safety" is long overdue. This claim is evident in framing of foundation discourse too. A Central Canadian city councillor suggested paid detail reduced transgressions in the city, however not if officers were inside private establishments:

> If you really want to address it [i.e., crime] have more officers walking the beat, that's the way that you have some kind of presence and at the time [it was argued that] we do have a presence because we have the paid detail ... I disagree with that because they're inside the bars a lot of the time (Central Canadian Councillor 1).

What does "the public" think about this safety being provided on their behalf? Are they queried and consulted about whether they feel safe and consequently wish it to continue? Are poor and racialized communities included in such communications and do they feel safe due to police officers standing next to holes in the street or sitting in cruisers next to construction sites?

Further into the Dark: Police Foundations and Commercial Paid Detail Brokers

Two trends that began to accelerate around 2016 discussed in previous chapters are perhaps the most troubling for the future. The first is the astonishing growth in police foundations in the US. The second is the equally stunning growth in US commercial paid detail broker contracts with departments, as seen in one large broker, and the aggressiveness of others.

Police Foundations

Police foundations will hide the possible influence of donors on a larger and larger number of departments going forward. Foundations' stunning growth, about which we found no evidence of stopping, will move private police funding further into the dark, situating most of their activities and arrangements further from public view. This means that as these organizations and networks grow in power, any exchanges the public would otherwise contend are disreputable will not only remain unknown but may increase along with the foundations themselves. It means privately funded purchases of armoured vehicles, drones, robots, military grade helmets, vests and shields, surveillance and communication technologies, mounted units, and SWAT, riot, or similar training for the police institution that smack of further militarization, and which tend to be used in and against racialized and marginalized communities, will proceed under the public radar, while a few community initiatives will be strategically displayed high in the sky. These special purchases will then suddenly appear in police hands in ways that lead to the violent trampling of a protestor in Houston, aid identifying and likely illegally pulling over a working journalist on a lonely Texas highway, render the longstanding, impoverished urban area in Vancouver more amenable to gentrification and corporate profits, and hide corruption and private influence in myriad other jurisdictions in between and beyond.

Commercial Brokers

Currently, the public has no way of knowing on whose behalf police officers are operating or who is funding their presence at any moment. These are officers who through tax dollars the public has paid to recruit, train and maintain through salaries and benefits. As one journalist succinctly put it, "officers equipped by the public wield their police powers to serve private clients" (Gilbert 2021). With the introduction of paid detail commercial brokers who manage this information, however, now no one can even use FOI to acquire this information. As more departments become enrolled in this kind of funding network, this funding becomes darker and darker.

Another unintended effect of the rise of these brokers, in one case in hundreds of police departments, is that paid detail becomes somewhat standardized as it is corporatized, since one broker will now handle multiple police departments in a network, and provide similar insurance coverage and oversight of officers, if any exists across different sites. Previously, each department was separate, dealing with external organizations a bit differently on their own. The paid detail networks consequently grow in size but not number. One interesting aspect to look for in the future is whether these corporations as they grow will advocate for more stringent standards for the police institution's members to eliminate their competitors. Thus, they serve as extensions of the police institution but as we suggested in previous chapters these private corporations still compete with others. This competition was evident in the case of Seattle's Finest, the complaints against which came not from the public, but a Washington State-based rival called Blucadia. These complaints allegedly led to the FBI investigation. Similarly, we were able to access information about two brokers when they submitted bids to the City of Orange County, NJ, a small city and department to take over the paid detail arrangements, with only one being ultimately chosen. Ironically, the introduction of paid detail commercial brokers potentially leads to more oversight too. One commercial paid detail broker explained:

> We have scheduling software where we make sure all the shifts are covered. We have 24/7 management and supervision, somebody awake and on duty 24/7. These are my managers and they'll go out and check on these officers at their assignments. That's something that a police department certainly doesn't do, but we go out there to make sure they're awake. We make sure they're standing where they're supposed to stand or park where they're supposed to be parked... and unfortunately we've come across some officers who, you know take a pillow and blanket and go to sleep and we have to fire them (Southern Broker 1).

However, this is narrow oversight since what is seen is only available to the commercial broker and – when the broker chooses to make them aware – the corporate funders. The officers caught sleeping, to which most "easy money" paid detail positions are conducive, are only fired for that assignment. They are not fired from their police department, which would never potentially learn of this infraction, nor are necessarily banned from providing a similar service for a different broker, or even the same broker, for a different client. This is at best a kind of market scrutiny where some information, controlled by the broker, could result in a funder choosing a different broker to arrange police funding. Ironically, as commercial brokers claim to offer more oversight of paid detail and generate more information about what officers are doing, the public learns less and less about whom police are working for and indeed which officers are providing a presence on their behalf. As with the police chief noticed by protestors and a journalist opening a gate for Kinder Morgan in Texas, when the journalist inquired, he found out there are not necessarily records kept of assignment logs, or if there are records, they are not necessarily available to the public other than perhaps a rudimentary agreement between the commercial broker and police and/or the local government.

The new brokered arrangements means it is possible police departments not only will be unaware of where their officers are at any moment, but also for whom they are providing a presence. This is now left to the police-friendly commercial broker, that has become an extension of the police institution. Like the spread of foundations, the onset of commercial paid detail brokers places private police funding into the darkest recesses of the funding gold mine, their activities, and arrangements further from public scrutiny. The fact that many owners and founders of these commercial broker firms are ex-police officers or are otherwise police affiliated and friendly (e.g., Off Duty Services 2021; Frizell Group 2021; Athos Group 2021), seems to be enough for smaller police departments – shown in Chapter Five to be signing up with brokers at a jaw-dropping rate. In some cases, the same prohibitions are in place to ensure their members are protected from morally unsavoury funders (a large oil and gas corporation further degrading the environment during the globe's climate emergency is apparently not deemed such).

No Monetary or Member Limits: A Greedy Institution's Dream

One massive hole in the eight department policies described in Chapter Two, as well as all the others concerning sponsorships, foundations, and paid detail was the lack of upward monetary limits on the institutional acquisition of private funding (other than to trigger a review by another body such as a City Council). We came across no policies that explicitly specified the police could accept only up to a certain amount of private funding overall or even as a proportion of their overall operating budget (like the 1% in the UK) and after that must halt it. There were no stipulations that the amount of sponsorship or transfers from foundations or revenue from paid detail policing was capped. This means there are no limits placed on this institution's greed and that, we contend, only encourages more and more unchecked greed and expansion. Having no limits on the monies or loyal members providing funding (e.g., the size of the network) is the greedy institution's dream. Nor are there restrictions on in-kind gifts such as firearms, surveillance technology, military vehicles and other equipment. We showed there are limits on the value of a donation that needs approval, with those reaching a certain size (which ranged dramatically from 0 to 500 to 20000 dollars as we showed) requiring a higher level of approval, sometimes a City or municipal council or a police board (that is usually controlled by the City with, for example, a mayor chairing it). There are no limits placed on the ultimate value of one donation or sponsorship arrangement or on the number of donations or sponsorships and thus new loyal funders. Vancouver Police can accept the $1 million earmarked for the Downtown Eastside discussed earlier with no barrier, which means even if such donations and sponsorships were deemed acceptable for some reason, several powerful players could influence police priorities. Based on the experience with forfeiture noted in Chapter Two, as well as Crime Stoppers partnerships (Lippert 2002), and other instances in previous chapters, there is every reason to believe such influence is occurring or soon will.

One finding regarding policies was that they tend to be more restrictive for individual officers than for the entire department. Individual officers are in most cases prevented from soliciting funds themselves without prior approval, and rules where they exist tend to be stringent on this as they should be. Similarly, individual officers are often restricted in the number of paid detail hours they can receive in a week or related period although those are not tight restrictions. If paid detail is not overseen by a department unit it is unclear whether there are any limits beyond fatigue and opportunity in other models (individual arrangements and commercial brokering) in part because there is little incentive to ensure these rules are followed in those networks since both stand to gain by not doing so. Where are the explicit limits on the value of sponsorships and partnerships as well as the solicitation of private corporations at the department level?

Sealing off the Dark Mine

The police institution has slowly but steadily dug a dark, rich mine. One response is to seal off the entrance to this mine entirely. This would render the idea of unmasking miners or trying to determine what if anything they received in return for extracted riches moot. This would mean watching the numerous policy holes for serious controversies to raise their ugly heads, like a high stakes whack-a-mole game, becomes unnecessary since the entire mine and its extensive channels and shafts are sealed. This would solve many problems and we contend this approach coheres with transforming the greedy police institution and might even serve as its catalyst.

Another way to render filling holes irrelevant is to simply prohibit any or all sponsorship, foundations, and paid detail practices we have documented. Prohibition of sponsorship and foundations and receipt of private funds is in place for higher level police agencies such as the Federal Bureau of Investigation. Prohibition is a viable policy option. It is also one that will be easier to implement sooner before this greedy institution becomes greedier, than later when more and more operations, not necessarily for public or community benefit, become dependent on private funds. If it was necessary for a department to receive private funds, a contention about which we have serious doubts given an abundance of public resources and which comes with serious issues, this funding could be channelled through a community foundation. This was why we mentioned community foundations in Chapter Two and which we discuss more below.

Foundations

Why are police, plainly part of the state, deemed a charity in the first place, and why have departments been permitted to create foundations that fuel this greedy institution's insatiable wants? If it is necessary for police to receive private funding beyond their public budgets, why can such funds not be filtered through an arms-length community foundation that determines the need for funds for myriad organizations related to community? The example of Baltimore above would give anyone pause, since when the Baltimore Police Foundation lost credibility it was this city's community foundation that arranged funding for the police department's secret and unproven mass aerial surveillance desires. Perhaps this could be prevented if this community foundation had mostly community members including those from racialized and marginalized communities on its board rather than police, corporate CEOs, elites with corporate ties, that we showed dominated foundation boards in Chapter Three, as well as elected councillors. This would help ensure the community is foremost served and that police are only one of many possible funding recipients. We also think any earmarking, if permitted at all, must be for community projects the community acknowledges as such beforehand, and not for police surveillance technologies, training, or operations leading to even more hard policing and militarization.

Paid Detail

A regular rationale for paid detail in the US especially is to provide police, sometimes relatively underpaid police officers in the US, with more income. One officer suggested this was partially the impetus for New York's formal paid detail program commenced in 1998 under then mayor Rudy Giuliani to allow lower salaries in the NYPD's collective agreements. This has two implications. One will be to increase salaries where they are not already in place, perhaps requiring more public monies annually. The second to offset this is to have fewer officers and more civilians in police departments, thus reducing the requirements. Another would be to revisit regulations or laws requiring paid detail to determine if, as in the case above regarding flaggers, they could be rescinded, thus allowing construction companies and movie production firms as well as event organizers to merely hire private security or make other security arrangements. Recall that police trainees, auxiliary, or officer volunteers (or even community group volunteers or staff in some cases) could serve a similar role, if necessary, as the TPSB report recommended, but which was not followed. We return to this point in the conclusion. Prohibiting paid detail is not without precedent. For example, US federal police agencies tend not to permit paid detail; if it works there it is unclear why it could not work in local departments.

If corporations and other businesses need extra security in, for example, retail sites, why can they not obtain it through private auspices and providers? There is a massive international private security industry from which to draw security guards and purchase security and surveillance technologies to serve private corporation's interests and protect their assets (see Walby and Lippert 2015; Walby and Lippert 2014). Why must private corporations be given access to publicly trained and equipped officers in the first place? Why not allow public police to police the public consistent with community priorities, especially if at first sign of serious violence police will be removed from private sites and events rather than present?

For events this was a huge hole, since it was unclear how these "negotiations" between police and event sponsors were conducted. While several police departments related some or all factors they apparently considered when determining how many paid detail officers were required for an event, the weight of any one factor in the calculus for funding was not provided. While it can be argued this provides flexibility, it also lends itself to greedily "requiring" more officers than needed and leaves too much discretion to police to profit from more officers receiving funds for these events. Many funders were unaware of what law or policy it was that compelled them to provide this mandatory funding though did not seem concerned about this either, loyal to the police institution as they were. We think requiring disclosure of the precise legal requirement and the calculus used for all such events to the funder but also the public on police department websites would help fill this hole as well.

Based on this evidence, we do think the best practice in this regard would be to close down access to the mine entirely. In the absence of sealing off the mine and its lucrative contents, there is good reason to at least prohibit overlapping funding channels given the possible influence of one on the other. If an external organization is permitted to fund paid detail, because that is discretionary in most departments, that same organization should not be permitted to donate or sponsor the department through other means. Conversely if an organization is already vetted to donate to or sponsor police, this could influence how many officers are "needed" or how these officers conduct themselves at a donor or sponsor site, and thus the organization should be prohibited from funding paid detail.

Conclusion

This chapter explored some controversies including those concerning corruption and the rule of law in relation to private funding of police in Canadian and US police departments. We showed this corruption and the rule of law violations are not hypothetical but instead have happened in some departments and are very likely happening in others. There have been documented criminal cases that show this occurs in several major US cities. Regarding a criminal case in Nassau County, New York, for example, local press uncovered "a March 2010 internal police department-wide memo stating foundation members were to be treated differently should police personnel come across them during their regular duties" (Long Island Press 2013). We do not know how prevalent it is and, worse, if it is becoming more difficult rather than easier to scrutinize whether it is occurring due to the funding networks becoming darker through corporate influence. Foundations and commercial brokers make these relations murkier all the time. Such influence is evinced in rapid police foundation creation and commercial broker paid detail arrangements rather than being subject to "sunny ways." Given the migration of other greedy institution developments from the US to Canada, as evinced in Crime Stoppers and civil forfeitures, and notwithstanding the lack of similar organizations pushing for their development, it is only a matter of time before the acceleration of these two trends commences in Canada. While holes can be watched or plugged, given the remarkably poor record of police reform in North America (Skogan 2018), in the next chapter we contend a more fundamental and structural transformation of the police institutional landscape away from greed and towards generosity is the preferred, long overdue ideal.

Note

1 Motorola is especially active in police foundation board membership, currently having its directors on the RCMP Foundation, LAP Foundation, Philadelphia Police Foundation, Phoenix Police Foundation, and National Police Foundation Network at the time of writing.

Conclusion

The Future of Private Sponsorship and Funding of Police

Greed to Generosity, Dark Money to Defunding, and Beyond

Introduction

Private sponsorship, foundations, and paid detail expand the institutional power and reach of police. The greedy institution is an endlessly growing black hole that consumes every kind of capital it can. To do this, police must accumulate social and cultural capital and align the interests of other large organizations with the police vision of the world. This is all occurring as governments, notwithstanding temporary pandemic-related spending, continue to underfund or cut community programs and social spending. We have argued that private sponsorship and funding of police is an overlooked dimension of police operations with far-reaching consequences. Further, we contend the acceptance of these funds and the emergence especially of police foundations to funnel them into policing is indicative of the greedy institutional character of police. This is the end of the book, but it is the beginning of seeing police in a new way for us and we hope for readers too. In this book, we have made several theoretical, methodological, and empirical contributions to criminology and criminal justice studies as well as police studies. We recount these contributions before moving on to some political implications of our findings and arguments, especially how all of this connects to debates about and the movement for police defunding. We conclude by drawing from several influences to sketch out what policing in a generous society might look like instead, something incumbent on us to reflect upon.

Theoretical

Regarding theoretical contributions, we have applied and extended the literature on greedy institutions (Cox 2016; De Campo 2013; Peterson and Uhnoo 2012; Coser 1974). We have adapted the notion of greedy institutions to police resource management by extending it from an inward to an outward focus. To see this entails looking at the frames, networks, and capital accumulation of police organizations as an endeavour to command loyalty and conformity, not only among police members but also the public. It is

DOI: 10.4324/9781003167914-9

a real achievement that police have managed to command so much public conformity. It is among the most effective institutions at persuading people to see the world as it does, a testament to its greedy status. People conform to the police worldview often without thinking about it. Authorities call upon us to be specific kinds of subjects for sure, as Althusser's old notion of ideology made clear, but a consequence is those authorities become more and more politically and economically powerful. This conformity is seemingly automatic (Karpiak 2010), but ultimately, we show it is dependent on police frames that are pervasive and persuasive. By applying greedy institution theory to police resource management, we have moved beyond conceptualizations of sponsorship and paid detail as a form of gift or ambiguous exchange (or as the narrower police-driven goal captured by the title of this book, "lengthening the arm of the law" (Ayling et al. 2009), the greedy police institution's mantra *par excellence*). Recall Ayling and colleagues (2009) refer to police resource management as gift giving and receiving. Instead of gift theory we have drawn from literature on disreputable exchange (Rossman 2014), moral regulation (Hunt 1997), nodes and networks (Luscombe et al. 2018; Lippert et al. 2016; Dupont 2006), and the greedy institution to make sense of these flows and forms of capital in police funding. We do not discount these exchanges mimic gifting, but thinking in gift terms tends to neglect institutional power and replication. The act of giving gifts requires a more generous rather than greedy worldview. Thinking in gift terms tends to neglect policing as a political project as well as calls for alternatives. A focus on obfuscation and disreputable exchange is needed. We have moved beyond the gift framework and drawn from greedy institution theory. We also contribute theoretically by discussing the implications of our analysis for concepts of police culture and rule of law used to understand and critique police conduct. Finally, we contribute to greedy institution theory by commencing an admittedly brief discussion of what an institution in a generous society might look like instead.

Our approach has been perhaps closer to the framework offered by Diphoorn and Grassiani (2016) who argue police networks are established and extended to protect and build police power. They use the idea of securitizing capital to advance this argument. Diphoorn and Grassiani (2016, 430) see "securitizing capital as a process whereby different forms of capital are, consciously and unconsciously, used to acquire legitimacy and power." These scholars have suggested focusing on police networks and exchanges of forms of capital instead of looking at exchanges in purely economic terms. As they explain:

> Rather than studying the 'state police' and/or the 'private security company' as single, independent institutions, we look at the various ways through which these entities are connected and disconnected and at the hierarchical relationships that develop from these multiple interactions (Diphoorn and Grassiani 2016, 431).

Drawing more directly from Bourdieu's thought, they argue the ultimate prize in these networks and exchanges is the translation of social and cultural capital into symbolic capital. As they argue, "[a]ctors who do not possess the right economic, political, cultural and/or social capital are unlikely to acquire symbolic capital" (436). Symbolic capital reproduces the status and authority of the institution who can translate social and cultural capital. Our arguments parallel this work by Diphoorn and Grassiani and we would suggest their approach and ours deserves more attention in future criminological, criminal justice and policing research. These networks and exchanges are about replicating the police as an institution as well as building and extending police power. Our focus on police and police foundations as greedy institutions is an extension of this approach. We have argued police foundations in the US and Canada have risen to prominence and taken on a specific form as a charity or non-profit. Police foundations in the US and Canada have become effective funnels for corporate monies while sheltering police from accusations of direct network ties to elites and corporations. However, corporate sponsorship of and donations to police is also an international phenomenon (see Chapter Four). In addition to capital and networks we have asserted framing is crucial for this accumulation because it allows police to not only keep officers behind the so-called 'blue wall,' even as it extends further and further, but also to persuade would-be partners and donors to view the world through police eyes beyond it (also see Cox 2016). In other words, although networks and capital are the material vessels and rewards gained in these exchanges, the rhetorical and symbolic work necessary for replicating the greedy institution or securitizing capital requires attention to framing and communication as well. We have suggested the rise and extension of public relations management in police services, police foundations, and police unions is also a key dimension of this need for framing.

All this means that the idea of dark money needs renovation too. There is untraceable money circulating in criminal justice, and corporate players try to influence the criminal justice sector in advantageous ways. This is an issue in policing, as we have shown. However, these are not one-way exchanges. Police are only open to these endeavours and exchanges to augment and extend the police footprint. This way police power and influence are not only susceptible to dark money but served by these exchanges. The replication of the greedy institution is furthered through these capital exchanges, and so a whole apparatus is created ranging from special foundations to paid detail offices and brokering firms to weak or absent internal policies to facilitate network expansion and proliferation of the exchanges that constitute and sustain them. We have examined these networks to show where the channels and seams of dark money are located, and how they are being arrogated. Below we also consider the need for these seams of monies to be recouped by community, for neighbourhoods, for families, for people, as part of a move towards fostering a more generous society.

Thinking through the Institutional Culture of Police

Our analysis and findings in this book also speak to and extend the widely used concept of police culture (Chan 2003). We have not used this concept to any extent to avoid some unfortunate baggage with which it arrives since it has multiple meanings (Chan 2003, 19–28). One we wish to laud, however, is Chan (2003), who reconceptualizes how police culture changes by acknowledging the efforts of police personnel to "make" police culture rather than only see it as perpetually and monolithically imposed on institutional actors, such as police administrators and rank and file officers. Thus, the framing we describe is accomplished by greedy institutional agents ranging from police foundation representatives to police executives to police unions to commercial brokers. We mean to refer to the notion of agency here, not to the individual level, as we noted in the book's introduction. Although beyond the scope of our study, we acknowledge framing does not appear as a matter of course in its calling for more donors and funders of paid detail gigs and at greater volumes. Nor does greed itself appear such. Greed is created in and represented through framing and exchanges into networks we have explored in this book.

The notion of a greedy institution describes a kind of institutional trajectory and organizational culture. Building on other applications of the greedy institution concept in policing studies (such as Cox 2016) we have argued these outside forms of police funding that flow in large part through police foundations create an outward trajectory. Police foundations are a strategic vehicle for scaling up the greedy institutional dimensions of public police. From robot dogs to police video game buses to tactical gear and surveillance cameras, the examples of gear purchased using police foundation funds reveal community development is not the name of the game for the greedy institution. We have been suggesting therefore that police institutional culture smacks of greed and that describing institutional changes – from sponsorships to for-profit paid detail brokers – only as corporatization – as valid as that may be compared to other terms like neoliberalism – is inadequate on its own. Rather, we contend greedy institutional outlooks and corporatization go hand and hand and are mutually constitutive; they feed and encourage the other to dig deeper and wider for desired riches rather than to fulfil real safety and security needs of communities and to allow no barriers – the rule of law, constitutional rights, viral pandemics, disadvantaged groups and community priorities, or even criminal law – to get in their way. Those who stand up and are unwilling to pledge loyalty to the police institution, for example, through protest or investigative journalism, may be suddenly trampled from behind or accosted on the highway for no apparent reason, or like most other citizens, kept in the dark about private funding of police through myriad means. Instead, like many others, they are expected to stay put, stay seated, and otherwise be mesmerized by and loyal to the police worldview, with its glossy community rhetoric. This is vital to note because otherwise discussing political implications of our analysis below becomes irrelevant or moot. If police culture arrives and stays fully formed it becomes unclear why one would bother to try to change it, or in our terms, to transform a greedy institution into something very different in a more generous society.

One idea raised by our analysis, which we can only speculate about here where paid detail is concerned, is that as police greed and footprints extend past the "blue wall" into private employment spheres, any aspects of police culture and rules that still protect communities can become "contaminated" there. For example, officers may become accustomed to contexts where physical violence and looking the other way for certain transgressions is more acceptable than during regular patrol duties. As noted in Chapter Five, the now former Minneapolis police officer Chauvin was present for the same paid detail nightclub assignment for many years where "he often pulled out mace and pepper spray" even though the nightclub owner "thought it was unwarranted" (Horn 2020). This raises the spectre of whether attending some, albeit relatively rare, paid detail assignments and the funding that make them possible can have detrimental effects on police institutional culture and norms of conduct. The point is not only whether such a culture of violence and rule avoidance in some paid detail positions mesh with the rule of law ideal, as explained more below. The question is also whether it has longer-term effects on police culture, on officers' normative conduct, due to their regular exposure to somewhat riskier nightclub and bar environments or to casually firing rubber bullets in rural areas at pipe-line protestors for private interests in ways far beyond department rules. Officers must follow up these paid detail "gigs" the very next day on regular patrol during which they are expected to consistently and fairly deal with a citizenry, obey the law, and use physical violence only as a last resort. There are other cases involving officer conduct and paid detail that raise the question of whether assignments, as proffered in Chapter Seven, rather than doing some policy hole filling, should be permitted at all.

Rule of Law

One of the most vital issues raised by police sponsorship and funding as elaborated in this book is the spectre of divergences from the rule of law. The centrality of the issue of the relation between police and the rule of law is longstanding and complex (Bayley 2002). This notion in liberal democracies refers to two accompanying notions that "everyone is subject to the law" and that "law treats everyone the same" (Brickey and Comack 1987, 100). Greedy institutions demand loyalty and conformity to what are deemed to be traditional practices more than adherence to broader principles. Any *quid pro quo* entailing police doing something because of sponsorship or donations rarely surfaces; the divergences are often more about what police "don't do." Thus, like the fictional Boston officer literally looking the other way in *The Town*, some transgressions are merely ignored or not sought out in the first place. For paid detail this is evident when officers do not lay charges or make arrests at the place of work. Our media analysis provided ample evidence of this avoidance; despite hundreds of thousands of these assignments occurring weekly we could locate only a handful of instances across North America and many years where a paid detail arrangement resulted in police discovering a crime and then acting upon it due to their presence on a paid detail job. There were more instances of police on paid detail being caught up and becoming potential victims in a shooting in a venue or even avoiding intervention than of police discovering transgressions about to happen, arresting, and laying charges there. As noted, this includes some major shooting incidents in recent years. It also includes FBI investigations of corruption in paid detail and sponsorship, providing more examples of police transgressing rules rather than others doing so. Our interviews and analysis of documents were similarly telling. The interviews with sponsors and paid detail funders did not reveal much evidence of police dealing with transgressions in communities as a result. Perhaps more troubling is the arrangement that sponsorship may result in police seeking out some kinds of transgressions of direct interest to sponsors (insurance fraud for the insurance company sponsor) not necessarily those of central and current community concern. The policy holes discussed in Chapter Seven revealed no special or direct attention to whether police would contravene the rule of law due to sponsorship or to a paid detail arrangement. It does not currently appear to be a major policy concern.

It is a matter of optics, however. As police find themselves lurching from legitimation crisis to legitimation crisis, they are not unaware of the potential problematic appearances of their private arrangements (as we showed in Chapter Two) for funding. Yet, for that reason, including violations of the rule of law, foundations have been erected for sponsorship or donations, and new mechanisms such as random assignment of officers to private gigs, has happened for paid detail, seeking to obfuscate any direct exchanges. Both are a means of obscuring the poor optics of police being funded by private entities to be somewhere to do something. Overall, we have considered the rule of law not to boost liberalism, but as a lens to assess the potential for negligence and nepotism in these dark money exchanges between corporations and in police foundation and paid detail networks.

Methodological

Concerning our methodological contribution, we have contributed to police studies by using Freedom of Information (FOI) requests combined with qualitative interviews, media analysis, and policy analysis. FOI requests in the social sciences are increasing (Luscombe et al. 2017a). As we have shown, it is possible to collect many documents and records that would never otherwise be disclosed to outsiders and which can systematically reveal the character and extent of specific police practices. We distinguish this method from journalistic one-off FOI stories, where documents are sought by media outlets in a way designed to be singular police "gotchas" more welcome during the current police legitimacy crisis before the media cycle quickly moves on to entirely different issue or institution for the next media crusade. Ours is systematic and purposeful. Through FOI, we have revealed the scope of some forms of police resource management. We have revealed the flow of capital exchanges that occur in paid detail policing. But FOI research has limits. For example, we have been unable to collect all sponsorship records using FOI because it only applies to public bodies, and police foundations and private employers of paid detail officers are not currently recognized as such. Police have increasingly funnelled sponsorships through private, not for profit or charitable police foundations, which renders them immune to FOI requests and other public scrutiny. Nonetheless, we gathered vital records using FOI regarding police resources, and have combined that approach with interviews, media analysis, and policy analysis. In the interviews, we learn a little bit about how police conceptualize these resource exchanges, how sponsors conceptualize these resource exchanges, and how paid detail funders conceptualize these resource exchanges.

Regarding media analysis, we have located examples of police framing of resource exchanges and police attempts to compel loyalty or persuade more and more people to donate resources. As shown in multiple chapters, sometimes these donations generate controversy and serious scandal. These only undermine police legitimacy and credibility further because of the real or perceived corruption and rule of law violations involved. Yet attempts to attract sponsorship and attempts to extend paid detail policing continue, which reinforces the notion of a greedy institution demanding and commanding more and more capital. We have also looked in Chapter Seven at holes in the policies for sponsorship and paid detail as the police institution is currently arranged, which point at a minimum to the need for greater municipal, state as well as provincial and federal regulation of these exchanges. The Council of Canadians, in fact, circulated a petition in September 2020, asking the Canadian federal government to stop sponsorship of police by private corporations using police foundations for this purpose altogether (Council of Canadians 2020). The petition failed to attract much attention and at the time of writing has not been addressed in the Canadian House of Commons. However, this petition suggests large gaps in policy that enable greedy institutions to proliferate are evident and should be addressed in future government deliberations.

Empirical

Concerning an empirical contribution, we have found that from the police to corporations the players view their exchanges as perfectly fine and necessary. This is happening when police budgets in Canada are at an all-time high on a per capita spending basis, and we have raised the question of whether these attempts to attract more funding are not merely responses to a police legitimation crisis. As we discussed, sponsorship differs from donation; the former involves an explicit exchange, whereas the latter tends to be framed as one-way philanthropic transfers. However, we have argued the police motivation is replication of the reach and power of the institution. Although police unions and police administrations do not always see eye to eye on replication and extension of policing as an institution (even if this is understood differently, such as bigger budgets versus more members), they tend to adopt the same framing to achieve this. In practice, differences between the two become obscure since donors may still reap unspoken benefits from their generosity such as special access to policing services. Our argument – that capital accumulation goes beyond economic capital to include social and political capital – follows this line of argumentation. These forms of resource exchange are partially about creating a political formation or bloc to support police power and its extension. The dollars and cents may fluctuate and contributions from cities and other levels of government may even decrease, but at the end of the day the greedy institution will be pleased if it is replicated, and if police power is extended. We contend this is in large part the ultimate endeavour of sponsorship and paid detail in their own ways. As Lawson (2021, 76) argues, imbalances in flows of capital are indicators of power and inequality. In this book, we have pointed to major imbalances of power in modern society further extended by a police-corporate symbiosis and the greedy operations of police foundations and paid detail brokers of several kinds.

To the extent police are being funded more through external private entities, as we have shown, it suggests a possible return to the early history of policing before public funding was systematically provided to police to ensure the rule of law. Yet, a greedy institution is unlikely to relinquish public monies in lieu of greater private funding; instead the police institution is empirically shown to merely seek and acquire more and more capital from almost *any* source, unless that source starkly contrasts with its equally strong drive for loyalty and conformity. These new and growing funding networks we have empirically documented in this book also raise key questions about police governance and accountability. The growing links and exchanges with nominally external institutions such as those above, means that the police institution is differently governed and accountable compared to how it is often framed with a chief and administrators and to a much lesser extent a board and/or higher-level oversight body calling the shots to serve communities. We have empirically shown that when it comes to governance of police funding and thus police priorities, as well as police practices shaped by them, various other nodal actors enrolled in police networks play a large and growing role that is often independent of community needs. We see police guarding pipelines and construction sites in Texas and Toronto and establishing secret invasive mass surveillance of disadvantaged communities in Los Angeles and Baltimore, neglecting serious transgressions of elites and corporations, and donning purchased military gear to confront public protestors, driven by these nodal agents of the growing police institution and their framing of issues and "needs." These loyal pro-police personnel of organizations ranging from foundations to commercial brokers to massive private corporations to police unions are found to play a role and wield influence, some increasingly so, as well. Though some scholars have previously acknowledged some but not all these nodes (e.g., police unions – see Burgess 2006), they have not done so in relation to funding and related priorities to any extent. We contend that scholars seeking a fuller empirical account of the workings of police networks and nodal governance of the police institution should consider these empirical realities going forward and embark on more study of them, especially in international contexts beyond North America.

The question of police legitimacy and its contestation raises questions and political debate requiring attention in this conclusion as well. We therefore next address the idea of the greedy institution and what it means for thinking through debates about defunding and abolition, followed by some preliminary thoughts on what policing in a generous society might look like. By doing so, we hope to further unpack the relevance of a greedy institution framework and show how it is relevant to political discussions and movements as well as possible alternatives in the 21st century.

Police as a Greedy Institution: The Political Implications

Let us begin by contrasting the idea of the greedy institution against other conceptualizations of police power in academic work and political movements. For example, one term used by activists, scholars and in social movements is the idea of a "police state" (Robinson 2019, 2018). This idea of a "police state," we would suggest, overlaps in some ways with the notion of a total institution. The total institution is one using force and containment strategies as a form of power (Moran 2014). No doubt police use detention and force in their encounters with people consistent with criminalization. However, police tend not to use these strategies on their own members, nor are they aimed to garner influence and legitimacy across society. Violence and force tend to have the opposite effect, pitting the police against the public. What we have argued is outward police communications and all manner of police fundraising activities better resemble what is called a greedy institution. What this means, we think, for scholars, activists and movements using the idea of a police state is that a focus should be added in social movement strategy on undermining this attempt to accumulate social and political capital by police. Simply focusing on the containment strategies and use of force the "police state" idea entails not only conflates politics and police but also neglects other elements of police power. It will not for example pinpoint the softer or more persuasion-oriented approaches entailed in police framing and expansion or make intelligible the multiple sources of the resources that allow police violence to persist, not in the "first instance" through state funding, but instead as calls for defunding grow in the "second private instance" beyond the state. We think the idea of a greedy institution is better oriented towards and captures these aspects. Social movement participants might find our elaboration and application of police as a greedy institution useful in some way.

We would likewise suggest the idea of a greedy institution has relevance for activists, scholars and others thinking through and mobilizing for the defunding and abolition of police. These discussions of police defunding and police abolition are not new, but they rose to prominence in 2020, after the police killing of George Floyd. There are many precursors of this movement. For example, Black feminists in the US (Ritchie 2017; Richie 2012) have been arguing for decades that police are destroying Black and other already marginalized communities through criminalization and have mobilized in response using community and social development to provide alternatives to police. These efforts have undoubtedly empowered communities and drawn attention to the racism and violence that often stems from policing there.

Purely academic interventions, such as Alex Vitale's (2019) book *The End of Policing* have emerged too. There, Vitale argues more training and technology for police will not fix the problems of accountability, transparency, or police violence that are increasingly a public concern. Vitale argues governments have already tried different technology and training for police for decades and it has not changed the institution. He elaborates this argument by looking at case studies from policing homelessness to sex work. Vitale argues we need to move to a model of community and social development to address transgression instead of simply reacting to transgression with force and criminalization through policing, because this does not actually address the causes of transgression. In fact, it makes transgression more likely because the police dislocate and disrupt community with force and criminalization. These arguments echo those of Black feminist abolitionists for decades in the US. These claims about policing entered the mainstream in 2020, so much so that some surveys have found over 50 per cent of young persons in Canada would like to defund the police (Ipsos 2020). There is some support across other age groups and across spectrums of society too.

The idea of abolishing and defunding the police institution is not easily avoided once it is heard or thought through because it is compelling. No doubt there is distress and transgression in our communities and neighbourhoods. The question is how to deal with them in ways that may prevent transgression and distress from reaching higher rates (McDowell and Fernandez 2018). This is why the argument for defunding the police and reinvesting in community and social development is so vital. One does not need a PhD in criminology or criminal justice to understand that high levels of transgression and distress deserve a response that will try to decrease high levels of transgression and distress and address the causes of those issues is the only hope of achieving real safety. We think the causes are lack of mental health outreach, lack of addictions outreach, lack of adequate housing, lack of economic opportunity, lack of integration in a healthy community, and a neglect of harmful acts by elites and corporate and governmental actors. There is a massive literature on these causes of transgression in criminology we will not revisit here. The point is these issues can be addressed by further public investment, and it makes sense to take monies from existing municipal and state and provincial government departments that are already the most highly funded, which usually are the police.

Police administrators have counterargued by pointing to the most harmful forms of transgression and suggesting these will become more frequent if police are inadequately funded. However, in general, if more funding for police decreased transgression, we should see transgression decreasing by this point in the history of policing and social control. Police have never received more of the budget pie of municipalities and provinces and states than currently, yet rates of transgression are still high and are rising in some spheres. This would suggest levels of police funding and intervention have little relationship to levels of transgression and that funding police more will not lessen transgression, at least not to the extent police tell us it will. If policing did decrease transgression and distress in our communities and neighbourhoods via criminalization, one would think one city and one police force somewhere in the Western world would be able to stand up and say, "we got rid of transgression and distress through policing." It has not happened. This is exactly the compelling point the defund police movement makes.

We have not written a book about police abolition or defunding. However, our arguments and the idea of a greedy institution have relevance for these discussions. Notably, we have suggested that as a greedy institution, police seek to expand their social and cultural influence as much as they try to attract additional economic capital. Even in endeavours such as police sponsorship, police foundations and paid detail policing, the economic dimension is merely one among several. The social and the political capital accumulation those endeavours entail is also significant. What this means is efforts at defunding or even abolishing the police institution must incorporate strategies to undermine those other forms of capital exchange, which are the broader basis of police power. It is one thing to reduce a police budget by 15 per cent, which we have seen happen already in some cities in North America since the police killing of George Floyd, which is remarkable social change. However, a budget cut alone does not erode police power. The reduction of the budget does not necessarily decrease the social and political capital of police. In fact, it could have the opposite effect. As some journalists and commentators pointed out during the summer of 2020 and has already been suggested by some police foundations, if governments defund police due to immense public pressure, police foundations are happy to acquire through persuasion and then direct corporate donations to police to fill in (Ramakrishna 2020). This underscores private corporation greediness too and underscores our point that the exchanges and networks police create and the relations they engender involve other greedy institutions, notably corporations. It also highlights that these external relations and networks make it difficult to ever eliminate the police institution entirely. In this way, we are arguing it is those mechanisms of social and political capital accumulation that are equally if not more important than the economic capital accumulation occurring in this domain.

This goes for related arguments regarding police abolition as well. All we can do here is suggest political advocacy and activism in this domain must focus on more than merely taking away economic resources of police because the basis of police power is broader. It extends to these forms of political and social capital accumulation we have pointed to. Police power is extended through the frames and networks of the police as a greedy institution turned outward. It is those mechanisms that must also be the focus of social movements against police. Perhaps these ideas have some relevance for other movements against other criminal justice sectors, for example, in the realm of prison abolition. Again, some movements have focused mainly on economic arguments and economic resources when fighting against the siting of public prisons or in the US private prisons and jails. Money matters, of course. But the legitimacy of the carceral is only possible because of the social, cultural, and political intelligibility of prisons and jails. Alongside making arguments against the economics of prisons and jails, perhaps it is necessary to also target those social networks and cultural ideas that make prison expansion possible.

We are neither social movement scholars nor leaders. If the events of 2020 have taught us anything, it is to try to learn from community leaders such as BIPOC persons mobilizing against criminal justice and police violence. We would simply, humbly, submit that it is vital to look beyond economic arguments when contesting the expansion of the police institution and contesting the expansion of police power in society. It is, in fact, the response of police to calls for defunding in 2020 that helped us to see these processes in this light. When we set out to write this book, the content was focused more on economic issues and formal policies. However, seeing the police departments and police foundations' response to the defund argument was a clue that this is about more than economics or money. It made us think about the function of police foundations and police communications more lucidly, and to reflect more genuinely on what police power is, how it is formed, how it is extended, and some of its serious detriments. Our arguments in this book were also shaped by seeing US municipal governments top police budgets back up after some defunding (see Goodman 2021), a development that underscores the historical difficulty of achieving police reform more broadly (Skogan 2018).

Police are a greedy institution, and the mechanisms of that greediness replicate the police as such. Even considering the violence they perpetrate and their failures to address transgression and distress in our society, police continue to replicate themselves. The economic exchanges they engage in are about demanding loyalty and conformity to the police vision of the world as much as they are about shoring up police economic resources. We think our approach sheds more academic and conceptual light on these processes. We hope our idea that this greediness pertains to economic capital accumulation as well as social and political capital accumulation will contribute to creating a future world where we are able to address transgression and distress in a more humane, helpful, way. Continued criminalization, violence, and expansion of police powers is not the way to create healthier neighbourhoods and communities in the 21st century. If greed is allowed to proliferate, to paraphrase Karl Marx, it will always rob humans of their own values and their own value.

Police in a Generous Society: What Might It Look Like?

We have already argued that community and social development would be beneficial and in large part could replace eventually some or even most of what the police institution currently claims to be doing. Yet it is obvious that in the interim police will remain. It is not true that regulation of transgression presents a direct affront to community and social development. Even some moments of true social revolt and transformation (the Paris Commune, Revolutionary Catalonia) entailed some means of regulating transgression, though they were totally community based. The need for reform while pushing for grander social change is implied in this book since we otherwise would not have bothered to have pointed to holes in policies if we do not think some benefit could come from filling them.

Having discussed the police as a greedy institution and the political implications of our analyses we would be remiss not to discuss what a different police institution might look like, including how it would be resourced. What would police in a generous society look like? Coser (1974) and those who have drawn on his work provide us with no clear examples and or guidance for this purpose, for example how to create generous institutions out of greedy ones or how to create a more generous, redistributive society overall. A generous society would not simply be a charitable one, and we are aware of the critiques of charity as a mechanism for upholding inequality. We instead are envisioning a society in which the public good and public interest genuinely trumps all other considerations. Such a shift would transform many of our current social institutions that have mutated and taken on fiscally and social conservative qualities, especially in the neo-liberal era. We do note the prevalence of community in Coser's treatise on greedy institutions, including use of "greedy community" (Coser 1974, 147–148), a point we return to below. We also draw on community policing ideals, an awareness of what became new left realism in critical criminological circles and its focus on community, and perhaps peculiarly, a little celebrated concept from the writings of Foucault (1988). The ideas exist and we merely combine them differently while also drawing from our combined 30 years of studying aspects of the police and criminal justice policy. Considering the sobering record of police reform in North America (Skogan 2018), we consider efforts and prospects of bringing a greedy institution into line with community or public good beyond our discussion of filling policy holes in Chapter Seven.

While defunding may be a necessary precursor to any redistribution of resources or creation of more generous institutions, there are other steps that can be taken at the same time. Below we sketch some features of what police in a generous society might look like. For this we draw from work on community policing, as it seems unimaginable, including given the efforts of Indigenous and Black communities to draw attention to police violence, to not embrace the notion of community, and not only due to Coser's (1974) engagement with it. This may be aggravating for those who would do away with the police institution entirely. What we have in mind is something that has more to do with community than with policing as we know it today.

We heed the lessons of the new left realists from Britain and to a lesser extent those writing in the US in the 1980s (Currie 2010; 2016; Lea 2010) who sought to temper the radical calls of some critical criminologists for a Marxist revolution when all transgressions and control structures would somehow disappear if our economic system radically changed. Transgression will remain. They noted the same communities where most incidents to which police are disproportionately called to respond, due to an array of factors that includes a lack of opportunity, entail much community violence. These transgressions and related victimizations (and other community violence such as right wing and white power violence against Black, Muslim, and Asian peoples) cannot be merely left to happen without regard for those tending to be harmed due to an ideological commitment to abolish the police institution instantly. Many changes suggested by the defunding moment should yield great neighbourhood benefits – eventually – and lead to dramatic reductions in victimization rates. But one lesson of the new left realist criminologists was that one cannot – morally or politically – simply abandon thinking about the role of police and criminal justice system in the interim, however flawed they are, because this would mean leaving working class as well as disadvantaged racialized communities without recourse to stop or curtail violent activity. Even as abolitionists such as Mariame Kaba argue, "we ain't ready," we do not have community capacity to reduce and respond to transgression at this time largely due to the defunding of social and community development since the 1970s. There will always be a need to remedy and confront community transgression, harm, and wrongdoing. The point is to think about doing so without reliance on greedy institutions and how to really empower communities to be safer and healthier to begin with.

Another idea from which we draw here, perhaps peculiarly so for some due to its link with post-structuralism, is the notion of pastoral power elaborated by historian and philosopher Michel Foucault in his discussions of "governmentality" (or rationality of government). While community policing has been discussed in its relations with neo-liberalism, or what some governmentality theorists such as Rose (1999) called "advanced liberalism," we would draw attention to a less discussed logic of governance, which continues today, and which could give life to and shape more generous relations. All institutions are imbued with and exercise power relations (recall that this is what we argued was the problem with seeing police sponsorship and donations as merely gift giving in Chapter One – doing so ignores power's presence). Since Foucaultian scholars have argued that pastoral power found its way into all sorts of historical institutions including schools, health care, and the welfare state (Foucault 1988). The welfare state according to Foucault was unimaginable without it. In 2020 it became easier to realize the importance of a welfare state after decades of relentless neo-liberal destruction in caring for those inflicted with COVID-19 and thrown out of paid work and preventing infliction in others. This kind of pastoral power in the public interest should focus on needs, not rights, and empowering rather than governing. Policing in a generous society would have to reflect this governmental logic of redistribution, social and community development, and robust social services, all of which would have to appear ahead of policing and criminalization as political and societal priorities. The community would become the shepherd seeking to care for members' needs, especially as it concerns preventing (as opposed to only reacting to, sometimes in unconstrained, violent, criminalizing, narrow, and even illegal ways) transgressions and victimization. So it is with generosity; institutional actors would not merely take or merely "give" in exchange for capital, but instead "give up" to satisfy community needs in the public interest.

Paid detail would no longer be lucratively paid through external funding or even formally be a detail or duty, but instead would be generous acts of volunteerism representing less the police and more the community. Winnipeg Police received more than $1 million CDN in unexpected funding to merely be present at key vaccination sites via paid detail assignments in that city during the COVID-19 pandemic (Pursaga 2021) and was undoubtedly not the only police department to do this in North America. Compare this arrangement with scores upon scores of volunteers, including medical and other professionals, across North America and globally who freely gave their time in their communities, often at greater risk to themselves, to make mass vaccinations possible. If there was ever a worthwhile opportunity to support and keep communities safer through volunteering a regulatory presence, that was it. Winnipeg Police graced these sites with their presence, but only if an organization loyally funded them at a rate of at least $119 CDN per hour, the highest paid detail rate in Canada and probably North America.

Yet sacrificing time and effort through volunteer policing is by no means a new idea either, as Dobrin (2017) asserts:

> Volunteer police have been part of western policing since the inception of the concept of police, and the practice currently continues. Of benefit to police organizations, modern volunteer police provide financial, personnel and strategic benefits to police agencies.

While it will undoubtedly be suggested that such volunteers are simply persons wanting to become paid police officers and are another example of the police institution imposing its worldview via enlisting more external agents in its narrow goals, this is not necessarily true. As Dobrin (2017, 722) remarks:

> A recent large survey of American Sheriff's Offices found that the primary motivation for volunteer officers was a sense of *community service*, with personal development, personal interest and offering useful skills following in importance (Wolf et al. 2015). Volunteer officers who do not wish to become full-time paid officers have wide-ranging motivations... Some volunteer for the sake of giving back to the community and the opportunity for personal fulfillment.

Volunteer officers and those who might fill such a role are not necessarily "poorly trained, aggressive and unaccountable police 'wanstables'" (Sleiman and Lippert 2010, 332), a popular label in relation to private security guards and urban 'ambassador' patrols. Many of these volunteers generously want to support their community for free. Such volunteers still need training, support, and some funding, but this is a far cry from demanding $119/hour CDN per officer from loyal funders. Because of greater integration with the community, and broken down blue walls for individuals, this would also mean there would be fewer restrictions on officers, and on what establishments and venues could be "worked," as well as less individual demand, since officers would not need to rely on such work (as noted there is some justification for paid detail if officers are to be restricted from any other secondary employment that other members of the community are not) as much as previously since they could engage in the same extra paid work the citizenry does. Many "gigs" would not need security as many of these are subtly or legally coerced by police before any approval of an event, parade, festival, rather than designated necessary by communities. Any other financial arrangements such as corporate sponsorship or donations not in the community interest or reflecting the public good would be seen as attempts to broker influence and to collect power and capital, rather than create healthier, safer neighbourhoods.

Let us state this starkly and unequivocally: we think community policing has neither been seriously embraced nor enacted since the emergence of this discourse first in North America and then across the globe decades ago. Its current iterations have little to do with community, the redistribution of resources, or the democratic control of social institutions. The idea of community policing has been deployed as rhetoric by police and government officials, used to extend some surveillance practices and to shore up police power as it is. Deukmedjian (2006) shows for example the "misalignment" between community policing and intelligence-led policing within the RCMP, Canada's largest police agency, where the embrace of community policing is minimal and dubious. This is happening *en masse*. Most programs introduced or operating under its banner, including those we have studied, such as Crime Stoppers (Lippert and Walby 2017; Lippert 2002) and community safety officers in Western Canada (Lippert and Walby 2019), are either hardly about community interests, or were temporary and so undernourished as to be doomed to fail from the outset in the few locales they were tried. Nor do we think community policing – if seriously and fully embraced – is a panacea for what ails the police as a greedy institution.

However, we do think embedded in many principles of community policing, hidden in earlier ideas especially, lie the seeds or even shallow roots from which a generous, as well as a civilian-centred, transformed policing institution controlled by communities could grow, as social and community development and its effects began to flourish alongside. It would be smaller, less expansive, and truly community-driven. Its expansion, replication, and power would never be put ahead of community and social development. Such an institution would serve at the pleasure of the community and look entirely different from what now exists, which is presently seeking to gobble up more and more resources, with limited effectiveness in reducing transgressions, having devastating effects of its own, and operating with little vision. Resources would be redirected to community and social development. While kindness might invoke "giving" and bringing us back to gift exchanges, perhaps even ignoring power relations, we mean something broader and deeper: a generous society oriented towards meeting diverse community needs. If the COVID-19 pandemic has taught us anything it is what seems like never changing arrangements "can" and "do," and that some generous acts that have happened in little enclaves, neighbourhoods, and via virtual exchanges, reveal potential and dire need for us to transform the orientation of our dominant institutions, including and especially the police, now, from greed to generosity.

References

Abbotsford Police. 2016. FOI Disclosure File 16-631 dated September 22.

ABC (American Broadcasting Corporation). 2020. "Houston Mayor apologizes to protester trampled by officer on horse" June KTRK 6/1/2020.

Association of Municipalities Ontario (AMO). 2015. *Building a New Public Safety Model in Ontario: AMO's Policing Modernization Report*. Toronto: AMO.

Altheide, D., and C. Schneider. 2012. *Qualitative Media Analysis*. Los Angeles: SAGE.

Athos Group. 2021. "Meet the team." https://www.athosgroup.com/about-us/meet-the-team/jeff-sweetin/.

Auditor General. 2010. *Toronto Police Service Paid Duty: Balancing Cost and Effectiveness*. Toronto: City of Toronto.

Austin Police Department. 2016. *Austin Police Department Policy Manual*. FOI Disclosure. Austin, Texas.

Ayling, J., and C. Shearing. 2008. "Taking Care of Business: Public Police as Commercial Security Vendors." *Criminology and Criminal Justice* 8 (1): 27–50.

Ayling, J., P. Grabosky, and C. Shearing. 2009. *Lengthening the Arm of the Law: Enhancing Police Resources in the 21st Century*. Cambridge: Cambridge University Press.

Aymaliev, I. 2017. "Corporate Motivations for Donating to the Police in Bulgaria." *East European Politics and Societies* 31 (4): 762–798.

Baines, D. 2010. "Neoliberal Restructuring, Activism/Participation, and Social Unionism in the Nonprofit Social Services." *Nonprofit and Voluntary Sector Quarterly* 39 (1): 10–28.

Banks, M. 2007. *Using Visual Data in Qualitative Research*. London: SAGE.

Barman, E. 2006. *Contesting Communities: The Transformation of Workplace Charity*. Stanford: Stanford University Press.

Barrett, D., and R. Mendick. 2012. "Private Firms Give UK Police Millions of Pounds to Investigate Crimes." *The Telegraph*. https://www.telegraph.co.uk/news/uknews/law-and-order/9061383/Private-firms-give-UK-police-forces-millions-of-pounds-to-investigate-crimes.html. February 5.

Bar-Nir, D., and J. Gal. 2010. "Who Has the Power? The Role of NPOs in Local Authorities." *Voluntas* 22: 1–25.

Barr, J. 2020. "Pipeline Exposed: Texas law enforcement moonlighting as Kinder Morgan pipeline security guards." https://www.kxan.com/investigations/pipeline-exposed-texas-law-enforcement-moonlighting-as-kinder-morgan-pipeline-security-guards/.

Baumer, E. 2008. "Evaluating the Balance Sheet of Asset Forfeiture Laws: Toward Evidence-Based Policy Assessments." *Criminology & Public Policy* 7: 245–256.

Bayley, D. 2002. "Law Enforcement and the Rule of Law: Is There a Tradeoff?" *Criminology & Public Policy* 2 (1): 133–154.

Bayley, D., and R. Perito. 2011. *Police Corruption: What Past Scandals Teach about Current Challenges*. United States Institute of Peace: Special Report. https://www.usip.org/sites/default/files/SR%20294.pdf.

BBC News UK. 2012. "Met Police got £22.7m from sponsors, FOI request finds." http://www.bbc.com/news/uk-20156574. November 1.

BC Local News. 2019. VIDEO: Delta Police Foundation returns with basketball tournament. https://www.bclocalnews.com/sports/video-delta-police-foundation-returns-with-basketball-tournament/. April 10.

Beaumont, H. 2021. "Revealed: Pipeline Company Paid Minnesota Police for Arresting and Surveilling Protesters." *The Guardian*. https://www.theguardian.com/uk-news/2021/oct/05/line-3-pipeline-enbridge-paid-police-arrest-protesters. October 5.

Beck, U. 1992. *Risk Society: Towards a New Modernity*. London: SAGE.

Before It's News. 2013. "Police Militarization Expo Urban Shield in Oakland." http://www.beforeitsnews.com/blogging-citizen-journalism/2013/10/group-gathers-to-protest-urban-shield-police-state-drill-in-oakland-nternational-war-games-in-california-to-train-police-and-corporate-mercenaries-to-massacre-americans-urban-sh-2449306.html. October 26.

Bell, D. 2014. "Ottawa Cops Rack Up Paid Duty Fees." *Ottawa Sun*. http://www.ottawasun.com/2014/09/02/ottawa-cops-rack-up-paid-duty-fees.

Bien, Y. 1997. "Bringing Strong Ties Back in: Indirect Ties, Network Bridges, and Job Searches in China." *American Sociology Review* 62: 366–385.

Bittle, S., and L. Snider. 2006. "From Manslaughter to Preventable Accident: Shaping Corporate Criminal Liability." *Law and Policy* 28 (4): 470–496.

Blatchford, C. 2009. "Police Ethics Advisor Quits Over Sponsors." *The Globe and Mail*. https://www.theglobeandmail.com/news/national/police-ethics-adviser-quits-over-sponsors/article4418828/. April 8.

Blomley, N. 2004. *Unsettling the City: Urban Land and the Politics of Property*. New York: Routledge.

Boetel, R. 2014. "Albuquerque Police Defend Camera Contract." *Albuquerque Journal*. https://www.officer.com/command-hq/news/11673464/albuquerque-police-defend-camera-contract. August 29.

Boise Police Department (BPD). 2015. *Boise Police Department Manual*. September.

Bollmer, G. 2018. *Theorizing Digital Cultures*. Los Angeles: SAGE.

Boston Municipal Research Bureau. 2008. "Paid detail in Boston should be changed." https://www.bmrb.org/wp-content/uploads/2014/10/Police1108.pdf. November.

Boston Police. 2004. "Rules and Procedures Rule 325 - PAID DETAILS." https://static1.squarespace.com/static/5086f19ce4b0ad16ff15598d/t/52af60cfe4b007c7c2257da2/1387225295091/Rule+325.pdf. August 16.

BPF. 2019a. "What is the Boston Police Foundation?" https://bostonpolicefoundation.org/what-is-the-boston-police-foundation/. November 27.

BPF. 2019b. "7th Annual Honoring our Heroes Night." https://bostonpolicefoundation.org/7th-annual-honoring-our-heroes-night/. July 30.

BPF. 2019c. "Outstanding Individuals of the Boston Police Department." https://bostonpolicefoundation.org/outstanding-individuals-of-the-boston-police-department/. February 21.

Bourdieu, P. 1989. "Social Space and Symbolic Power." *Sociological Theory* 7 (1): 14–25.

Brady, M., and R. Lippert (eds.). 2016. *Governing Practices: Neoliberalism, Governmentality, and the Ethnographic Imaginary.* Toronto: University of Toronto Press.

Brickey, S., and E. Comack. 1987. "The Role of Law in Social Transformation: Is a Jurisprudence of Insurgency Possible." *Canadian Journal of Law and Society* 2: 97–119.

Brighenti, A. 2007. "Visibility: A Category for the Social Sciences." *Current Sociology* 55: 323–342.

Broadwater, L., and D. Donovan. 2016. "Council Plans Hearing on Police Surveillance – Mayor and Governor Also Unaware of Aerial Video." *The Baltimore Sun.* NewsBank. August 26.

Bromley, P., and J. Meyer. 2017. "'They Are All Organizations': The Cultural Roots of Blurring Between Nonprofit, Business, and Government Sectors." *Administration & Society* 49 (7): 939–966.

Bruser, D., and D. Brazao. 2009. "Cops as Props? Off-Duty Police Cash in on Private 'paid Duty'." *Toronto Star.* December 9, A1.

Bullock, K. 2018a. "(Re) Presenting 'Order' Online: the Construction of Police Presentational Strategies on Social Media." *Policing and Society* 28 (3): 345–359.

Bullock, K. 2018b. "The Police Use of Social Media: Transformation or Normalisation?" *Social Policy and Society* 17 (2): 245–258.

Burpo, J. 1971. *The Police Labor Movement: Problems and Prospects.* Springfield: Charles Thomas Publisher.

Burris, S., P. Drahos, and C. Shearing. 2005. "Nodal Governance." *Australian Journal of Legal Philosophy* 30: 1–43.

Burgess, M. 2006. "Police Unions as Network Participants." In J. Fleming and J. Wood (eds.), *Fighting Crime Together: The Challenges of Policing and Security Networks.* Sydney: New South Wales Press, 150–169.

Burt, R. 1983. *Corporate Profits and Cooptation: Networks of Market Constraints and Directorate Ties in the American Economy.* New York: Academic Press.

Butler, D., and P. Delaney. 2010. "Starting a Police Foundation—Lessons Learned." *Police Chief,* LXXVII, http://www.policechiefmagazine.org/magazine/index.cfm?fuseaction=display_arch&article_id=2006&issue_id=22010.

Button, M., and A. Wakefield. 2018. 'The Real Private Police': Franchising Constables and the Emergence of Employer Supported Policing." In A. Hucklesby and S. Lister (eds.), *The Private Sector and Criminal Justice.* London: Palgrave Macmillan, 135–159.

Campeau, H. 2015. "'Police Culture' at Work: Making Sense of Police Oversight." *British Journal of Criminology* 55: 669–687.

Canadian Broadcasting Corporation (CBC). 2020a. "Toronto Police Seize $18M in Drugs, 65 Guns in Largest Single-Day Recovery." https://www.cbc.ca/news/canada/toronto/toronto-police-large-drug-gun-seizure-1.5844119. December 16.

Canadian Broadcasting Corporation (CBC). 2020b. "Derek Chauvin, Ex-cop Charged in George Floyd's Death, Faces 9 Tax Evasion Charges." https://www.cbc.ca/news/world/chauvin-tax-evasion-charged-1.5659867. July 23.

Canadian Broadcasting Corporation. 2000. "Toronto Cops Tone Down Operation True Blue?" February 1. https://www.cbc.ca/news/canada/toronto-cops-tone-down-operation-true-blue-1.245681.

Canadian Crime Stoppers. 2021. "About Us." https://www.canadiancrimestoppers.org/aboutus.

Canadian Justice Review Board. 2017. "Civil Forfeiture in Canada." https://www.canadianjusticereviewboard.ca/reports-papers/civil-forfeiture-in-canada.

Canadian Government News. 2014. "Police Sunglasses Raise Funds for Community Outreach Programs," June 19.

Canadian Press. 2014. "Tour Oakwood Heights: The Detroit 'ghost town' that Marathon Oil Created." https://financialpost.com/news/the-detroit-ghost-town-that-canadian-oil-helped-build. April 14.

Canadian Television Network (CTV). 2019. "Police Week Launches and Bail or Jail Returns." https://windsor.ctvnews.ca/police-week-launches-and-bail-or-jail-returns-1.4415948?cache=yes%3FautoPlay%3Dtrue%3FclipId%3D104062.

Cardoso, T., and M. Hayes. 2020. "Canadian Cities' Police Spending Ranges from One-10th to Nearly a Third of Total Budgets, Globe Analysis Finds." *Globe and Mail*. August 16.

Carman, J. 2015. "What You Don't Know Can Hurt Your Community: Lessons from a Local United Way." *Nonprofit Management & Leadership* 21 (4): 433–448.

Carriere, K., and R. Ericson. 1989. *Crime Stoppers: A Study in the Organization of Community Policing*. Toronto: Centre of Criminology, University of Toronto.

Carroll, W., N. Graham, and M. Shakespear. 2021. "Mapping the environmental field: Networks of foundations, ENGOs and think tanks." *Canadian Review of Sociology* 58 (3): 284-305.

Carter, A. 2013. "Group Protests Enbridge Donations to Hamilton Police." *CBC News*. http://www.cbc.ca/news/Canada/Hamilton/group-protests-enbridge-donations-to-Hamilton-police-1.1308945. June 5.

Carter, M., and S. Miletich. 2017. "Seattle City Light has Paid $7.8M to off-Duty Cops in 'Unusual Relationship'." https://www.seattletimes.com/seattlenews/seattle-city-light-has-paid-7-8m-to-off-duty-cops-in-unusual-relationship/.

Casey, L., and P. Loriggio. 2015. "Critics Want to see Changes to 'Rent-a-Cop' Programs in Canadian Cities." Canadian Broadcasting Corporation. http://www.cbc.ca/news/canada/toronto/critics-want-to-see-changes-to-rent-a-cop-programs-in-canadian-cities-1.3077503.

Chan, J., C. Devery, and S. Doran. 2003. *Fair Cop: Learning the Art of Policing*. Toronto: University of Toronto Press.

City of Boise. 2016a. FOI Disclosure 3439-1000-M7893.

City of Boise. 2016b. FOI Disclosure 3980-1000-M9554.

Clear, T. 2009. *Imprisoning Communities: How Mass Incarceration Makes Disadvantaged Neighborhoods Worse*. London: Oxford University Press.

Cleveland Foundation. 2021. "An idea whose time has come." http://www.clevelandfoundation100.org/timeline/?hide=#view-event-3483.

Coleman, S. 2004. "When Police Should Say "No!" to Gratuities." *Criminal Justice Ethics* 23 (1): 33–44.

Conti, N. 2006. "Role Call: Preprofessional Socialization into Police Culture." *Policing & Society* 16 (3): 221–242.

Conti, N. 2009. "A Visigoth System: Shame, Honor, and Police Socialization." *Journal of Contemporary Ethnography* 38 (3): 409–432.

Cope, N. 2004. "'Intelligence Led Policing or Policing Led Intelligence?' Integrating Volume Crime Analysis into Policing." *British Journal of Criminology* 44 (2): 188–203.

Copeman, J., and D. Banerjee. 2020. "Actual and Potential Gifts: Critique, Shadow Gift Relations and the Virtual Domain of the Ungiven." *Anthropological Theory* 21 (1): 28–49.

Coser, L. 1974. *Greedy Institutions: Patterns of Undivided Commitment*. New York: Free Press.

Côté-Lussier, C. 2013. "Narratives of Legitimacy: Police Expansionism and the Contest Over Policing." *Policing and Society* 23 (2): 183–203.

Council of Canadians. 2020. "Say no to Big Oil Funding Police." https://canadians.org/action/big-oil-funding-police.

Cox, A. 2016. "Mechanisms of Organizational Commitment: Adding Frames to Greedy Institution Theory." *Sociological Forum* 31 (3): 685–708.

CPYF. n.d. "Calgary Police Cadet Corps." https://www.yycyouthfoundation.ca/calgary-police-cadet-corps/.

Crank, J. 1994. "Watchman and Community: Myth and Institutionalization in Policing." *Law & Society Review* 28 (2): 325–352.

Crawford, A. 2006. "Networked Governance and The Post-Regulatory State? Steering, Rowing, and Anchoring the Provision of Policing and Security." *Theoretical Criminology* 10 (4): 449–479.

Creed, W., J. Langstraat, and M. Scully. 2002. "A Picture of the Frame: Frame Analysis as Technique and as Politics." *Organizational Research Methods* 5 (1): 34–55.

Crime Stoppers International. 2021a "Regions." https://csiworld.org/about-us.

Crime Stoppers International. 2021b. "About us." https://csiworld.org/about-us.

Crime Stoppers USA. 2021. "Locate a Program." https://www.crimestoppersusa.org/wp-content/uploads/2019/06/CSUSA-2019-Member-Programs-as-of-6.20.2019-1.pdf

Crump, J. 2011. "What Are the Police Doing on Twitter? Social Media, the Police and the Public." *Policy & Internet* 3 (4): 1–27.

CTV News. 2007. "Officer leaves OPP amid conflict questions at OLG." https://www.cbc.ca/news/canada/toronto/officer-leaves-opp-amid-conflict-questions-at-olg-1.653264. March 15.

Cunningham, W., J. Strauchs, and C. Van Meter. 1990. *The Hallcrest Report II: Private Security Trends (1970 to 2000)*. McLean, Virginia: Hallcrest Systems Inc. https://www.ojp.gov/pdffiles1/Digitization/126681NCJRS.pdf.

Currie, E. 2010. "Plain Left Realism: An Appreciation, and Some Thoughts for the Future." *Crime, Law and Social Change* 54 (2): 111–124.

Cwiek, S. 2013. "$8 Million Gift Nets Detroit's New Police, EMS Vehicles." *Michigan Radio*. https://www.michiganradio.org/post/8-million-gift-nets-detroit-new-police-ems-vehicles. August 22.

Dart, T. 2016. "Eye in the Sky: Billionaires' Surveillance Project Raises Privacy Fears in Baltimore." *The Baltimore Sun*. NewsBank. October 15.

Daurio, J. 2020. "Jersey City Brings Back Off-Duty Police Job Program Once Rife with Corruption." https://www.njspotlight.com/2020/12/nj-jersey-city-off-duty-police-jobs-program-shut-down-2018-federal-investigation-corruption-charges-revamped/. December 2.

Davis, R. 2010. "Thoughts on Starting a Police Foundation." *Police Chief*. http://www.policechiefmagazine.org/magazine/index. March.

De Campo, M. 2013. "Contemporary Greedy Institutions: An Essay on Lewis Coser's Concept in Times of the 'Hive Mind'." *Czech Sociological Review* 49 (6): 969–987.

Delaney, P. 1987. *About the New York City Police Foundation*. Honor: The 1987 Journal of the New York City Police Foundation.

Delaney, P. 2007. "Partnerships in 21st Century Policing." *Police Chief*. http://www.policechiefmagazine.org/magazine/index. August.

Delaney, P. 2010. "The Case for Police Foundation." Subject to Debate. http://www.policeforum.org/assets/docs/Subject_to_Debate/Debate2010/debate_2010_jun.pdf. June.

Delaney, P. 2011. "National Police Foundations project: Establishing private sector partnerships." The E-Newsletter of the COPS Office, 4. https://cops.usdoj.gov/html/dispatch/06-2011/NationalPoliceFoundationsProject.asp.

Dellora, C., and L. Beck. 2021. "Imposing Fees for Police Services in Australia." *Griffiths Law Review*. Online First.

Denzin, N., and C. Keller. 1981. "Frame Analysis Reconsidered: A Review of Goffman's Frame Analysis." *Contemporary Sociology* 10 (1): 52–60.

Department of Justice, US Attorney's Office. 2018. "Press Release: Former Jersey City Chief Of Police Admits Fraud Involving Off-Duty Work Assignments." https://www.justice.gov/usao-nj/pr/former-jersey-city-chief-police-admits-fraud-involving-duty-work-assignments. January 5.

Department of Justice. 2011. *Investigation of the New Orleans Police Department*. United States: Department of Justice Civil Rights Division.

Deukmedjian, J. 2006. "From Community to Intelligence: Executive Realignment of RCMP Mission." *Canadian Journal of Criminology and Criminal Justice* 48 (4): 523–542.

DiMaggio, P., and W. Powell. 1983. "The Iron Cage Revisited: Collective Rationality and Institutional Isomorphism in Organizational Fields." *American Sociological Review* 48: 147–160.

Dimant, E., and G. Tosato. 2018. "Causes and Effects of Corruption: What Has Past Decade's Empirical Research Taught Us? A Survey." *Journal of Economic Surveys* 32 (2): 335–356.

Diphoorn, T., and E. Grassiani. 2016. "Securitizing Capital: A Processual-Relational Approach to Pluralized Security." *Theoretical Criminology* 20 (4): 430–445.

Dobrin, A. 2017. "Volunteer Police: History, Benefits, Costs and Current Descriptions." *Security Journal* 30 (3): 717–733.

Donovan, D. 2016a. "Private Fund Public Mistrust – Charitable Donations to Baltimore Police Have Been Followed by Criticism of Secrecy." *The Baltimore Sun*. NewsBank.

Donovan, D. 2016b. "Donors Support More Than Just Aerial Video – Laura, John Arnold Gave Millions to Area Universities." *The Baltimore Sun*. NewsBank.

Dreschel, A. 2015. "Dreschel: Enbridge Pulls Plug on Police Grants." *Hamilton Spectator*. https://www.thespec.com/opinion/columnists/2015/11/09/dreschel-enbridge-pulls-plug-on-police-grants.html.

Druley, L. 2002. "Cop Cars for Ads." Minnesota Public Radio. http://news.minnesota.publicradio.org/features/200212/10_druleyl_squadads/.

Duncan, J. and K. Walby. 2022. "Police Union Political Communications in Canada." *British Journal of Criminology* 62 (1): 90-105.

Duffin, C. 2013. "Police Commissioner Wants Private Firms to Sponsor Cars and Stations." *The Telegraph*. https://www.telegraph.co.uk/news/uknews/crime/10031215/Police-commissioner-wants-private-firms-to-sponsor-cars-and-stations.html. May 2.

Dupont, B. 2004. "Security in the Age of Networks." *Policing and Society* 14 (1): 76–91.

Dupont, B. 2006. "Delivering Security through Networks: Surveying the Relational Landscape of Security Managers in an Urban Setting." *Crime, Law & Social Change* 45 (3): 165–184.

Eikenberry, A., and J. Kluver. 2004. "The Marketization of the Non-Profit Sector: Civil Society at Risk?" *Public Administration Review* 64 (2): 132–140.

Ellis, J., and A. McGovern. 2016. "The End of Symbiosis? Australia Police–Media Relations in the Digital Age." *Policing and Society* 26 (8): 944–962.

Ellison, G., and M. Brogden. 2012. *Policing in an Age of Austerity: A Postcolonial Perspective*. London: Routledge.

England, K. 2019. "Maine State Police K9 Dallas to Get Donation of Body Armor." *Department of Public Safety – Maine State Police*. https://www.maine.gov/dps/msp/media-center/public-releases/maine-state-police-k9-dallas-get-donation-body-armor. November 7.

EPF. 2018a. ":#TBFYEG: True-Blue Friends Investing in a Safer Edmonton." http://truebluefriendyeg.com/true-blue-friends-investing-in-a-safer-edmonton. October 23.

EPF. 2018b. "#TBFYEG Doug's Story." http://truebluefriendyeg.com/dougs-story. October 10.

Ericson, R. 2007. *Crime in an Insecure World*. London: Polity.

Ericson, R., and K. Haggerty. 1997. *Policing the Risk Society*. Toronto: University of Toronto Press.

Federman, A. 2015. "Kinder Morgan Paid Pennsylvania Police Department to 'Deter Protests'." *Earth Island Journal*. https://www.earthisland.org/journal/index.php/articles/entry/kinder_morgan_paid_pennsylvania_police_department_to_deter_protests/. May 21.

Extra Duty Solutions. 2021. "Company History." https://extradutysolutions.com/history-growth/.

Extra Duty Solutions. 2020a. "Client List." http://www.ci.orange.nj.us/Reso_356_2020_Extra_Duty_(amended).pdf.

Extra Duty Solutions. 2020b. "Cover letter from EDS to Purchasing Agent for City of Orange Township for Bid dated February 25." http://www.ci.orange.nj.us/Reso_356_2020_Extra_Duty_(amended).pdf.

Fenton, J., and D. Donovan. 2016. "Use of Local Foundation Allowed Baltimore Police Surveillance Project to Remain Secret." *The Baltimore Sun*. http://www.baltimoresun.com/news/maryland/baltimore-city/bs-md-ci-community-foundation20160824-story.html.

Fernandez, K., and J. Tremblay-Boire. 2021. "Raising Money for Government and Connecting Community: The Isomorphic Rise of Nonprofit Police Foundations Across the US." *Public Performance & Management Review* 44: 1–33.

Financial Fraud Action UK. n.d. "Dedicated Cheque and Plastic Crime Unit." http://www.financialfraudaction.org.uk/police-the-dcpcu.asp?genre=police&pagecontent=0

Fleming, J., M. Marks, and J. Wood. 2006. "'Standing on the Inside Looking Out': The Significance of Police Unions in Networks of Police Governance." *Australian & New Zealand Journal of Criminology* 39 (1): 71–89.

Fleury-Steiner, B., and K. Wiles. 2003. "Use of Commercial Advertisements on Public Police Cars in the United States, Post 9/11." *Policing and Society* 13 (4): 441–450.

Foucault., M. 1988. *Politics Philosophy Culture: Interviews and Other Writings 1977-1984*. New York: Routledge.

Fridman, D., and A. Luscombe. 2017. "Gift-Giving, Disreputable Exchange, and the Management of Donations in a Police Department." *Social Forces* 96 (2): 507–528.

Frizell Group. 2021. "About Us." https://frizellgroup.com/about-us/

Gallaher, C. 2016. *The Politics of Staying Put: Condo Conversion and Tenant Right to Buy in Washington D.C.*. Philadelphia: Temple University Press.

Gallant, M., C. King, and C. Walker. 2014. "Civil Processes and Tainted Assets: Exploring Canadian Models of Forfeiture." *Dirty Assets: Emerging Issues in the Regulation of Criminal and Terrorist Assets. Farnham: Ashgate*, 165–181.

Gallant, M., and C. King. 2013. "The Seizure of Illicit Assets: Patterns of Civil Forfeiture in Canada and Ireland." *Common Law World Review* 42 (1): 91–109.

Gans, J. 2000. "Privately Paid Public Policing: Law and Practice." *Policing and Society* 10 (2): 183–206.

Garda Inspectorate. 2015. *Changing Police in Ireland: Delivering a Visible, Accessible and Responsive Service*. Dublin, Ireland: Garda Inspectorate.

Giacomantonio, C. 2014. "A Typology of Police Organizational Boundaries." *Policing and Society* 24 (5): 545–565.

Gibson, G., and D. Wilber. 2004. "Norris Enters Plea of Guilty to Corruption." *The Baltimore Sun*. http://www.baltimoresun.com/bal-te.md.norris09mar09-story.

Giddens, A. 1991. *Modernity and Self-Identity: Self and Society in the Late Modern Age*. Cambridge, UK: Polity Press.

Gill, P. 2006. "Not Just Joining the Dots but Crossing the Borders and Bridging the Voids: Constructing Security Networks after 11 September 2001." *Policing and Society* 16 (1): 27–49.

Gilbert, D. 2021. "Cops for $1,000 a day: How Seattle spends millions hiring off-duty police officers but does little to monitor their moonlighting." https://www.seattletimes.com/seattle-news/times-watchdog/as-off-duty-police-reforms-languish-a-for-profit-force-rises/ April 11.

Godbout, J., and A. Caillé. 1998. *The World of the Gift*, trans Donald Winkler. Montreal: McGill-Queen's University Press.

Goff, C., and C. Reasons. 1978. *Corporate Crime in Canada: A Critical Analysis of Anti-Combines Legislation*. Scarborough: Prentice-Hall of Canada.

Goffman, E. 1961. *Asylums: Essays on the Social Situation of Mental Patients and Other Inmates*. New York: Anchor Books.

Goffman, E. 1981. "A Reply to Denzin and Keller." *Contemporary Sociology* 10 (1): 60–68.

Goodman, J. 2021. "A Year After 'Defund." *Police Departments Get Their Money Back. New York Times*. https://www.nytimes.com/2021/10/10/us/dallas-police-defund.html. October 10.

Grabosky, P. 2007. "Private Sponsorship of Public Policing." *Police Practice and Research* 8 (1): 5–16.

Grant, M. 1977. "Relationship of Moonlighting to Job Dissatisfaction in Police Officers." *Journal of Police Science and Administration* 5 (2): 193–196.

Haggerty, K. 2003. "From Risk to Precaution: Rationalities of Personal Crime Prevention." In R. Ericson and A. Doyle (eds.), *Risk and Morality*, Toronto: University of Toronto Press, 193–214.

Hamilton Spectator. 2013. "Police have 60 days to comment on Enbridge." https://www.thespec.com/news/hamilton-region/2013/08/16/police-have-60-days-to-comment-on-enbridge.html. August 16.

Hauff, B. 2018. "Longboat Police Get Donation for New Traffic Cameras, Cruiser Computers." *Your Observer*. https://www.yourobserver.com/article/longboat-police-get-donation-for-new-traffic-cameras-cruiser-computers. February 13.

Henderson, G. 2000. "Questioning Contract Cops." *Windsor Star A3*. September 9.

Holcomb, J., T. Kovandzic, and M. Williams. 2011. "Civil Asset Forfeiture, Equitable Sharing, and Policing for Profit in the United States." *Journal of Criminal Justice* 39 (3): 273–285.

Holcomb, J., M. Williams, W. Hicks, T. Kovandzic, and M. Meitl. 2018. "Civil Asset Forfeiture Laws and Equitable Sharing Activity by the Police." *Criminology & Public Policy* 17 (1): 101–127.

Horn, A. 2020. "George Floyd and Derek Chauvin Were Once Co-Workers, Ex-Club Owner Tells TV Station." https://www.npr.org/2020/05/29/865803157/george-floyd-and-derek-chauvin-were-co-workers-says-former-club-owner. May 29.

Houston Chronicle. 2021. "Woman Trampled by Mounted Houston Police Officer at Black Lives Matter Demonstration Sues HPD, City." https://www.houstonchronicle.com/news/houston-texas/houston/article/Woman-trampled-by-mounted-Houston-police-officer-15922701.php. February 3.

Houston Police Foundation. 2021a. "Our Recently Funded Projects." https://www.houstonpolicefoundation.org/funding.

Houston Police Foundation. 2021b. "Applying for a Grant." https://www.houstonpolicefoundation.org/grants.

Houston Police Foundation. 2021c. Tactical Village. "The Houston Police Foundation's Newest Project." https://www.houstonpolicefoundation.org/funding/tactical-village.

Hu, X., K. Rodgers, and N. Lovrich. 2018. "We Are More than Crime Fighters: Social Media Images of Police Departments." *Police Quarterly* 21 (4): 544–572.

Huey, L. 2007. *Negotiating Demands: The Politics of Skid Row Policing in Edinburgh, San Francisco, and Vancouver*. Toronto: University of Toronto Press.

Huey, L., J. Nhan, and R. Broll. 2012. "'Uppity Civilians' and 'Cyber-Vigilantes': the Role of the General Public in Policing Cyber-Crime." *Criminology and Criminal Justice* 13 (1): 81–97.

Hunt, A. 1997. "Moral Regulation and Making-Up the New Person: Putting Gramsci to Work." *Theoretical Criminology* 1 (3): 275–301.

Hunt, A. 1999. *Governing Morals: A Social History of Moral Regulation*. Cambridge: Cambridge University Press.

IACP. 2017. "Police Foundations Section." http://www.iacp.org/Police-Foundations-Section.

Ingraham, C. 2015. "New report: In tough times, police start seizing a lot more stuff from people." https://www.washingtonpost.com/news/wonk/wp/2015/11/10/report-in-lean-times-police-start-taking-a-lot-more-stuff-from-people/.

International Conference for Police and Law Enforcement Executives (ICPLEE). 2014a. International Conference for Police and Law Enforcement Executives. http://www.internationalpoliceconference.com/home. August 27.

International Conference for Police and Law Enforcement Executives (ICPLEE). 2014b. "Trade Show and Sponsorship opportunities." http://www.internationalpoliceconference.com/files/brochures/trade%20show%20brochure.pdf. August 27.

Ipsos. 2020. "Canadians divided on whether to defund the Police: 51% Support the idea, 49% Oppose It." https://www.ipsos.com/en-ca/news-and-polls/Canadians-Divided-On-Whether-To-Defund-Police.

Jacques, I. 2019. "Delta police reach out to youth through basketball." *Delta Optimist* April 18. https://www.delta-optimist.com/local-news/delta-police-reach-out-to-youth-through-basketball-3097887

Jagodzinski, J. 1998. "Deconstructing the Master Signifier of Community: Between the Pre-Modern and Modern Community of Organic Solidarity and the Postmodern Community of Technological Dissemination in Cyberspace." *Journal of Social Theory in Art Education* 18: 4–20.

Jancsics, D. 2014. "Interdisciplinary Perspectives on Corruption." *Sociology Compass* 8 (4): 358–372.

Jancsics, D. 2015. "'A Friend Gave Me A Phone Number': Brokerage in Low-Level Corruption." *International Journal of Law, Crime and Justice* 43 (1): 68–87.

Jancsics, D., and I. Jávor. 2012. "Corrupt Governmental Networks." *International Public Management Journal* 15 (1): 62–99.

Jaywork, C. 2017. "Burgess Seeks to Clamp Down on Police Moonlighting." https://www.seattleweekly.com/news/burgess-seeks-to-clamp-down-on-police-moonlighting/. September 27.

Jenks, D. 2009. "Police Corruption or Police Productivity? Officers Perceptions of Moonlighting in U.S. Agencies." *Critical Issues in Justice and Politics* 2 (2): 87–104.

Johnson, K. 2012. "Police Group Receives Donation from Taser Stun-Gun Maker." *USA Today*. https://www.usatoday.com/story/news/nation/2012/10/21/taser-police-chiefs/1627299/. October 21.

Johnson, K. 2011. "Police museum Donors Are Contract Recipients." *USA Today*. http://usatoday30.usatoday.com/news/nation/story/2011-11-13/law-enforcement-museum-corporate-donations/51190170/1. November 14.

Johnston, L. 2007. "'Keeping the Family Together'. Police Community Support Officers and the 'Police Extended Family' in London." *Policing and Society* 17 (2): 119–140.

Jolowicz, C. 1994. *Seconded Police Officers: The Experience of the North East Region*. London: Police Research Group. http://www.ncjrs.gov/app/publications/abstract.aspx?ID=149294.

Juris, H., and P. Feuille. 1973. *Police Unionism: Power and Impact in Public-Sector Bargaining*. Lexington: Lexington Books.

Kania, R. 1988. "Should We Tell the Police to Say "Yes" to Gratuities?" *Criminal Justice Ethics* 7 (2): 37–49.

Kappeler, V., R. Sluder, and G. Alpert. 1998. *Forces of Deviance: Understanding the Dark Side of Policing*. Long Grove: Waveland Press.

Karpiak, K. 2010. "Of Heroes and Polemics: 'The Policeman' in Urban Ethnography." *PoLAR: Political and Legal Anthropology Review* 33: 7–31.

Kern, L. 2011. *Sex and the Revitalized City: Gender, Condominium Development, and Urban Citizenship*. Vancouver: UBC Press.

Kilborn, P. 2003. "Police Superintendent Resigns in Maryland After Indictment." *New York Times*. http://www.nytimes.com/2003/12/11/us/police-superintendent-resigns-in-maryland-after-indictment.html.

Kleinig, J. 2002. "Rethinking Noble Cause Corruption." *International Journal of Police Science and Management* 4 (4): 287–314.

Kringen, A., and M. Novich. 2018. "Is It 'Just Hair' or Is It 'Everything'? Embodiment and Gender Repression in Policing." *Gender, Work & Organization* 25 (2): 195–213.

Kupferman, S. 2014. "Paid-Duty Policing: Toronto's Perennial Scandal." *Toronto Life*. https://torontolife.com/city/paid-duty-policing-torontos-perennial-scandal/. May 12.

Kuypers, J. 2005. "Framing Analysis." In J. Kuypers (ed.), *The Art of Rhetorical Criticism*. Boston: Allyn & Bacon, 186–211.

Kuypers, J., and S. Cooper. 2005. "A Comparative Framing Analysis of Embedded and Behind-the-Lines Reporting on the 2003 Iraq War." *Qualitative Research Reports in Communication* 6 (1): 1–10.

LaFleche, G. 2009. "Hiring of Officers for Special Events Under Review." *St Catharines Standard*. May 9.

LAPD. n.d. "Equipment/Technology." https://www.supportlapd.org/what-we-do/equipment-technology.

Lawson, J. 2021. "Lines of Work, Corridors of Power: Extraction, Obstruction, and Counter-Obstruction along Fossil Fuel Production Networks Regime of Obstruction." In W. K. Carroll (ed.), *Regime of Obstruction: How Corporate Power Blocks Energy Democracy*. Edmonton: Athabasca University Press, 61–90.

Lazar, K. 2007. "For Cruisers, and Ad-on." *The Boston Globe*. http://archive.boston.com/news/local/articles/2007/11/30/for_cruisers_an_ad_on/. November 30.

Lazare, S. 2013. "Urban Shield: 'The Epitome of State Repression' Coming to Town Near You." *Common Dreams*. https://www.commondreams.org/news/2013/10/24/urban-shield-epitome-state-repression-coming-town-near-you. October 24.

Lea, J. 2016. "Left Realism: A Radical Criminology for the Current Crisis." *International Journal for Crime, Justice and Social Democracy* 5 (3): 53–65.

Lea, J. 2010. "Left Realism, Community, and State-Building." *Crime, Law and Social Change* 54 (2): 141–158.

Lee, M., and A. McGovern. 2013. "Force to Sell: Policing the Image and Manufacturing Public Confidence." *Policing and Society* 23 (2): 103–124.

Lewis, M. 2017a. "Memo: Seattle Cop Bragged that "Mini-Mafia" Controlled Off-Duty Contracts." http://mynorthwest.com/760494/memo-seattle-copbragged-that-mini-mafia-controlled-off-duty-contracts. September 22.

Lewis, M. 2017b. "Seattle Cops Off-Duty Work Comes Under Investigation." https://mynorthwest.com/756169/off-duty-seattle-officers/ September 20.

Little Sis/Color of Change and Public Accountability Initiative/Little. 2021. "Police foundations: A corporate-sponsored threat to democracy and black lives." Report. October 21. https://policefoundations.org.

Lippert, R. 2002. "Policing Property and Moral Risk Through Promotions, Anonymization, and Rewards: Crime Stoppers Revisited." *Social & Legal Studies* 11 (4): 475–502.

Lippert, R. 2006. *Sanctuary, Sovereignty, Sacrifice: Canadian Sanctuary Incidents, Power and Law*. Vancouver: UBC Press.

Lippert, R. 2019. *Condo Conquest: Urban Governance, Law and Condoization in New York City and Toronto*. Vancouver: UBC Press.

Lippert, R., and Newell, B. 2016. "Debate Introduction: the Privacy and Surveillance Implications of Police Body Cameras. *Surveillance & Society*, 14(1): 113–116.

Lippert, R., K. Walby, and P. Taylor. 2016. "Capital Exchanges, Security Networks, and User Pays Policing." *Criminology, Criminal Justice, Law and Society* 17 (2): 18–33.

Lippert, R., K. Walby, and B. Wilkinson. 2016. "Spins, Stalls, and Shutdowns: Pitfalls of Qualitative Policing and Security Research." *Forum Qualitative Sozialforschung/Forum: Qualitative Social Research*. 17 (1).

Lippert, R., and K. Walby. 2017. "Funneling through Foundations and Crime Stoppers: How Public Police Create and Span Inter-Organisational Boundaries." *Policing and Society* 27 (6): 602–619.

Lippert, R., and K. Walby. 2019. *A Criminology of Policing and Security Frontiers*. Bristol: Bristol University Press.

Lippert, R., and B. Wilkinson. 2010. "Capturing Crime, Criminals and the Public's Imagination: Assembling Crime Stoppers and CCTV Surveillance." *Crime, Media, Culture* 6 (2): 131–152.

Loader, I. 2016. "In Search of Civic Policing: Recasting the 'Peelian' Principles." *Criminal Law and Philosophy* 10 (3): 427–440.

Loader, I., and N. Walker. 2001. "Policing as a Public Good: Reconstituting the Connections Between Policing and the State." *Theoretical Criminology* 5 (1): 9–35.

Loftus, B. 2010. "Police Occupational Culture: Classic Themes, Altered Times." *Policing and Society* 20 (1): 1–20.

Long Island Press. 2013. "New Revelations in Nassau County Police Department Conspiracy Case." https://www.longislandpress.com/2013/02/01/new-revelations-in-nassau-county-police-department-conspiracy-case/.

Luscombe, A., K. Walby, and R. Lippert. 2018. "Police-Sponsorship Networks: Benign Ties or Relations of Private Influence?" *Policing and Society* 28 (5): 553–569.

Luscombe, A., K. Walby, and R. Lippert. 2017a. "Brokering Access beyond the Border and in the Wild: Comparing Freedom of Information Law and Policy in Canada and the United States." *Law & Policy* 39 (3): 259–279.

Luscombe, A., K. Walby, and R. Lippert. 2017b. "Readers' Comments as Popular Texts: Public Opinions of Paid Duty Policing in Canada." *Canadian Journal of Communication* 42 (5): 745–765.

McCarthy, N. 2017. "How Much Do U.S. Cities Spend Every Year on Policing?" *Forbes*. https://www.forbes.com/sites/niallmccarthy/2017/08/07/how-much-do-u-s-cities-spend-every-year-on-policing-infographic/?sh=623cb2b2e7b7.

McDonald, T. 2017a. "What We Know About the Federal Probe of Jersey City police." https://www.nj.com/hudson/index.ssf/2017/01/what_you_should_know_about_the_jersey_city_off-dut.html.

McDonald, T. 2017b. "Jersey City Cop Admits Taking $55K in Off-Duty Jobs Scheme." https://www.nj.com/hudson/index.ssf/2017/06/jersey_city_cop_pleads_guilty_to_federal_bribery_c.html.

McDonald, T. 2017c. "3 More Cops Face Prison in Federal Probe of Jersey City Police." https://www.nj.com/hudson/2017/07/number_of_guilty_pleas_in_federal_probe_of_jersey.html. July 27.

McDonald, T. 2018a. "Ex-Jersey City police chief admits stealing $31K from city's housing authority." https://www.nj.com/hudson/index.ssf/2018/01/ex-jersey_city_police_chief_admits_stealing_31k_fr.html.

McDonald, T. 2018b. "Ex-Jersey City Police Chief Says he Warned City About Off-Duty Jobs Scam." https://www.nj.com/hudson/index.ssf/2018/01/exjersey_city_police_chief_says_he_warned_city_of.html.

McDonald, T. 2018c. "Jersey City mayor faces police ire over halting off-duty jobs." https://www.nj.com/hudson/index.ssf/2018/01/jersey_city_mayor_faces_police_ire_over_halting_of.html.

McDonald, D. 2014. "Public Ambiguity and the Multiple Meanings of Corporatization." In D. McDonald (ed.), *Rethinking Corporatization and Public Services in the Global South*. London: Zed Books, 1–30.

McDonald, T. 2019. "Eleventh Jersey City Cop Admits Guilt in Off-Duty Jobs Scheme." *Jersey Journal*. Eleventh Jersey City cop admits guilt in off-duty jobs scheme - nj.com.

McDowell, M., and L. Fernandez. 2018. "'Disband, Disempower, and Disarm': Amplifying the Theory and Practice of Police Abolition." *Critical Criminology* 26 (3): 373–391.

McEvoy, J. 2020. "At Least 13 Cities Are Defunding Their Police Departments." *Forbes*. https://www.forbes.com/sites/jemimamcevoy/2020/08/13/at-least-13-cities-are-defunding-their-police-departments/?sh=748351d629e3.

MacDonald, C., M. McDonald, and W. Norman. 2002. "Charitable Conflicts of Interest." *Journal of Business Ethics* 39 (1-2): 67–74.

Macintyre, S., and T. Prenzler. 1999. "The Influence of Gratuities and Personal Relationships on Police Use of Discretion." *Policing and Society* 9 (2): 181–201.

MacMahon, M., and D. Wong. 2021. "$1M Donation to Vancouver policing Inappropriate, Critics say." https://www.citynews1130.com/2021/02/22/critics-donation-vancouver-policing/ February 22.

Maddox, J., and R. Firstenberg. 1975. *Private Sector Assistance to the Cleveland Police Department*. Cleveland: Cleveland Foundation.

Maier, F., M. Meyer, and M. Steinbereithner. 2016. "Non-Profit Organizations Becoming Business-Like: A Systematic Review." *Non-profit and Voluntary Sector Quarterly* 45 (1): 64–86.

Manning, P. 2008. "Performance Rituals." *Policing: A Journal of Policy and Practice* 2 (3): 284–293.

Marathon Michigan Refining Division. 2014. "Community Update May 2014. Wide Range of Topics at Recent Community Meeting." http://www.detroitrefinery.com/external/content/document/6025/2169422/1/newsletter percent20-percent20issue percent205 percent20 percent28may percent202014 percent29 percent20v1.pdf. May.

Marketwire Canada. 2011. "London Drugs Pays Tribute to the Vancouver Police Foundation." *Comtex New Network*. June 24.

Marshall, R. 2009. "Police Chiefs' Links With Taser Sniffy." *Winnipeg Free Press*. https://www.winnipegfreepress.com/opinion/analysis/police-chiefs-links-with-taser-sniffy-64689642.html. October 18.

Martin, J. 2013. "Informal Security Nodes and Force Capital." *Policing and Society* 23 (2): 145–163.

Matier, P. 2019. "Businesses Hiring Real SF Copes on OT to Keep Crime Down, Employees Safe." *San Francisco Chronicle*. https://www.sfchronicle.com/bayarea/philmatier/article/Businesses-hiring-real-SF-cops-on-OT-to-keep-14365181.php. August 21.

Matheny, K. 2016. "Enbridge Hit with a $177M Bill for Michigan, Illinois Oil Spills." *Detroit Free Press*. July 20 https://www.freep.com/story/news/local/michigan/2016/07/20/enbridge-reaches-177m-settlement-oil-spills/87336380/.

Matthews, T. 2018 "Outside the Box Grant Sources for Law Enforcement." *Police 1*. https://www.police1.com/police-grants/articles/outside-the-box-grant-sources-for-law-enforcement-kWAcBJmymHq2R258/. December 10.

Matthews, T. 2019. "Outside-the-Box Funding for Police Fleets." *Police Grants Help*. https://www.policegrantshelp.com/columnists/digital-edition/articles/outside-the-box-funding-for-police-fleets-T6LYNW7x0lDTXIq9/. October 24.

Mau, S. 2019. *The Metric Society: On the Quantification of the Social*. London: John Wiley and Sons.

Mawby, R., and S. Worthington. 2002. "Marketing the Police: From a Force to a Service." *Journal of Marketing Management* 18 (9-10): 857–876.

Mawby, R. 2013. *Policing Images: Policing, Communication and Legitimacy*. London: Willan.

Mayer, J. 2016. *Dark Money: The Hidden History of the Billionaires Behind the Rise of the Radical Right*. New York: Anchor Books.

McKaig, W. 2006. *Review of Contract Duty Policing Issue for the Windsor Police Services Board*. Windsor, Ontario: Sullivan-Mahoney, LLP.

McLelland, E. 2016. "Britain's Private Police Force: How More than 1,100 Officers Have Been Funded by Millions in Contributions from Schools, Businesses And Councils." *Daily Mail*. http://www.dailymail.co.uk/news/article-3383407/Britain-s-private-police-force-1-100-officers-funded-millions-contributions-schools-businesses-councils.html. January 4.

Meijer, A., and M. Thaens. 2013. "Social Media Strategies: Understanding the Differences between North American Police Departments." *Government Information Quarterly* 30 (4): 343–350.

Meijer, A., and R. Torenvlied. 2016. "Social Media and the New Organization of Government Communications: an Empirical Analysis of Twitter Usage by the Dutch Police." *American Review of Public Administration* 46 (2): 143–161.

Miami-Dade Police Department. 2016. *Community Relations Section: Standard Operating Procedures.*. Miami, Florida: FOI Disclosure.

Miami-Dade Police Department. 2021. "Off-Duty Police Services." https://www.miamidade.gov/global/service.page?Mduid_service=ser1508436203916940.

Miletich, S., and M. Carter. 2017. "Seattle police officials concerned about officers' off-duty work before FBI probe." https://www.seattletimes.com/seattlenews/crime/seattle-police-officials-concerned-about-officers-off-duty-work-before-fbi-probe/.

Miller, G., and R. Presley. 1973. "Multi-Jobholding by Fireman and Policemen Compared." *Public Personnel Management* 2 (4): 283–289.

Miller, M., and L. Selva. 1994. "Drug Enforcement's Double-Edged Sword: An Assessment of Asset Forfeiture Programs." *Justice Quarterly* 11: 313–335.

Miller, S., K. Forest, and N. Jurik. 2003. "Diversity in Blue: Lesbian and Gay Police Officers in a Masculine Occupation." *Men and Masculinities* 5 (4): 355–385.

Milmo, C., and D. Kirby. 2019 "'Officers for Sale': Budget Airline Easyjet among Companies Funding Police as Forces Raise Millions from Private Contracts." *iNews UK*. https://inews.co.uk/news/uk/officers-for-sale-police-forces-raising-millions-a-year-from-private-contracts-with-companies-including-major-airline-and-supermarket-276754. April 5.

Moores, E. 2009. "Reforming the Civil Asset Forfeiture Reform Act." *Arizona Law Review* 51: 777.

Mopas, M., and P. Stenning. 2001. "Tools of The Trade: The Symbolic Power of Private Security: An Exploratory Study." *Policing and Society* 11 (1): 67–97.

Moran, D. 2014. "Leaving Behind the 'Total Institution'? Teeth, Transcarceral Spaces and (Re) Inscription of the Formerly Incarcerated Body." *Gender, Place & Culture* 21 (1): 35–51.

Mota, C. 2017. "Seventh Jersey City Cop Pleads Guilty in Off-Duty Work Scheme." https://www.nj.com/hudson/index.ssf/2017/09/seventh_jersey_city_cop_pleads_guilty_to_federal_c.html.

Mulone, M. 2011. "When Private and Public Policing Merge: Thoughts on Commercial Policing." *Social Justice* 38 (1/2): 165–183.

Mulvany, L., and G. Gordon. 2014. "Motorola spreads its money and influence far and wide." *McClatchy DC Bureau*. https://www.mcclatchydc.com/news/nation-world/national/economy/article24765652.html.

Murthy, D. 2008. "Digital Ethnography: An Examination of the Use of New Technologies for Social Research." *Sociology* 42 (5): 837–855.

New York. 1972. *The Knapp Commission Report on Police Corruption*. George Braziller. New York City Police Department (NYPD) 2016. "Paid Details." http://www.nyc.gov/html/nypd/downloads/pdf/public_information/nypd-258_paid_details_2016-06-16.pdf.

New York City Police Department (NYPD). 2021. "Crime Stoppers." https://www1.nyc.gov/site/nypd/services/see-say-something/crimestoppers.page.

News12 Staff. 2018. "Jersey City Puts End to Police Officers Working Off-Duty Jobs." https://newjersey.news12.com/jersey-city-puts-end-to-police-officers-working-off-duty-jobs-37409999.

NOPJF. 2019. "The Baby is Back!" https://nopjf.org/the-baby-is-back/. January 10.

NYCPF. 2017a. "40 Year History." http://www.nycpolicefoundation.org/about-us/40-year-history/.

NYCPF. 2017b. "Real Time Crime Center." http://www.nycpolicefoundation.org/programs/real-time-crime-center/.

NYCPF. 2020a. "NYPD Holiday Sleigh Ride." https://www.nycpolicefoundation.org/sleighride/. December 23.

NYCPF. 2020b. "Police Foundation Partners with NY Giants." https://www.nycpolicefoundation.org/togetherblue/. August 27.

NYCPF. 2020c. "New NYPD Bullet-Resistant Vest Pilot." https://www.nycpolicefoundation.org/vestpilot/. December 23.

NYCPF. 2018. "2018 Gala." http://www.nycpolicefoundation.org/2018-gala/. May 18.

Nicholson-Crotty, S., J. Nicholson-Crotty, D. Li, and S. Mughan, 2020. "Race, Representation, and Assets Forfeiture." *International Public Management Journal* 24(2): 1–20.

O'Brien, F. 2020. "Developers hope to Reclaim Vancouver's Downtown Eastside." https://www.vancouverisawesome.com/real-estate/developers-reclaim-vancouver-downtown-eastside-2666897. August 26.

O'Connor, C. 2017. "The Police on Twitter: Image Management, Community Building, and Implications for Policing in Canada." *Policing and Society* 27 (8): 899–912.

O'Hara, P., and V. Sainato. 2015. "Monetizing the Police: Corruption Vectors in Agency-Managed off-Duty Work." *Policy and Society* 34 (2): 151–164.

O'Malley, P., and S. Hutchinson. 2007. "Converging Corporatization? Police Management, Police Unionism, and the Transfer of Business Principles." *Police Practice and Research* 8 (2): 159–174.

O'Reilly, C. 2015. "The Pluralization of High Policing: Convergence and Divergence at the Public–Private Interface." *British Journal of Criminology* 55 (4): 688–710.

O'Reilly, C. 2010. "The Transnational Security Consultancy Industry: A Case of State-Corporate Symbiosis." *Theoretical Criminology* 14 (2): 183–210.

Oelberger, C. 2018. "Cui Bono? Public and Private Goals in Non-Profit Organizations." *Administration & Society* 50 (7): 973–1014.

Off Duty Services. 2021. "History." https://www.offdutyservices.com/about-us/history.

Office of Police Secondary Employment (OPSE). 2021. "Office Of Police Secondary Employment." https://www.nola.gov/opse/.

OACS. 2021. "Our Sponsors." https://ontariocrimestoppers.ca/about-us/our-sponsors.

Ottawa Police. 2017. "Paid Duty Assignments." Policy No. 3.16. January 23.

Ottawa Police. 2018. "Paid Duty Program Costing Update." *Finance and Audit Committee*. Ottawa Police Service. November 18.

Ottawa Police. 2021. "Hire Police for an Event." Ottawa Police Service. https://www.ottawapolice.ca/en/contact-us/hire-police-for-an-event.aspx.

Palmater, P. 2016. "Shining Light on the Dark Places: Addressing Police Racism and Sexualized Violence against Indigenous Women and Girls in the National Inquiry." *Canadian Journal of Women and the Law* 28 (2): 253–284.

Pamplin, T. 2020. "Detroit Police Spread Holiday Cheer with Annual Sergeant Santa Event." *Click On It News Detroit*. https://www.clickondetroit.com/news/local/2020/12/17/detroit-police-spread-holiday-cheer-with-annual-sergeant-santa-event/. December 17.

Parker, R. 2014. "LAPD Chief Beck Admits His Involvement in Department Horse Deal." *Los Angeles Times*. http://www.latimes.com/local/lanow/la-me-ln-lapdchief-beck-admits-horse-deal-20140806-story.html.

Peel Police. 2021. "Paid Duty Officer." https://www.peelpolice.ca/en/services/paid-duty-officer.aspx.

Pennings, J. 1980. *Interlocking Directorates: Origins and Consequences of Connections among Organizations' Board of Directors*. San Francisco: Jossey-Bass.

Peterson, A., and S. Uhnoo. 2012. "Trials of Loyalty: Ethnic Minority Police Officers as 'Outsiders' within a Greedy Institution." *European Journal of Criminology* 9 (4): 354–369.

Phillips, S. 2016. "Myths, Militarism and The Police Patrol Rifle." *Policing and Society* 26 (2): 185–196.

Pfuhl, E. 1992. "Crimestoppers: The Legitimation of Snitching." *Justice Quarterly* 9 (3): 505–528.

Police Executive Research Forum. 2019. *The Workforce Crisis, and What Police Agencies Are Doing about It*. Washington, DC: Police Executive Research Forum. https://www.policeforum.org/assets/WorkforceCrisis.pdf.

Police Foundation. 2021. "Evidence-based policing." https://www.policefoundation.org/publication/evidence-based-policing/?gclid=EAIaIQobChMIiOSlvpep8gIV1W1vBB2PnguAEAAYASAAEgKQdfD_BwE.

Police Foundation. 2017. "A Review of the Baltimore Police Department's Use of Persistent Surveillance (Baltimore Community Support Program)." https://www.policefoundation.org/wp-content/uploads/2017/02/PF-Review-of-BCSP-Final.pdf. January 30.

Ponce, A., and A. Bonafiglia. 2013. "Chicago Proposal would Allow Private Sponsorship of Police." *NBC Washington*. https://www.nbcwashington.com/news/national-international/chicago-proposal-would-allow-private-sponsorship-of-police/2046996/. April 4.

Powell, B. 2015. "Paid-Duty Policing Suspended at Muzik after Multiple Shooting." *Toronto Star*. August 10.

Prenzler, T., and P. Mackay. 1995. "Police Gratuities: What the Public Think." *Criminal Justice Ethics* 14 (1): 15–25.

Prenzler, T., A. Beckley, and S. Bronitt. 2013. "Police Gifts and Benefits Scandals: Addressing Deficits in Policy, Leadership and Enforcement." *International Journal of Police Science & Management* 15 (4): 294–304.

Pueblo Lands. 2013 "William J. Bratton: Motorola's High-tech Super Cop." https://darwinbondgraham.wordpress.com/2013/01/13/william-j-bratton-motorolas-hi-tech-super-cop/. January 13.

Punch, M. 2000. "Police Corruption and Its Prevention." *European Journal on Criminal Policy and Research* 8 (3): 301–324.

Pursaga, J. 2021. "Vaccination Site Shifts Boost Police Revenue." *Winnipeg Free Press*. https://www.winnipegfreepress.com/local/vaccination-site-shifts-boost-police-revenue-574617712.html. June 12.

Raghu, V. 2018. "Sponsored Police Station Boards Draw Flak, to Be Removed Soon." *DTNEXT*. https://www.dtnext.in/News/City/2018/02/14013035/1061850/Sponsored-police-station-boards-draw-flak-to-be-removed-.vpf.

Ramakrishna, S. 2020. "Giving Back to Themselves: Police Foundations Exemplify the Logic of Racial Capitalism." *The Baffler Magazine*. June 22.

Ransley, J., and L. Mazerolle. 2009. "Policing in an Era of Uncertainty." *Police Practice and Research* 10 (4): 365–381.

Ranzal, E. 1972. "Fund Begun to Aid Police Programs." *New York Times*. p. 30. June 4.

Rasmussen, D. 2018. "Documented Abuses and Uncertain Benefits of Civil Asset Forfeiture." *Criminology & Public Policy* 17: 97–100.

Ratcliffe, J. 2008. *Intelligence-Led Policing*. London: Willan Publishing.

Rector, K., and L. Broadwater. 2016. "Secret Aerial Surveillance by Baltimore Police Stirs Outrage." *The Los Angeles Times*. http://www.latimes.com/nation/la-na-baltimore-aerial-surveillance-20160825-snap-story.html.

Reel, M. 2016. "Since January, Police Have Been Testing an Aerial Surveillance System Adapted from the Surge in Iraq." *Bloomberg Business Week*. https://www.bloomberg.com/features/2016-baltimore-secret-surveillance/.

Regina Police. 2021. "Regina Police Service Special Duty Policing request form." https://reginapolice.ca/resources/special-duty-request-form/.

Reiner, R. 1992. *The Politics of the Police*, 2nd ed. London: Harvester Wheatsheaf.

Reiss, A. 1988. *Private Employment of Public Police*. Washington, DC: U.S. National Inst. of Justice.

Reiss, A. 1991. "Private Employment of Public Police." In W. Gormley, ed., *Privatization and Its Alternatives*. Madison: University of Wisconsin Press, 226–240.

Reuters. 2017. "Protecting Trump Tower Cost NY City $24 Million from Election to Inauguration." https://www.reuters.com/article/us-usa-trump-nyc-idUSKBN16203Q.

Rich, E. 2004. "Norris Sentenced to Six Months in Prison." *Washington Post*. http://www.washingtonpost.com/wp-dyn/articles/A59127-2004Jun21.html\.

Richie, B. 2012. *Arrested Justice: Black Women, Violence, and America's Prison Nation*. New York: New York University Press.

Ritchie, A. 2017. *Invisible No More: Police Violence against Black Women and Women of Color*. Boston: Beacon Press.

Robertson, J. 2013. "Police Cost a Sour Note at Concerts." *Sydney Morning Herald*. https://www.smh.com.au/national/nsw/police-cost-a-sour-note-at-concerts-20130831-2sxfa.html. September 11.

Robinson, W. 2018. "The Next Economic Crisis: Digital Capitalism and Global Police State." *Race & Class* 60 (1): 77–92.

Robinson, W. 2019. "Accumulation Crisis and Global Police State." *Critical Sociology* 45 (6): 845–858.

Rosemont, H. 2014. "Private Sector Engagement in the UK's Counter-Terrorism Strategy: A New Agenda." *Behavioral Sciences of Terrorism and Political Aggression* 6 (2): 147–161.

Rose, N. 1999. *Powers of Freedom: Reframing Political Thought*. Cambridge: Cambridge University Press.

Rossman, G. 2014. "Obfuscatory Relational Work and Disreputable Exchange." *Sociological Theory* 32 (1): 43–63.

Royal Newfoundland Constabulary 2015. (Personal Communication with A. Luscombe). December 15th.

Ruiz, J., and C. Bono. 2004. "At What Price a "Freebie"? The Real Cost of Police Gratuities." *Criminal Justice Ethics* 23 (1): 44–54.

Sanders, C., C. Weston, and N. Schott. 2015. "Police Innovations, 'Secret Squirrels' and Accountability: Empirically Studying Intelligence-Led Policing in Canada." *British Journal of Criminology* 55 (4): 711–729.

Santa Clara. 2017. "City Manager's Direction (CMD) No. 70." FOI Disclosure.

Schilke, O., and G. Rossman. 2018. "It's Only Wrong If It's Transactional: Moral Perceptions of Obfuscated Exchange." *American Sociological Review* 83 (6): 1079–1107.

Scott, C. 2006. "Establishment of the Winnipeg Police Foundation: A Framework for Enhanced Success," MA Thesis, Athabasca University http://dtpr.lib.athabascau.ca/action/viewdtrdesc.php?cpk=569&id=22965.

Seattle's Finest. 2020. "Proudly Providing WA State with Security and Traffic Control Since 2002 with over 1,000,000 Hours Completed." https://www.seafinest.com/.

Seattle Police. 2015. "Seattle secondary employment policy 5.120" (2014), Section V (7 & 8).

SPF. 2020. "Picnics in the Precincts." https://www.seattlepolicefoundation.org/events/precinct-picnics.

SPF. 2021. "Blue Tie Ball." https://www.seattlepolicefoundation.org/events/2021-blue-tie-ball.

SPF. 2019. "January 2019 Newsletter." https://www.seattlepolicefoundation.org/lp1/messages-and-newsletters/january-2019-newsletter. February 1.

SPF. 2018. "September 2018 Newsletter." https://www.seattlepolicefoundation.org/lp1/messages-and-newsletters/september-2018-newsletter. December 6.

Seattle Times. 2017. "FBI Investigating Off-Duty Work by Seattle Police at Construction Sites, Parking Garages." https://www.seattletimes.com/seattle-news/crime/fbi-investigating-off-duty-work-by-seattle-police-at-construction-sites-parking-garages/.

Segal, M. 1986. "The Military and the Family as Greedy Institutions." *Armed Forces and Society* 13 (1): 9–38.

Seven-Eleven. 2012. "7-Eleven Announces Gift of New T3s to Dallas Police Department." https://franchise.7-eleven.com/franchise-press-releases/03-09-2012-7-eleven-announces-gift-of-new-t3s-to-dallas-police-department.

Shearing, C. 2005. "Nodal Security." *Police Quarterly* 8 (1): 57–63.

Shearing, C., and L. Johnston. 2010. "Nodal Wars and Network Fallacies: A Genealogical Analysis of Global Insecurities." *Theoretical Criminology* 14 (4): 495–514.

Silbey, S., and P. Ewick. 1998. *Common Place of Law: Stories from Everyday Life*. Chicago: Chicago University Press.

Sillince, J., and A. Brown. 2009. "Multiple Organizational Identities and Legitimacy: The Rhetoric of Police Websites." *Human Relations* 62 (12): 1829–1856.

Silvestri, M. 2017. "Police Culture and Gender: Revisiting the 'Cult of Masculinity." *Policing: A Journal of Policy and Practice* 11 (3): 289–300.

Skogan, W. 2018. "The Commission and the Police." *Criminology and Public Policy* 17 (2): 379–396.

Sleiman, M., and R. Lippert. 2010. "Downtown Ambassadors, Police Relations and 'Clean and Safe' Security." *Policing and Society* 20 (3): 316–335.

Smith, D. 2018. "Law Enforcement's Secret Weapon." *The Philanthropy Roundtable*. https://www.philanthropyroundtable.org/philanthropy-magazine/article/winter-2018-law-enforcement percent27s-secret-weapon.

Stalder, F. 2018. *The Digital Condition*. London: John Wiley and Sons.

Stand with Those Who Serve (SWTWS). 2021. "2016 Sponsors." https://swtws.org/2016-sponsor/.

Statistics Canada. 2020. "Police Resources in Canada, 2019." https://www150.statcan.gc.ca/n1/pub/85-002-x/2020001/article/00015-eng.htm.

Stenning, P. 2009. "Governance and Accountability in a Plural Policing Environment-The Story So Far." *Policing: A Journal of Policy and Practice*. 3 (1): 22–33.

Stone, K. 2013. "Cash Donation Taints Hamilton Police." *Hamilton Spectator*. https://www.thespec.com/opinion/contributors/2013/06/16/cash-donation-taints-hamilton-police.html. June 16.

Stoughton, S. 2017. "Moonlighting: The Private Employment of Off-Duty Officers." *University of Illinois Law Review* (1): 1847–1900.

Sullivan, J. 1987. "Legal Issues in Private Security: The Moonlighting Police Officer." *Journal of Security Administration* 10 (1): 29–37.

Sylvestre, M., N. Blomley, and C. Bellot. 2019. *Red Zones: Criminal Law and the Territorial Governance of Marginalized People*. London: Cambridge University Press.

Sweetin, J. 2021. "Why Police Executives Are Outsourcing Their Off-Duty Programs." *Police Chief*. https://www.policechiefmagazine.org/why-police-executives-are-outsourcing-their-off-duty-programs/.

Tampa Bay Times. 2019. "They promise to help families of fallen officers. But they're mostly paying telemarketers." https://www.tampabay.com/investigations/2019/12/27/they-promise-to-help-families-of-fallen-officers-but-theyre-mostly-paying-telemarketers/. December 27.

Taylor, P. 2011. "Who Will Pay for an End to Paid-Duty Policing?" *The Record*.

Terpstram, J. 2008. "Police, Local Government, and Citizens as Participants in Local Security Networks." *Police Practice and Research*. 9 (3): 213–225.

Terreri, J. 2014. "Derenda Bans Work by Off-Duty Officers at Bars in Wake of Molly's Pub Assault." *Buffalo News*. 23 May.

Toronto. 2019. "Response to Member Motion 5.17: Protecting the Viability of Street Festivals." https://www.toronto.ca/legdocs/mmis/2019/ex/bgrd/backgroundfile-134981.pdf. June 19.

Toronto Crime Stoppers. 2021a. "About Us." https://www.222tips.com/about/.

Toronto Crime Stoppers. 2021b. "Sponsors." https://www.222tips.com/sponsor/.

Toronto Crime Stoppers. 2021c. "Partners." https://www.222tips.com/partner/.

Toronto Police Services Board. 2009. Meeting minutes. https://tpsb.ca/component/jdownloads/send/22-2009/347-minutes-jan22-09-pub. January 22.

Toronto Star. 2021. "What Cities have Defunded the Police?" Toronto Star. https://www.thestar.com/local-oshawa/news/2021/08/17/what-cities-have-defunded-the-police.html#:~:text=New%20York%2C%20Los%20Angeles%2C%20Chicago,have%20all%20defunded%20their%20police. August 17.

Trottier, D. 2012. "Policing Social Media." *Canadian Review of Sociology* 49 (4): 411–425.

Trujillo, J. 2019. "Do Cops Serve the Rich? Meet The NYPD's Private Piggy Bank." *Gothamist*. https://gothamist.com/news/do-cops-serve-the-rich-meet-the-nypds-private-piggy-bank. October 24.

Tyler, T. 2004. "Enhancing Police Legitimacy." *The Annals of the American Academy of Political and Social Science* 593 (1): 84–99.

Urban Institute. 2021. "Criminal Justice Expenditures: Police, Corrections, and Courts." https://www.urban.org/policy-centers/cross-center-initiatives/state-and-local-finance-initiative/state-and-local-backgrounders/criminal-justice-police-corrections-courts-expenditures.

US Securities and Exchange Commission. 2010. "Motorola Solutions announces new board of directors effective Jan. 4." https://www.sec.gov/Archives/edgar/data/68505/000110465910060618/a10–22005_1ex99d2.htm.

Valverde, M. 2003. *Law's Dream of a Common Knowledge*. Princeton: Princeton University Press.

Valverde, M. 2006. *Law and Order: Images, Meanings, Myths*. New Brunswick: Rutgers University Press.

Vancouver. 1976. "Vancouver Police Foundation minutes," City of Vancouver Archives.

Vancouver Police Department. 2016. "Policy 2.6.3 and 2.6.4" FOI Disclosure.

VPF. 2021a. "VPF Receives Amazing $1 Million Gift to Support Public Safety." https://www.vancouverpolicefoundation.org/2021/01/vpf-receives-incredible-1-million-gift. January 14.

VPF. 2021b. "The Healing Path Initiative." https://www.vancouverpolicefoundation.org/2021/06/the-healing-path-initiative/. June 28.

VPF. 2021c. "National Volunteer Week: A Conversation With VPF Chair. Dr. Sherri Magee." https://www.vancouverpolicefoundation.org/2021/06/the-healing-path-initiative-part-two-a-closer-look/. April 24.

VPF. 2021d. "Project 529 Reduces Bike Theft in Vancouver By 40%." https://www.vancouverpolicefoundation.org/2021/04/project-529-reduces-bike-theft-in-vancouver-by-40/. April 27.

VPF. 2020a. "Above and Beyond: VPD K9 Calendar Team." https://www.vancouverpolicefoundation.org/2020/04/above-and-beyond-vpd-k9-calendar-team/. April 27.

VPF. 2020b. "National Police Week: Celebrating our VPD." https://www.vancouverpolicefoundation.org/2020/05/national-police-week-celebrating-our-vpd/. May 12.

VPF. 2020c. "Above and Beyond: Sgt. Lorna Berndsen." https://www.vancouverpolicefoundation.org/2020/11/above-and-beyond-sgt-lorna-berndsen/. November 12.

VPF. 2020d. "Beyond the Blue." https://www.vancouverpolicefoundation.org/2020/04/beyond-the-blue/. April 17.

VPF. 2019a. "VPD Cadets Class 6." https://www.vancouverpolicefoundation.org/2019/09/vpd-cadets-class-6/. September 18.

VPF. 2019b. "Grants Season Officially Begins." https://www.vancouverpolicefoundation.org/2019/03/grants-season-officially-begins/. March 8.

VPF. 2018a. "Outfitting Youth With the Right Stuff." https://www.vancouverpolicefoundation.org/2018/12/outfitting-youth-with-the-right-stuff/. December 21.

VPF. 2018b. "Seniors' Health & Safety Fair 2018." https://www.vancouverpolicefoundation.org/2018/07/seniors-health-safety-fair-2018/. July 9.

Vancouver Newcondos. 2021. "Strathcona Village by Wall Financial." https://www.vancouvernewcondos.com/properties/theheatley/

VanGorp, B. 2007. "The Constructionist Approach to Framing: Brining Culture Back In." *Journal of Communication* 57: 60–78.

Van Maanen, J. 1975. "Police Socialization: A Longitudinal Examination of Job Attitudes in an Urban Police Department." *Administrative Science Quarterly* 20 (2): 207–228.

van Stokkom, B., and J. Terpstra. 2018. "Plural Policing, The Public Good, and the Constitutional State: An International Comparison of Austria and Canada-Ontario." *Policing and Society* 28 (4): 415–430.

Vancouver Police. 2021. "Organization." https://vpd.ca/police/organization/index.html.

Vaughn, M., and L. Coomes. 1995. "The Liability of Moonlighting: Are Police Officers Employed as Security Guards Acting Under Color of Law?" *Police Liability Review* 6: 6–9.

Villanova, P. 2018. "Ex-Jersey City cop sentenced for off-duty jobs scheme." https://www.nj.com/hudson/index.ssf/2018/03/ex-jersey_city_cop_sentenced_for_off-duty_jobs_sch.html

Vitale, A. 2017. *The End of Policing*. New York: Verso Books.

Vuga, J., and J. Juvan. 2013. "Work–family Conflict between Two Greedy Institutions–the Family and the Military." *Current Sociology* 61 (7): 1058–1077.

Ward, C. 2005. "CPRC Taser Review Released." *A. Cameron Ward and Company*. http://www.cameronward.com/2005/08/cprc-taser-review-released/. August 22.

Walby, K., and C. Gumieny. 2020. "Public Police Philanthropy and Twitter Communications in Canada." *Policing: An International Journal* 43 (5): 755–768.

Walby, K., and A. Luscombe. 2019. *Freedom of Information and Social Science Research Design.* London: Routledge.

Walby, K., A. Luscombe, and R. Lippert. 2018. "Going to the Dogs? Police, Donations, and K9s." *Policing: An International Journal of Police Strategies & Management* 41 (6): 798–812.

Walby, K., R. Lippert, and A. Luscombe. 2018. "The Rise of the Police Foundation: Public Police's Dark Money." *British Journal of Criminology* 58 (4): 824–844.

Walby, K., R. Lippert, and B. Wilkinson. 2014. "'The Right People to Do the Right Job…': Legitimation Work of Municipal Corporate Security Personnel." *Australian & New Zealand Journal of Criminology* 47 (2): 259–275.

Walby, K., and R. Lippert. 2015. *Municipal Corporate Security in International Context.* New York: Routledge.

Walby, K., and R. Lippert. 2014. *Corporate Security in the 21st Century: Theory and Practice in International Perspective.* New York: Palgrave MacMillan.

Walker, S., and C. Archbold. 2013. *The New World of Police Accountability.* London: SAGE.

Walsh, D., and V. Conway. 2011. "Police Governance and Accountability: Overview of Current Issues." *Crime, Law and Social Change* 55 (2-3): 61–86.

Washington, D.C. Police Foundation (WDCPF). 2019. "Annual Report 2019." https://www.dcpolicefoundation.org/uploads/2/6/3/5/26357602/dcpf_2019_annual_report.pdf.

Weisbrod, B. 1997. "The Future of the Non-Profit Sector: Its Entwining with Private Enterprise and Government." *Journal of Policy Analysis and Management* 16: 541–555.

Weissenstein, M. 2003. "Budgets Tightening, Police Departments Turn to Private Money." http://www.nycpolicefoundation.org/news.asp.

Police. West Vancouver. 2016. "Donations and Gifts to the Department." WVPD Administrative Policy.

Whelan, C., and B. Dupont. 2017. "Taking Stock of Networks across the Security Field: A Review, Typology and Research Agenda." *Policing and Society* 27 (6): 671–687.

White, A. 2012. "The New Political Economy of Private Security." *Theoretical Criminology* 16 (1): 85–101.

Wilber, D. 2003. "A Career and Legacy Suffer Under Accusations." *The Baltimore Sun.* http://www.baltimoresun.com/bal-te.md.profile11dec11-story.html.

Williams, P. 2002. "The Competent Boundary Spanner." *Public Administration* 80 (1): 103–124.

Williams, C. 2008. "Constables for Hire: The History of Private 'Public' Policing in the UK." *Policing and Society* 18 (2): 190–205.

Williams, M. 2002. "Civil Asset Forfeiture: Where Does the Money Go?" *Criminal Justice Review* 27 (2): 321–329.

Williams, M., J. Holcomb, T. Kovandzic, and S. Bullock. 2010. "The Abuse of Civil Asset Forfeiture." Institute for Justice. http://www.ij.org/images/pdf_folder/other_pubs/assetforfeituretoemail.pdf.

Winnipeg Foundation. 2021. "Winnipeg Police Service Endowment Fund." https://www.mycharitytools.com/gift/wpgfdn/donate?fund=379.

Winnipeg Police. 2016. "Donations and Sponsorship policy." FOI Disclosure.

Winnipeg Police. 2015. "Winnipeg Special Duty Policy" (Amended 2015), Section 7, E(7).

Winston, A., and D. Graham. 2014. "Private Donors Supply Spy Gear to Cops." *ProPublica.* https://www.propublica.org/article/private-donors-supply-spy-gear-to-cops.

Wolf, R., S. Holmes, and C. Jones. 2015. "Utilization and Satisfaction of Volunteer Law Enforcement Officers in the Office of the American Sheriff: An Exploratory Nationwide Study. *Police Practice and Research*. 17 (5): 448–462.

Wolfson, M. 2006. "New Contract Rules for Cops: Officers Randomly Chosen for Night Club, Festival Duty." *Windsor Star*. A3. July 27.

Wood, J. 2004. "Cultural Change in the Governance of Security." *Policing and Society* 14 (1): 31–48.

Wood, D. 2002. "Your Ad Here: Cop Cars as the Next Billboards." *The Christian Science Monitor*. https://www.csmonitor.com/2002/1003/p01s01-ussc.html. October 3.

Wood, M. 2020. "Policing's 'Meme Strategy': Understanding the Rise of Police Social Media Engagement Work." *Current Issues in Criminal Justice* 32 (1): 40–58.

Worrall, J. 2001. "Addicted to the Drug War: The Role of Civil Asset Forfeiture as a Budgetary Necessity in Contemporary Law Enforcement." *Journal of Criminal Justice* 29 (3): 171–187.

York Regional Police (YRP). 2016. "Directive on Solicitations, Donations, and Gifts." FOI Disclosure.

York Regional Police (YRP). 2015. "Command Directive (#7262), Section E (Excluded Paid Duty Activities)." York Regional Police. Ontario.

Young, D., and L. Salamon. 2002. "Commercialization, Social Ventures, and For-Profit Competition." In L. Salamon (ed.), *The State of Non-Profit America*. Washington: Brookings Institution Press, 423–446.

Zytaruk, T. 2021. Chief Constable Says a Surrey Police Foundation Should Be 'full on' by Early 2022. *Surrey-Now Leader*. https://www.surreynowleader.com/news/chief-constable-says-a-surrey-police-foundation-should-be-full-on-by-early-2022/. February 18.

Archival

Seattle Archives, 5287-01 Box 18, File 2 "Police Department Off Duty Employment 1972."

Vancouver Archives, 753C File 3 "Gratuities to Officers" 1929–1930.

Legislation

Conflict of Interest Act. SNL Chapter C-30.1. (Newfoundland and Labrador, Canada).

Winnipeg by-law no. 138/2013- A By-law of THE CITY OF WINNIPEG to authorize the establishment of a Winnipeg Police Service Endowment Fund and to regulate the use of its income.

Cases

Pierre v. City of New York, et al., 2020 (New York State, US).

Toronto (Metropolitan) Police Force v. Bromell, 2000 (Ontario, Canada).

Index

www.ingramcontent.com/pod-product-compliance
Lightning Source LLC
LaVergne TN
LVHW021124300926
849160LV00010B/860
9780367766481